MAAMIE
AND
PARPI DALEY
OF
MONTSERRAT

(Meet the Daleys)

Dorine S. O'Garro

Order this book online at www.trafford.com
or email orders@trafford.com

Most Trafford titles are also available at major online book retailers.

Maamie and Parpi Daley of Montserrat is a work of fiction. Names, characters, places and incidents are
either a product of the author's imagination, or are used fictitiously. Any resemblance to any actual persons,
living or dead, events, or locales is entirely coincidental.

Printed in Victoria, BC, Canada.

ISBN: 978-1-4269-2938-0 (sc)
ISBN: 978-1-4269-2939-7 (hc)

Library of Congress Control Number: 2010903752

*Our mission is to efficiently provide the world's finest, most comprehensive book publishing
service, enabling every author to experience success. To find out how to publish your book, your
way, and have it available worldwide, visit us online at www.trafford.com*

Trafford rev. 6/15/2010

Trafford
PUBLISHING®   www.trafford.com

North America & international
toll-free: 1 888 232 4444 (USA & Canada)
phone: 250 383 6864 ♦ fax: 812 355 4082

Acknowledgements:

I would like to thank my pastor, the Rev. Joy P. Clarke of St. Peters Lutheran Church, Springfield Gardens, NY, for her editing and for her encouragement.

I would also like to thank Mrs. Gloria Allen of Brooklyn, NY, Mrs. Nellie Hugh of South Carolina, and Mrs. Christine Hughes of Jamaica, NY whose help I sought because, they were born or raised in New York of Montserratian mothers, and are socially and emotionally involved in its culture, especially in its cuisine.

They, too, are very concerned about the volcanic eruptions that have devastated two thirds of the island.

Dorine S. O'Garro

Foreword

Is Montserrat truly burning? Is it doomed? To hear some folks tell it, they should have evacuated the island from the start. Yes, the Soufriere Hills volcano began to erupt on July 18, 1995, and changed the face of Montserrat's scenery forever. One of the hardest years was 1997 when all hell broke loose in the Emerald Isle of the Caribbean. Yet, many hardy and patriotic Montserratians decided to hold fast to their homeland. Some migrated to foreign soil, but returned home later to deal with the erupting monster.

None of their children and grandchildren abroad could convince my grandparents, with whom I spent many summers in my childhood and early adolescence, to leave Montserrat. My grandmother, Magdalene Elizabeth Daley, for whom I was named, seldom used the Montserrat lingo, but she told me plainly, "A ya me barn, a ya me reah and a ya me a go dead."[1] My grandfather, Gabriel Emanuel Daley, nodded silently in acquiescence to his beloved wife's point of view. Maamie and Parpi Daley, speaking now from an adult point of view, I applaud your patriotism.

Montserrat, we the offspring of your native sons and daughters will cherish your memory as long as God lends us breath. We are the Allens, the Barzeys, the Brades, the Branns, the Brinns, the Brambles, the Brumbles, the Buffonges, the Cabeys, the Cassells, the Corbetts, the Daleys, the Daniels, the Dorsetts, the Duberrys, the Dyers, the Dyetts, the Edgecombes, the Farrells, the Fentons, the Ferguses, the Fagans, the

---

1   I was born here, I was raised here, and I'll die here.

Francises, the Galloways, the Greenaways, the Greers, the Griffiths, the Harneys, the Herberts, the Hixons, the Howes, the Irishes, the Jeffers, the Kellys, the Kelsicks, the Kennedys, the Kirnons, the Lees, the Lewises, the Lindseys, the Lynches, the Maloneys, the Markhams, the Martineaus, the Martins, the Meades, the Molineaux, the Missetts, the Nantons, the O'Briens, the O'Garros, the Osbornes, the Perkins, the Peters, the Phillips, the Pipers, the Ponds, the Ponteens, the Reids, the Rileys, the Roaches, the Ryans, the Ryners, the Sempers, the Sergeants, the Silcotts, the Skerritts, the Tonges, the Tuitts, the Wades, the Webbs, the Weekes, the Willocks, and many not mentioned here. These are some of the major names of Montserratians. We are bound to you by flesh and blood, and as long as we live, Montserrat you will never die.

Montserratians had always placed Americans on pedestals. The island was not as progressive then as it is now, and the seemingly "rich foreigners and returning natives" lent a noted contrast, and the hope that some day soon they, too, would travel abroad to seek their fortune. Most poor Montserratians also revered family members and their children who returned home from "America" on holiday.

However, the Daley family saw it quite differently. Parpi and Maamie Daley treated their vacationing grandchildren just as they had treated their children. We were praised or punished according to our behavior.

Please read and learn as I, Magdalene Elizabeth Daley, II, a first generation Montserratian-American, tell their story.

I have determined that the title of this novel will be **Maamie and Parpi Daley of Montserrat,** because like Montserrat, they will live forever on my mind and in my heart.

Chapter I

Meet the Daleys

I started going to my father's homeland, Montserrat, West Indies, when I was six, but I was eight before I began to appreciate my annual summer vacations there. Dad took my brother, Syd Murray and me, Magdalene Elizabeth Daley II, called Maggie or Mags, and left us. Either he or Mom returned for us at the end of our summer vacation. As we grew older, we traveled in the care of the flight attendants.

Maamie and Parpi Daley were hard-working people. He was a farmer, and she was his helper and a consummate housewife. Maamie and Parpi Daley had six children, five of whom migrated to Barbados, England, and North America.

Their children, in order of their birth, were Uncle Bernard, nicknamed Bern. He migrated to Canada when he was a young man and returned to the Island occasionally. He married Rebecca, Becky Ferguson of St. Croix. They had two children, Vincent and James.

Auntie Eleanor, Ellie, married Christopher Ford of Barbados and settled there. They had three children, twin girls, Yolanda and Christa, and a boy, Marc. They settled in St. Philip's, Barbados, where Uncle Chris was a schoolmaster.

Uncle Solomon, Sol, migrated to the United States, and sponsored my father. Later, he married Anne Marie Simpson of East Orange, New Jersey. They had three children, Nathaniel, Rosalie and David. We visited each other regularly, because he lived on Convent Avenue at 145th Street in the Village of Harlem, and we lived only a few blocks away at the Dunbar Apartments, 149th Street between Seventh and Eighth Avenues. When we were little, they divorced, and Auntie Anne and the children moved to North Carolina. Uncle Sol visited them often, but we did not see our cousins after they moved. Auntie Anne remarried two years later, and relocated to California. Uncle Sol bought a home in South Orange, New Jersey, and we visited him regularly.

Uncle Paul went to London to study, fell in love with England, and remained there. He married Alexandra Bridgewater. They were the proud parents of Verona and Darius. Early on, we knew them from their photos.

Anthony, Tunny, my Dad, was the fairest of them all. He migrated to New York, having been sponsored by Uncle Sol. He was handsome, tall, arrogant and intelligent. He married my mother, Lisa Evelyn Murray, of the Bronx, New York. My brother, Syd Murray and yours truly, were their only children for a while. When I was going on thirteen, my parents had a baby boy. They named him Emanuel Jay, but nicknamed him Ejay. Mom said she had gotten careless, but she still welcomed her bundle of joy.

Dad decided to move from Harlem, but they chose to move to Queens. They bought a home in St. Albans. Dad bought a car, and we visited Uncle Sol often, especially on his birthday in early September when he had a fiesta in his yard.

According to the island's custom, the youngest daughter stayed at home to take care of her aging parents. Generally, she remained unmarried. However, Auntie Vera, Vee, the youngest daughter, married Simeon Duberry, Sym, of Cork Hill, Montserrat. They had two children, Sadie and Keith. Sadie was my age and Keith was Syd's age.

Auntie Vee and her family shared the family's residence, called the Big House, with Maamie and Parpi Daley. Parpi Daley had attached a three-bedroom flat to the house when Auntie Vera got married. They shared a common entrance, and seldom locked the door that separated the flats. Auntie Vera fully accepted the Montserrat tradition and dutifully stayed close to her parents.

Auntie Vee was in an enviable position. Her brothers were so pleased with her dedication to their parents that they richly rewarded her and her family. They sent them many gifts, annually. Her children, Keith and Sadie, dressed as well as Syd and I did, in the latest American, British, and Canadian fashions.

You have met the Daleys. Now, let us take a peek into their lives.

I must say that Syd and I, the little Americans, were not happy campers at first, but Maamie and Parpi Daley were affectionate, and we soon fit into the swing of things. We looked forward to going back to Montserrat year after year. We joined our cousins and friends, spent our free time at the beach, climbing trees, racing in the open fields, studying anthills,-(ants nests-in Montserrat) and having fun.

As I grew older, I realized that Syd and I were as lucky as Auntie Vera and her family were. We had our own adventures by day, and by night, especially when the moon and stars seemed so close to earth that one felt he could reach out and touch them. We also joined in our family's productions of songs, and story telling.

All the adults told us stories that were told to them in their youth, but Maamie Daley was our primary story teller. Parpi still listened intently as if he were still a child sitting at his mother's knees.

Maamie and Parpi Daley were quite tall for their generation. They were slim and good-looking people, who were well groomed. Uncle Sym cut Parpi's hair weekly, and Parpi shaved daily. When they were dressed in their Sunday best, they looked elegant. Maamie had long thick hair. She washed it once a week with the cactus pear, called "prickly" pear in Montserrat, and dark brown soap. She used homemade coconut oil that she applied generously to her scalp, combed and brushed her hair well, and made one large Congo[2] braid that she stuck under her straw hat on farm days. She wore a French roll on Sundays. She was of a darker complexion than Parpi, with a sharp nose and puckered lips. Parpi had short curly black hair intermingled with gray. He had large brown eyes, and a tan complexion. He was soft spoken, but could be very stern when provoked. They had raised their children to fear God, love and help one another, and stay out of trouble. All the Daley males had one or more trades, but each had knowledge of carpentry. The girls were seamstresses.

Maamie Daley, lovingly called "Shug" by Parpi Daley her eternal Boy, lived as if they were born brother and sister. Someone once told Maamie Daley that she resembled Parpi. She laughed excitedly, but said nothing.

---

2   cornrow

Chapter II

The Big House and Its Environs

The Daleys named their home The Big House. It was built on a plateau with a clear view of the Caribbean Sea to the west, the serrated mountains to the east, and the harbor of Plymouth, the capital of the island, to the northwest. Dad told me that the Daley boys took advantage of their lofty heights to announce the arrival of ships to the harbor. He demonstrated that ploy by cupping his mouth and shouting, "Man o'-War ahoy! Man-o'-War ahoy!" He said that Parpi Daley often told him that he had the "biggest mouth" of all his boys.

The soil was fertile, and the family took full advantage of its fertility. The Daleys had multiple trees of all the fruits that were known to the island, and some exotic ones, such as the Java plums.

The Big House was made of wood, island stone and concrete. Maamie and Parpi had started with a three-room structure, and added rooms as their family grew and their financial situation allowed it. Its mahogany floors sparkled. They used the seal wax that anglers collected on the far shores of the Caribbean.

The Big House was spacious. The Daleys and Duberrys shared the front and back verandahs, the dining room, and, later, the indoor kitchen. Auntie Vera's dining room was just a showpiece. It, too, was elegantly furnished. When flush toilets replaced the latrines in the island, Uncle Bern returned from Canada, hired local workers, and built four bathrooms in the Big House. He built two bathrooms in each flat, with a bidet in each of the private bathrooms adjoining the master bedrooms. We had never seen bidets before, so Maamie Daley showed me how to use it, and told Syd it was not for him.

When I was small, I wished I were in Montserrat when Uncle Bern was there. I thought he resembled Dad very closely, although he was slightly shorter.

They had no hot water heater. I did not like the coldwater showers, so I showered around 9:00 a.m. in the outdoor shower that Maamie and Parpi Daley had built in the yard. It was a roofless hovel with a flat stone for its floor, and an overhead faucet with an attached sprinkler. The water was steaming hot by midday, and lukewarm in the early evening, because the pipes were exposed to the tropical sun, the mighty heating force. On rainy and cloudy days, I took quick showers indoors.

During our first years at the Big House, the kitchen was a separate structure. At first, it was huge with thatched roof, two doors and four windows. There was a rather large stone oven just below the kitchen. They used wood to "fire" it. Keith and Sadie showed Syd and me how to bake sweet corn and sweet potatoes in the hot ashes swept from the oven. Normally, they "fired" it on Friday afternoons. The kitchen and the stone oven were not far from the front door of the house. Auntie Vera and Maamie Daley baked bread, cakes, coconut tarts, and sweet biscuits (cookies) weekly. They used an oar-like large wooden spatula to place things in the oven and to retrieve them. It had a five-foot or longer wooden handle. When the men were not around, Maamie Daley and Aunty Vee handled the oar skillfully. Parpi Daley had made a separate cupboard for the baked goods, when their children were little. They called it a safe. It was made of cedar and very fine wire mesh. The mesh served as a protector from flies, and as a vent for the baked goods. Dad told me that they kept it locked to prevent petty theft among the children. They kept it in Maamie and Parpi Daley's dining room in the Big House.

Occasionally, we ran out of baked goods during the week, because Maamie Daley always entertained folks who dropped in to visit us by offering them cake, sweet biscuits, or coconut tart, and a beverage. It was then that they used the Charley-Man oven. It was the size of our stove and oven in New York. It was made of heavy-duty aluminum sheets, was well insulated and was encased in wood. Uncle Bern and Parpi Daley had made it.

They placed a charcoal pot in the compartment at the bottom to heat it, and then put the cakes and pies on removable racks. It baked everything slowly. They knew how to regulate the heat although it had no gauge. Neither Maamie nor Parpi Daley knew why they called it a "Charley-Man" oven, but I learned later that it was named for the man who first made one in Montserrat.

5

I liked the Charley Man oven. They had made the top in the shape of a large tray. They placed the hot baked goods in it to cool them. There were large brass rings on both sides of the tray for the potholders. Uncle Sym had placed it on wheels, so that they could change its location to suit their need.

"Boy had made me a Charley Man oven after we got married, Mags, Sweetie," Maamie told me. "It was older than Bern. This is not our original kitchen, Mags, Sweetie. The first one burnt to ashes, and destroyed my Charley Man oven. The wowla [3] roof had caught fire."

"Why did they rebuild the kitchen with a wowla roof?" I asked.

"It was the style back then, and we couldn't afford the full galvanized roofing, Mags, Sweetie."

"But one part of the roof is galvanized, Maamie Daley?"

"Have you noticed that it's there that Boy put our corned pork to dry? The galvanized area attracts the heat. We also dry the coco and coffee beans on that part of the roof, before we parch and grind them."

"I like speaking to you, Maamie Daley. One of these days, I'm going to write down everything you're telling me now."

"That would be nice, Mags, Sweetie," she said.

Early on, Nathaniel, Natty Daley, Parpi Daley's father, Parpi Daley, and their helpers had built two cisterns, the largest one on the farm. Its overflow watered the young banana and dasheen plants. The dasheen is my favorite root vegetable. During the dry season, the Daleys had enough water for their animals and plants.

The smaller cistern supplied the water for the Big House. It was above the kitchen, under a large calabash tree. It had a steel trapdoor, as did the one on the farm. They kept both cisterns locked. Parpi Daley and Uncle Sym maintained the cisterns. They permitted the neighbors who did not have pipes to get water there in times of drought. The poorer villagers had to depend on the government reservoirs and public water fountains for their water. They arrived with pails and large scrubbed kerosene oil cans, called "tinnins". They filled their containers with the water that they carried easily on their heads.

However, in spite of the running water in the big yard, Parpi Daley took two kegs of drinking spring water from his favorite spring near his farm to The Big House every night. He filled the calabash and clay goblets

---

3   thatched

that they kept inside the house, and left the rest in the kitchen for Maamie Daley. I preferred the water from the calabash goblet. It was naturally cool and mellow.

One year, when Syd and I returned to the island, we found that they had built an archway from the Big House to the kitchen, and connected a water pipe to the indoor sink. The stone oven remained on the outside, due to the heat that it generated, of course. They had replaced the thatched roof with heavy gauge aluminum panels. While they liked their modernizations, Syd and I did not appreciate most of them. We hoped they would never close the separate kitchen. We wanted to find the real Montserrat in the Island of Montserrat when we returned each summer. They wanted to modernize.

Maamie Daley explained the archway to Syd and me. "I was weary of getting wet while going from my house to the kitchen, in the rainy season, Syd and Mags, Sweetie."

Maamie Daley bragged that she had running water in her kitchen. The coldwater faucet produced hot water around midday, because its pipe, too, was exposed to the blistering tropical sun. Parpi Daley and Uncle Bern had built two benches, each about six feet long, and Auntie Vera made cushions for them. Maamie Daley and Auntie Vera made the colorful kitchen curtains. It was a little house by itself, with its large windows and clay floor. Maamie Daley had ordered huge straw mats that covered much of the clay floor. There was a large cedar round table with ten mahogany chairs. Parpi Daley, Uncle Bern and my father had built them. Maamie Daley kept her large stainless steel pots, gifts from her children in England and North America, as ornaments. They shone like a looking glass or a mirror. She never abandoned her cast-iron cooking utensils. They were perfect for cooking on the potbelly wood stove.

The kitchen also served as a dining room. When they had invited guests, they used Maamie Daley's dining room. The linen and embroidered tablecloths were the prettiest I had ever seen. Maamie Daley told us that they were in the family for generations. They were properly laundered and returned to their storage place in a cedar trunk.

When I got older, I realized why Mom often said, "If Maamie Daley goes before me, I would like to have at least one of those linen tablecloths. Linen like that just does not exist any more."

When I told Maamie Daley what my mother had said, she sent her a linen tablecloth one year. Mom could hardly thank her enough.

I liked being in the kitchen with Maamie Daley. They had no refrigeration at the time, so they "corned" loins of pork to preserve them. The corning process was a lively ritual. They washed the meat to be cured with lemon juice, lemon leaves and sage. Maamie Daley had previously prepared pounds of diced onions, sage, garlic, thyme and scallions that Montserratians called "hubbs and chibble", ground cloves, curry, cumin, tumeric, dark brown sugar and salt. They used the coarse sea salt from the salt ponds of the Caribbean. Maamie Daley mixed the condiments and herbs well in a deep earthen dish that dated back to her mother's time, filled her right hand with the mix, and rubbed it into the loins of pork. Her movements resembled those of a masseuse. Parpi Daley and Uncle Sym then put them in burlap sacks, called crocus bags, tied them securely, and hung them on hooks to drip. After a certain time, they placed them in the sunlight for many days on the galvanized roof, and then on large hooks in the storage room in the kitchen. By then, they were fully cured.

Of course, Maamie Daley saved and sent corned pork for her baby boy, Tunny, every summer when we returned to New York. My Mom liked it, too. She called it Daley ham. Naturally, Uncle Sol learned about Tunny's treat, and demanded his, too. He got it.

Chapter III

Prepared to Meet Life Head On

All of the Daley brothers were jacks-of-all-trades, but Uncle Bern was the true artisan. Parpi Daley himself, a jack-of-all-trades, made his sons learn carpentry. He explained that a man who knew carpentry could earn a shilling anywhere in the world. At first, I did not know that the shilling was a monetary unit, but he seldom spoke of the modern coins.

Uncle Bern proved that Parpi Daley was right when he migrated to Canada. He worked as a handyman carpenter at first and earned enough money to pursue his study of plumbing and electricity. He got his certificates in all of them. He studied French formally, and practiced it with Auntie Becky, because he served a bilingual community in Montreal.

If Auntie Becky had liked the United States, they would have made a mint there. Born in the Island of St. Croix, she was an American citizen by birth, but migrated to Canada with her father following the death of her mother, and became a naturalized Canadian citizen. She spoke French, because her father was originally from the Island of Martinique, and he had taught his children the language when they were little. .

Uncle Paul was the only brother who held a university degree. He was an accountant, but he also dabbled in carpentry. Auntie Alexandra had written to Maamie and Parpi Daley and told them that if Paul did not get out of his workroom, she would pick up her children and leave.

She wrote, "With your son, it is from bed to work, and from work to his workshop. Then he reverses it; from work to his workshop, and from the workshop to bed. He eats like a wolf, rushing to get to his workshop. Can't he spend an hour with the children and me, especially after dinner? We have all the desks and tables we need. He might as well be married to his workshop. It gets his full attention. What upsets me most is that my boy, Darius, is just like him. Parpi Daley, you have created a carpentry monster."

Maamie and Parpi Daley wrote to Uncle Paul, and that summer, he took his family to Egypt for their mid-summer holiday. Auntie Alexandra wrote and thanked them. When their children grew up, she joined a woman's club, and socialized with her friends. Uncle Paul never complained.

Uncle Sol mended everything that broke in his house. He bragged that he never called a repairman. He had taken up with a much younger woman after his divorce, and they liked to dance, so he was seldom at home in the evenings. However, he found time to tinker with wood. He had learned a little tailoring when he was a teenager. When he became disgruntled with the slacks on the market, he made his own.

My father, Tunny, was a treasure around our house. He taught Syd and Ejay what he knew about carpentry, and sewing. He and Uncle Sol had actually taken some lessons in tailoring with one of the island's famous tailors at the time, Mr. Hezekiah Piper. Dad made some fancy slacks and jackets. He taught Mom and me how to sew, but Mom took to it more seriously than I did.

The Daley daughters were not carpenters, but they learned to sew, because Maamie Daley had taught them. Auntie Ellie and Auntie Vera were very good at it. They were especially adept at making curtains, bedspreads, and drapes. Their cushions were every bit as professionally made as those available in the finest boutiques in New York City. Auntie Ellie had customers in Barbados, and some as far away as Trinidad and Tobago. One year, Maamie Daley and Auntie Vera sent two bedspreads with matching pillowcases and shams to "Tunny and family, and also to Sol."

Chapter IV

The Fisher's Tale

Uncle Sym, Auntie Vera's husband, was a fisherman by trade, but he, too, knew a little carpentry. He kept his boat, the **Dub-Me-On**, in good repair, and made some of the finest seines in the island.

His greatest joy was the tall fish tales he told us after dinner. He was definitely a fine representative of the Caribbean tradition of adults telling stories at the family's evening gatherings. That was their way of bonding with their children and grandchildren.

Uncle Sym and his partners brought the fish ashore at the bay. Sadie and I went to the bay in the late afternoon when the *Dub-Me-On* docked. Uncle Sym and his men parceled the fish in sets of five or six, according to their sizes, and placed them in wire baskets.

They had large wooden mallets that they used to club the live fish on their heads after the hagglers had made their choices. I liked to hear the villagers barter for fish. A large scale hung from its hook on the boat, but Uncle Sym hardly used it. He guessed the weight, named his price, and seldom changed it, in spite of his disgruntled customers. Their clients liked to haggle, but Uncle Sym often ignored them, so they muttered profanities as they paid him.

A disgruntled elderly man shouted, "Sym Duberry, why in hell do you have a scale? Is it to weigh your conscience after you rob arwe (us)? If you say tree[4] dollurs a pound, and the fish them weigh *tree* pounds, then me could undoostand. Every Tarm, Dick and Harry know you a rob arwe[5]."

Uncle Sym shouted, "Next!"

---

4   three
5   us

"Sym Duberry," a toothless old woman said, "You are one damn tief; a one damn tief you be."

"That's okay, Mrs. Dyer," he said, answering her in kind in the Montserratian lingo. "If me dead out a sea, you a go still bawl foo me."[6]

"A one liar you be, too, Sym Duberry," she said. "Wait 'till you need castor oil," she added. "Me a go make sure you get the one with the extra gripe." The people laughed.

I stared at her. "So that's Lizzie Dyer, the famous castor oil lady," I said to Sadie.

"How did you guess?" she asked.

"My Dad's name is Tunny Daley," I said. "Remember?"

She laughed. Then she told me that it took Maamie and Parpi Daley to hold down her Uncle Tunny and my Auntie Vera for their annual doses of castor oil. It was the late August "purge" before their return to school after the mid-summer holiday. They didn't have flush toilets back in those days.

We laughed out loud one day, when an elderly man, after he had paid Uncle Sym for his fish, said, "Simeon Duberry, Lizzie Dyer is right. You are a damn thief. It's time you live and let live. Look at your damn bang (big) belly."

"Thank you Mr. Tarmy Misset," Uncle Sym said.

Sadie whispered in my ear, "Maggie, don't think Dada is so easy, you know. If we weren't here, he would cuss them, bad. He is very conscious of his stomach. I don't think he believes that the pile of food he eats morning, noon, and night really matters. Check out his plate tonight."

I promised Sadie that I would.

The fishermen had strung and set fish aside for their families, while they were at sea. It was fascinating to watch Uncle Sym and the other fishermen string the fish together by running a fine wire through their gills. Sadie and I took our fish home. Caribbean fish were unlike any that we had seen in the markets in New York. They were multicolored, like the rainbow. I liked the silvery garl and ballahoo, fried dry in Montserrat's own cottonseed oil, and served in a hot pepper, vinegar, and sliced raw onions and scallions mix.

Sadie and Keith were adept at eating fish with bones, but Syd and I were not. Uncle Sym filleted the fish for us just before Maamie Daley prepared them for cooking. Sadie and Keith laughed at us. We stared at

---

6   If I die at sea, you'll still mourn for me.

them as they attacked the fish heads, sucking out their brains with gusto. Sadie said that she also liked to suck the eyes out of the heads.

After dinner, Uncle Sym wore a mischievous smile while he weaved his tales. Maamie Daley said that she had never known anyone with a split between his upper front teeth who was not a liar, "So Sym Duberry must be a liar." That was my cue, but I was very gullible.

"The other day," he began, "just off Redonda, we caught a huge shark."

Uncle Sym opened his arms as large as Montserrat to demonstrate the size of the shark. He was a poker face joker, if ever there was one.

He continued, "That villain chuckled as he fought us. It damn near sunk **Dub-Me-On**. It took all our wit to outsmart him. When we split it open, we found a man's finger with this on it."

He pulled a gold ring from his pocket and placed it on the table.

"Who was the man?" I asked alarmed.

"Only the shark knows, but he'll never talk."

"Suppose it was a woman, Uncle Sym," I said.

"No, Maggie," he assured me. "No woman has a size fourteen finger, but man or woman, it doesn't matter. We had the most delicious shark steaks for dinner that night."

My bowels did a somersault. I felt nauseous. I remembered how I liked the shark steaks, fried crisp in Montserrat's cottonseed oil, and topped with braised onions, garlic, vinegar and green peppers.

Syd said, "Size fourteen? He must have been a giant, Uncle Sym."

Uncle Sym said, "Yes, Syd. But that shark was a Montserratian."

"How do you know that, Uncle Sym?" Syd asked.

"It had a tattoo on its belly. "I'm from Montserrat."

The more I glared at Uncle Sym, the more my mouth watered, so I ran outside. The thought that I had eaten steak from a shark that had eaten a man made me sick. I could hear Sadie and the boys laughing.

The following day, while we were playing, Sadie said, "Maggie, why do you believe Dada's fish stories? They are lies. All fishermen lie. You are a 'doondoo; a real chupitah!' Just think, 'A Montserratian shark with a tattoo on its belly?' I guess you'll believe the one about the mermaids on Redonda, too."

Sadie seldom spoke in the Montserrat lingo, but she called me a "doondoo[7] and a chupitah."[8]

---

7   fool
8   dummy

I defended myself, by saying, "Mermaids? I know they're fantasies. "Besides, marine biologists sometimes mark endangered species to keep track of them."

"Really?" Sadie asked, 'it's a wonder Dada didn't say, 'the shark said, I am a Montserratian.' Trust me. Dada is no marine biologist. Everybody knows Dada is a real joker. Only you believe him. Sometimes, we have turtle for dinner. Maybe the turtles Dada catches are Americans like you and Syd, Maggie. I like turtle."

"Turtle! Shark! Do turtles eat people, too?"

Sadie smiled. "No," she said.

"Where is Redonda?" I asked.

"Don't you remember the rock island in the sea that we see when we travel north to St. John's? That's Redonda."

"Do people live there?"

"No. They get wild donkeys and goats there. Dada and his partners do not fish off Redonda. The barracudas that swim near there are usually poisonous because they eat from the phosphate deposits on the rock."

"Thanks, Sadie," I said.

"Ask Uncle Tunny when you go home about the time he helped Parpi Daley and Uncle Bern catch a donkey on Redonda. Mama said. 'That jackass was so wicked they called him 'Satan'. Satan would take them to a precipice and try to dump them. However, Parpi Daley tamed him."

"Dad told us they had a jackass named Satan, but he did not tell us how they had gotten it," I said.

"You say you want to write about your Montserratian experiences some day, Maggie. Dada has more stories like the one he told last night."

Chapter V

Parpi Daley, Our Ancestors and the Farm

Parpi Daley's farm was located near the mountain under the Soufriere Hills volcano, and on farm days, we joined him there. Maamie Daley also went there, except on Friday mornings, when she had "business" in Town, and on Saturdays when she was a vendor in the public market. Parpi Daley called the volcano "The Mighty Watchman." He said that he was lucky to inherit the land from his grandfather and father, because farms located near the Mighty Watchman were very fertile.

Year after year, we heard the tales of the Daley jumbies.[9] No one ever stole Parpi Daley's produce. It seemed that the farm had a reputation of being haunted. People claimed that my great-grandfather and great-great-grandfather walked the land from dusk to daybreak. Of course, Parpi credited the safety of his farm to the presence of the Mighty Watchman. Sometimes, the volcano let off little puffs of sulfur, and rained pebbles that came rolling down the hill. Upon noting the phenomenon, the people, being very superstitious, claimed the Daley jumbies were stoning them. Parpi helped to prolong the myth.

Seeing a jumbie was the one experience that I longed to have in Montserrat. I would really like to tell my parents that I had seen a jumbie, any jumbie, on one of my returns home.

On farm days, I dressed like Sadie and Maamie Daley, in a loose cotton frock and a broad straw hat. Maamie Daley was happy to make my

---

9   Corrupt for zombies

farm dresses. I helped her for the practice. Auntie Vera and Sadie made Sadie's farm dresses. The boys wore caps, khaki shorts, and short-sleeve cotton shirts, as did Parpi Daley. All of us wore sandals.

Parpi and the boys left for the farm quite early. We joined them there later. We weeded the rows, transplanted some plants, and prepared lunch. We had our lunch in the barn, and lazed about for an hour after lunch. The mid-day sun was scorching, and Maamie Daley tried to avoid it. The men proved to be hardier than we women were.

Parpi Daley taught Syd and me how to separate the weeds from the young plants. I liked to harvest beans, peas, sweet potatoes, tomatoes, and balanjays[10]. We did not use gloves. My hands became rough in a short time. They introduced us to freshly squeezed limejuice as a moisturizer, and I used it regularly.

Like other Montserratian farmers, Parpi Daley also raised animals: sheep, goats, and pigs. Goats were essential, because goatwater, a rich stew, had always been the national dish of Montserrat. Parpi Daley's dogs, Friend and Foe, guarded the huge animals' pen. Their kennel, located behind the stone wall, near the entrance to the pen, had two rooms, one for Friend and the other for Foe. Parpi kept the sheep and goats separated by a fence that divided the pen in two parts. Each part had its own gate. A stone wall enclosed a chain-link fence that surrounded the pen. I walked among the sheep, and played with their lambs. Only Keith was brave enough to challenge Vicious, the boldest ram goat, and the other goats. They were rambunctious and crazy.

I supposed that the Mighty Watchman also protected the animals. There were no intrusions or thefts from the pen. However, Friend and Foe also had a bad reputation. Parpi had learned the art of training dogs from his father and grandfather, and passed it on to his sons and Keith. He trained his dogs to be cross, insisting that they were guard dogs; not pets. No intruders ever got past them, and Parpi Daley liked it that way. However, several signs on the fences reminded all potential thieves of their impending encounter with danger: Vicious Dogs would attack fiercely without warning.

The pigsty was behind the sheep and goat pens. That year, the sows had litters, so they had about twenty pigs. Parpi Daley bragged that he never lost any of his piglets. Many Montserratians abroad still hankered for their gifts of corned pork from home.

---

10   eggplants

When the dogs died, Parpi Daley replaced them. However, Syd and I learned that he always named them Friend and Foe. We told Dad about it, and we had to listen to his story.

"Maggie and Syd," he said, "The present Friend and Foe, would be the great-great-great-grand dogs of those of my childhood. Here is how they got their names. Originally, Parpi had one dog, 'Friend.' One afternoon, Parson Philpotts came to find out why we boys had been absent from confirmation class for two weeks. As they said in Montserrat, 'our arses rang diamond,' which means Parpi tore up our butts, in the Parson's presence. You know the bit about sparing the rod. Parson watched as we got our comeuppance. When the parson was leaving, Bern hid in the cellar and sicced Friend on him. Friend bit him on his calf. This is the first time I'm mentioning it to anyone except my brothers. Bern will still deny it. Parpi was devastated. He believed that not even a dog should touch the Lord's anointed. He grabbed Friend to beat him, but Parson Philpotts objected firmly, saying, 'Dogs are man's best friends, Gabriel.'

"'Who are children, Parson Philpot's?' I wondered.

"Parpi said, 'That may be so, Parson Philpotts. Friend, get out of my sight!' Friend barked hard and left.

"Parson Philpotts said, 'Gabriel, this dog treated me not as a friend, but as a foe.' Although our butts were sore, we had a good laugh that day. When we got the second dog, Parpi named him Foe.

"When we were kids, we dared not mess with the clergy, our teachers, and adults in general. Vera was bold. She shot off with her mouth and took her lumps. Ellie was the saint."

"So you were really bad, Dad?" I asked.

"No, Maggie. I prefer to say as Maamie did, 'Tunny is the most mischievous of my children.' Dad laughed until his eyes filled with tears.

Parpi Daley had one permanent employee, a young man named Percy Matthews, who helped him on the farm. Together, they slaughtered the animals. The slaughter slab was nailed into two large cement stakes not far from the cistern. Parpi Daley kept large barrels of rainwater, caught from spouts that overflowed from the cistern, near the slaughter slab. He and Percy washed the blood away thoroughly with a fowl-smelling disinfectant after each slaughter. I could not stand the smell of the disinfectant. I never learned its name.

Syd and I liked to help Sadie and Keith take the goats and sheep to greener pastures near the farm, and feed the pigs in their sty. In the afternoons, we returned the sheep and goats to their pens. Other goatherds and shepherds had larger flocks than Parpi Daley. They provided meat for the butchers at the weekly market in Plymouth, the capital of the Island, called Town. Parpi sold livestock and meat from time to time, especially during the festive seasons, Easter, Christmas and at Harvest time. After they had explained Harvest to us, we likened it to our Thanksgiving in the U.S.A. However, the church was the focus of their celebration of Harvest.

Syd and I never experienced Harvest in Montserrat because of our school calendar. Sadie told us that the farmers, bakers, and chefs donated their best produce, pastries and dishes to the church. Other members gave their finest fruits, some, exotic.

She salivated as she explained, "We cannot wait to eat Mrs. Bramble's Java plum jam."

At harvest time, the churches donated baskets of vegetables, fruits, baked goods and precooked meals to the sick, the elders, and the shut-ins, and sold the rest of the produce in the churchyard.

One year, one of Mom's colleagues, Veronica Arnold, invited us to her church for their Harvest at the St. Thomas Liberal Catholic Church in Harlem. Caribbean people had brought that part of their culture with them to the Village of Harlem. It was a rousing service. The chancel choir was outstanding. The hymns, "We Plow the Fields and Scatter," and "Come Harvest Time," still linger in my memory. They had many of the fruits and vegetables we knew in the Caribbean, and the largest bread I had ever seen. They had made it in the shape of a cross, and placed it on the altar. I had many slices of it with Maamie Daley's butter and guava jelly. We also bought sugar cane and guinips.

Syd and I learned that there was no dog food in the island, when we saw Maamie Daley collect the scraps from the table for Friend and Foe. She cooked green bananas in their skin, crushed them with gravy, and added them to the scrap. At slaughtering time, Parpi Daley gave them the large bones after he had done his special cuts of meat.

Speaking of organic, everything was fresh, and truly organic, on Maamie Daley's table in the Big House and on the farm. Even Friend and Foe ate organic food. The only thing preserved for the family was the corned pork, that they considered a delicacy.

Maamie Daley prepared hot lunches for us at the farm, every day except on Fridays. She cooked on an open fire, using firewood when the weather was good, and on the indoor grill, using charcoal, when it rained. We ate roast potatoes, roast ripe plantains, roast corned pork, or cooked crayfish. Montserratians roasted chickens. They seldom used the word "baked." Maamie Daley kept a bottle of Montserrat's cottonseed oil at the farm. She also had thyme, garlic, onions, chives, and other fresh herbs at her disposal. The food was always delicious. I learned to identify many of the savory plants. After eating fish, I liked to use sage and lemon tree leaves to deodorize my hands, and then fresh-squeezed limejuice to moisturize them. We chewed on bits of ginger as a breath freshener.

On Friday mornings, while Maamie Daley was in Town on business, we were on our own at the farm. Parpi often took slices of corned pork with him. He said we would roast some sweet potatoes and corn. Keith and Sadie placed the pork on the outdoor grill. While it sizzled, the hissing sound and aroma invaded the farm. I prepared the salad with lettuce, cucumbers, tomatoes, and the fresh salad dressing that Maamie Daley had taught me how to make with cottonseed oil, diced green sweet peppers, limejuice, thyme leaves, diced onions and garlic, a teaspoon of brown sugar, salt, and water, blended together in a glass jar.

"Keith, Parpi Daley said that we would have baked potatoes. The salad is ready, and the pork is almost ready. Where are the potatoes?" I asked.

"They are almost ready, too, Maggie," he said.

"Then, where are they?" I insisted.

"Don't you smell them?" Keith asked.

I breathed deeply, and I inhaled the aroma of baked sweet potatoes.

Sadie led me to a ten-inch deep pit. They had dug the pit, gotten some dried cow dung from a small pile in a corner, lit it, and placed six large sweet potatoes in the pit. They also placed lighted dung on the top, and covered them tightly with a clay dish. The potatoes baked smoothly. I knew I would not eat mine, but Syd joined the others, peeled his, and cut biting portions that he devoured.

Upon seeing my apprehension, Parpi Daley said, "Maggie, dry cow dung is one of the finest fuels we know. It is light, and catches fire fast. It's no wonder the Indians worship the cow. We use her dung for fertilizing and for baking. It hardly smokes. We also know about the cow's milk and her meat. It's a remarkable animal. It is a fine fuel to heat the iron we call the goose."[11]

---

11   A precursor to the steam iron, the goose was made of cast iron and loaded with charcoal.

Syd said, "What about bull dung, Parpi Daley?"

"Son, learn early on that it's a woman's world. They rule everything. Just don't tell my Shug what I said." He laughed heartily.

They watched quietly as I ate my potato.

Percy Matthews had made fresh lemonade with spring water, brown sugar, and fresh squeezed limejuice. Percy's lime drink was delicious. However, they called it "lemonade." Each of us had a tin cup, on which Parpi Daley had soldered handles. It took a number of cups full to quench my thirst. We had no ice, but we did not miss it. I heard that Montserrat had gained fame for its limejuice among the British sailors of long ago. The elder Montserratians taught them how to use it to cure their scurvy.

There was a home garden behind the kitchen of the Big House. Maamie and Parpi Daley sold the food grown on the farm, but kept the homegrown vegetables for the house. Maamie Daley also gave some to the poor and elderly villagers. Because of the lack of refrigeration, we ate fresh-cooked food three times a day. Later on, I had a solid explanation from Maamie Daley why refrigerated food could never be considered fresh.

Caribbean carrots were the worst tasting vegetables I ever ate. They were bitter. Maamie Daley did not scold Syd or me when we pushed food aside on our plates. Just one stern look and we got the message. Therefore, we ate them unwillingly. She said Montserrat's carrots were better than any carrots we could buy in America, because of the rich chemicals produced by the volcano that stood high above Parpi's farm. It also spewed sulfuric gases that Maamie claimed were good for our health, like the carrots. I was not sure that she was right, but I did not argue with her.

Sadie and I took turns getting the vegetables for dinner. I liked when it was my turn. Readers, as you know, I was named Magdalene Elizabeth Daley, II for Maamie Daley. My family called me Mags or Maggie, but Maamie Daley added "Sweetie," her special name for all her granddaughters.

"Mags, Sweetie, go fetch me a cabbage."

I started to leave. "Wait! Think, Maggie, Sweetie. There are Boy, Sym and Vera, Sadie, Keith, Syd, you and I; eight of us, and you know that I prepare a dinner for Percy Matthews six days a week. 'Time was,' she added reminiscing, 'when there were more than eight at my table, my six little Daleys, Boy, me, and any stray that Tunny Daley would invite to dinner.' Bring the biggest head of cabbage, please."

"Maamie Daley, are you talking about my Dad?"

"Who else? Anthony 'Tunny' Daley, my youngest boy, always had uninvited guests for dinner."

"He does the same thing in New York. Sometimes, Mom walks out of the kitchen and lets him finish the cooking. But, Dad can cook."

"Of course, he can. All my sons know how to cook. Boy and I taught them."

Sadie said, "When Uncle Sol visited us from America, he made lasagna. Keith and I ate so much that they thought we would burst. However, Dada cooks, too. Most Montserrat men can cook. Dada cooks the best shark in Montserrat, but you must drink plenty of water. He adds more pepper to Maamie Daley's pepper sauce."

Maamie said, "He learned that from Boy. Thank God, neither Sym nor Boy indulges in too much rum. They get their kick from my hot pepper sauce. Sym's father, Duby, has serious drinking woes."

Sadie became sad, upon hearing her grandfather's name, and Keith stared blankly at the ground.

Chapter VI

"Boy" and "Shug"

"Maamie Daley, why do you call Parpi, Boy?" I asked. I did not expect a lengthy explanation.

"We have known each other since we were little. We, the Corbett family, and the Daley family, were neighbors. My grandfather, Kirnon Corbett, willed the land to my father, Jeremiah Corbett. Papa always wondered about 'that Gabriel Daley. He is too damn polite, to be true. I don't trust him.' Mother would say, 'Corbett, leave the young people alone. Either they are too damn rude, or too polite. Gabriel Daley is a fine young man.'

"Boy began to call me 'Shug' when we were courting under the watchful eyes of my father, and I called him 'Boy.'"

"What's Shug?"

"It's short for Sugar, Mags, Sweetie," she said smiling. "Now, go get the cabbage, Sweetie." She was really laughing, then. Afterwards, she added, "Since I had no brothers, we joined the Corbett's' land with the Daley's land, after our parents died."

"Didn't you have any relatives, Maamie Daley?"

"Not any connected with Kirnon Corbett's land. He had bought it with his own money. My mother was an Alleyne, but they disowned her when she married my father, because they were among the high mucky mucks. What was all that fuss about? Aren't they all dead now? They were merchants in Town, but they were originally from somewhere up the island, and left Montserrat after the 1928 hurricane. It seemed they had lost everything. I warned my children that they must share. When I die, if they fight over any land we own, I'll ask the Lord for the power to haunt them. Remember, children, the word is 'Share!'"

We said in a chorus, "Yes, Maamie Daley."

I found the biggest head of cabbage and took it to Maamie Daley. She washed it in vinegar and cold water, cut it in quarters and then in eighths and showed me how to cut each piece in tiny spaghetti-like strips. She placed them in a large skillet with two teaspoons of red butter, cottonseed oil, diced onions, sliced tomatoes, fresh garlic, one teaspoon of brown sugar and salt. She mixed it well after she had added some ground spices, covered it tightly, and pushed the charcoal aside. It steamed to a crispy delicacy on the hot grill. I could have eaten it, forever. It was that good.

I mentioned coleslaw to Maamie Daley, but she did not know what it was. At that time, mayonnaise was not popular in Montserrat.

In the early afternoon, Percy dropped Maamie Daley, Sadie and me home, to get the dinner started. He returned to the farm. Parpi Daley, Keith and Syd remained there until around 6:00 p.m.

We ate fish often: fried, baked, stewed, or steamed. Maamie Daley served poultry, mainly chicken, but sometimes duck once a week. Occasionally, at the farm, we ate wild rabbit when Percy and Parpi Daley were lucky to trap one. My stomach longed for a hot dog with sauerkraut and a juicy hamburger with relish and ketchup.

When I complained about the frequent fish dinners, Maamie Daley said, "I'll have you know, Maggie, Sweetie that fresh fish is the healthiest food we can eat. All my friends, who have been to America and back, talk of the twice dead frozen fish you eat up there. 'You buy it stale,' they say, 'and then you freeze it.' When you return home, you will be healthy and strong. Learn to pick fresh fish. If the eyes are red and the gills are not healthy looking, do not choose them. Let your nose be your guide, too. Above all, don't freeze stale fish. Anyhow, you may never eat twice dead fish again, Mags, Sweetie."

Syd never fussed about eating fish. He liked it. I grew to like it, too, especially Maamie Daley's fried garl and ballahoo. When I asked for ketchup, nobody knew what I meant. Soon, I learned to eat my fish with the hot pepper sauce that Maamie made with sliced onions, whole cloves, green tomatoes, bird peppers, brown sugar, vinegar and mustard that Mom had sent her from America. Her preparation of hot pepper sauce was a sinus cleanser. We sneezed as if we were the members of a sneezing chorus. Nobody bothered to say, "God bless you!"

Early on, Maamie Daley had warned us, "My little American darlings, in this house we cook one pot. We are mainly fish eaters. On Sundays, we eat meat, or roast chicken, and now and then, I stew a fowl. On festive occasions, I make goat water. We have to learn to 'cut and contrive'. We do not ask for what is not on our table. We give thanks to God for what He has provided. Some day, you'll appreciate these fresh meals."

"What is cut and contrive, Maamie Daley?" I asked.

"It means to 'make do,' Mags, Sweetie. Remember, we eat what the Lord provides, and we must be grateful for it."

"I never heard Dad use that saying, Maamie Daley. His favorite is 'One fall down is good enough for monkey; two are too much.'"

"Yes, he learned that early on, when he never gave up on his tricks, until he was caught."

"Maamie Daley, Dad said that a monkey never falls twice from the same limb, no matter how large the forest is," Syd said. "Is that true?"

"Yes, Syd. Your father spent some weeks in St. Kitts with his godparents. He used to join his friends and go to tease the little monkeys in their rain forest, called the River. They teased the monkeys whose aim was good enough to hit them with green mangoes."

"Maamie Daley, when we misbehave and don't listen to Mom, Dad says, 'Children, obey your mother. Pickny who no hear what Maamie say drinks pepper water, lime and salt.' We laugh. Mom laughs too. She thinks Montserrat's sayings are hysterical," I said, laughing.

"Just think of it Mags, Sweetie. Would you like to have a drink made of pepper, water, lime and salt?"

"No way!" I said.

"It's a saying that means 'Those who do not obey will suffer.'"

"I figured it out, Maamie Daley," I said.

I thought I would welcome Sundays when they cooked meat, but upon seeing it, I remembered the slaughtering slab where Parpi Daley and Percy killed the animals in plain view. They tied the feet and mouths of the animals, placed them on the thick slab, and slaughtered them. I was horrified at the sight of blood spurting from the wounds and running like streams. I swore I could never eat meat at the Big House. However, Maamie Daley' stews were so good! The aroma permeated the air and made the kitchen and the big yard smell like a chef's paradise. To smell them was to crave them!

They caught the blood of the hogs when they slaughtered them. It was one of the ingredients in their black or blood pudding. It resembled our sausage, but had many herbs, cassava bread or rice and ground lean pork stuffed in the intestines of the hogs. I refused to eat it, but Syd looked forward to eating it.

"Maggie," he said, "you do not know what you are missing."

"That's okay, Syd," I said.

I knew when Maamie Daley would cook chicken on Sundays. Keith and Syd ran down the chickens for Sunday dinner on Tuesdays or on Wednesdays. They tied them in the shade of one of the trees. They fed them only spring water, thereby purging them for the kill. Keith was the master at wringing[12] the chickens' necks, dumping them in boiling water, and plucking their feathers. He removed the liver and gizzards, and threw the rest of the intestines into the large kerosene tin where Maamie washed them, and cooked them with breadfruit and Callao for the pigs. My dear brother, Syd, learned the task of killing chickens quickly.

I liked when Maamie Daley served baked chicken. Her stuffing was the best in the world. She made cassava bread stuffing that was unique in aroma and flavor. Soon, I ate the stews and baked or fried chicken without thinking of the poor animals that had died so mercilessly. I was fast becoming a true Montserratian.

Maamie Daley saved the chicken feet and heads for the broth in which the vegetables were cooked. Everyone got an enamel cup of the broth with his dinner. I just accepted it since I was six years old. They also used the enamel cups to serve hot "coco tea" and "coffee tea" at breakfast time. In Montserrat, all hot drinks served at breakfast are known as "teas." They also had bush tea, made from aromatic weeds that grew abundantly around the big yard. My favorite bush teas were anise seed, fever grass, and ram goat bush. We grew mint in our backyard in St. Albans, Queens, New York, so mint was not exotic to me.

The only bush tea I did not appreciate was the eucalyptus tea. One summer, I caught a cold, and Maamie Daley made me a cup of eucalyptus tea. It was the worst thing I ever drank. I hated anything bitter. However, the moment I drank it, I felt the clearing of my sinuses, and then I coughed up the mucous on my chest. I had to drink the insipid brew for three days.

---

12   twisting

Maamie told me, "You have to drink it, Maggie, Sweetie. It will not kill you, but it may cure you;" and cure it did.

My mother always wanted to know what we had learned from being with Parpi on his farm, particularly, and about our summer vacation in general. The cow dung fuel was at the top of my list, that year. Mom could not believe it. I was surprised to hear Dad's explanation to her.

"Lisa, cow dung is one of the finest fuels on earth. When I was a boy, we stored it for cooking on raining days. It makes a damn good fertilizer, too. The next time we go to Montserrat, I'll bake you some potatoes."

He said exactly what Parpi Daley had told us. Mom cringed as she thought of Dad's promise.

Mom said, "No, thank you, Love. I wouldn't eat them. Honey", she asked, "What about bull dung?"

Dad said, "In the world of dung, the cow is the queen. Nobody ever speaks of bull dung."

I thought of how much my father was like my grandfather, Parpi Daley. Then it hit me, nobody ever used cow dung as an expletive. We hear, "Bull sh...!" I suppose that's in its wet state.

Maamie Daley told us tales too. One day at the farm, I stopped to look at a flock of black doves in flight. Maamie Daley used that incident to tell us about her mother's funeral. She said that after the gravediggers had placed the last shovels of dirt on the box, two black doves circled the area. They scrutinized the mourners and then flew out to sea. When the family got home, they saw a flock of black doves circling their land. Then, two of them separated from the flock and circled their house. They dove down, flew through the open door and out an open window.

"What did that mean, Maamie Daley?" Sadie asked. Evidently, she, too, was hearing the story for the first time.

"Sadie, Sweetie, I was too sad to consider what it meant at that time, but later at the wake, I heard the older folks saying that Mummah had joined with Pupah and was stating their presence. Whenever I see black doves in flight, I remember my parents."

"Do you believe what the old folks said, Maamie Daley?" I asked.

"Oh yes, Mags, Sweetie. They told the tales, as they knew them. Remember, I am an old woman now. I have to tell you about these things."

That sounded funny to me. Maamie Daley was just Maamie Daley. I never thought of her as being old. I looked at her face and saw the clearest, unwrinkled skin. I did not know, then, how old she was, and I did not ask, because it did not really matter.

Maamie and Parpi Daley did not spoil Syd and me. They had many grandchildren, and we were just two of them. Besides, Mom had warned Maamie and Parpi not to indulge us. For reasons unclear to me, then, the islanders revered their American-born relatives, especially the children. They liked to hear our Yankee accent, and were alarmed when we spoke their lingo. Our Canadian cousins also spoke like us. They sounded like New Yorkers.

But in America, when I was in elementary school, a family migrated to our neighborhood from England, and everyone was agog over their British accent. Maybe criticizing or liking foreign accents is a people thing.

Chapter VII

Our Canadian Cousins

Speaking of our Canadian cousins, I remember the year when Uncle Bern's sons, Vincent and James Daley of Montreal, visited Montserrat. They were handsome, well-dressed young men with money to spend. Maamie Daley did not take their money from them. They were too old for that. They were girl crazy, and Maamie Daley was not pleased with their behavior. They asked Parpi Daley and Uncle Sym to introduce them to all the girls in the village. They brought their ten-speed bicycles with them. Uncle Bern had suggested to the boys that they take their bicycles to Montserrat. Maybe he thought that his sons wanted to explore the island. They left after breakfast, around 6:30 a.m., and did not return until dinnertime. The neighbors began to gossip about them. Then, Vincent showed his martial arts training when he beat up two brothers, because he had made a move on their girlfriends and sisters, and they challenged him.

Maamie Daley wrote to Uncle Bern, and asked him to write to them. He did, but they pursued the girls in a more covert manner. They went out partying every weekend and did not return until the roosters crowed. Going to church was out of the question for them. Syd and Keith left the backdoor open for them, after the rest of us had fallen asleep. Vincent and James bribed them to be their accomplices. Auntie Vera scolded them, but never in Uncle Sym's presence, because he would have defended them. I overheard one of their little discussions concerning Vincent and James. The doors between the flats were wide open.

"Vee, the boys are on holiday," he told her. "Let them have their fun."

"Fun? Fun? Is that what you think they're having?"

"I had a long chat with them, and they know the ropes. Trust me, Vee. They can take care of themselves."

"What about the young ladies? Suppose they were your daughters?"

"Young women who are up and out carousing at those ungodly hours, are not ladies. Every night, before my parents went to sleep, they checked our beds. They didn't trust me and they watched my sister, Lydia, like a hawk. When Sebastian Duberry was in his prime, even I didn't challenge him."

"I don't care what you say, Sym Duberry. They should respect their grandparents' home."

"Have they brought any of their young women here, Vee?" Uncle Sym asked.

"That would be the last straw," she said fuming. "I would personally help them to pack."

"Vee, Vincent is almost twenty and James is over eighteen. They are not exactly little boys."

"Thank you for your observation, Sym," she said.

However, Auntie Vera took it upon herself to write to her brother, and told him, "Bern, if you want to spare your mother's life, keep Vincent and James in Montreal. Montserrat is too small to contain them."

Uncle Bern wrote to the boys telling them what their aunt had said, and they told it to Syd and Keith. Keith said they thought it was the funniest thing they had ever heard.

They did go with us to the farm one Wednesday. They rode on one of Parpi Daley's donkeys, while Syd and Keith rode their bicycles. They moved around, found one of the little lakes, and swam butt naked there. They asked Syd and Keith to join them, but they did not. Syd and Keith accompanied them on their climb to the summit of Chances Peak, Parpi's Mighty Watchman, because Keith was very familiar with the path. They enjoyed the view of the Island from there. They photographed all they had seen. They had lunch with us, and left, saying that some young ladies had planned a picnic for them on Fox's Bay. Sadie reminded me that Wednesday was half-day in Montserrat, and that all the stores and businesses had shut down at midday.

Vincent and James hugged Sadie and me, kissed Maamie Daley, shook hands with Parpi and the boys, mounted their bicycles, and sped away. Maamie Daley shook her head as they raised the dust on the unpaved road. Parpi Daley, no doubt saw a reflection of himself as a young man in them, and just smiled at their antics.

Syd and Keith asked Vincent and James to leave their bicycles with them, and they promised to do so. On the eve of their return to Montreal, they praised Maamie Daley for her hospitality. Maamie had prepared the famous Montserrat goat water for them.

"Maamie Daley, you are the greatest. The goat water was delicious, Vincent said hugging and kissing her. "We just loved being here with you, and we'll be back next year. We may even return at Christmas. The girls told us about the festive times. Your girls are fine," he added, with a longing in his eyes. "I had a hard time choosing just one." He winked at Auntie Vera, who stared at him.

Maamie Daley pursed her lips, but said nothing.

James said, "Maamie and Parpi Daley, you'll be seeing a lot of me. We had a blast. Dad didn't tell us that Montserrat is so fine. Vin is right. We'll be back. Parpi Daley, I'd like to have a sleepover with some friends in your cabin up there in the hills. We'll break out some bottles of rum and beer and raise hell. When it gets too hot to handle, we'll jump in one of those nearby ponds, and cool off."

Parpi laughed, and Maamie Daley glared at him. He wiped the laughter off his face so quickly, I thought his poor face would crack. Auntie Vera blushed. Uncle Sym put on his deadpan face, like the shark he had caught, but Syd and Keith laughed heartily.

I knew Maamie Daley would have her say. "Vincent and James, stand still so I can fix your features in my mind. You are Daleys, all right. You spent three weeks in Montserrat, but I can't say I know you, because you were seldom here. However, I am happy you came. I pray that you are not leaving any trouble[13] behind," she concluded.

"Trouble?" James asked.

Vincent said hurriedly, "No, Maamie Daley. We are too smart for that. We know how to avoid trouble."

That did it. Parpi Daley and Uncle Sym laughed, rose and patted James and Vincent on their backs, and hugged them.

Maamie's speech did not prevent them from having their last-night trysts. However, they returned "at a reasonable time," most likely around midnight. We were up on time to say good-bye to them that morning. They emptied their pockets, spread all of their unspent Eastern Caribbean money on the table, kissed us, and went to the car that was waiting

---

13   Babies. Like us in New York, Vincent must have heard his dad speak of "not leaving any girl pregnant behind.

for them. Sadie said she recognized the young woman who came to get them.

"That was Mathilde Pierre Rostand, one of our French teachers," she quipped.

They shouted from the open window of the car, "Love you Daleys and Duberrys. So long!" They blew us kisses as they rode away.

I shouted, "Au revoir Vin and Jim. Bon voyage!"

Auntie Vera told us that Jim and Vin returned at Christmas, but Auntie Becky was with them. They didn't have their trysts at Parpi's cabin. However, they ran the girls down. They met two young women from LaSalle, Quebec, who were also vacationing in Montserrat, and they exchanged addresses and telephone numbers. Auntie Becky told Auntie Vera that they studied hard, got excellent grades, worked part time, and earned quite a bit of money. They were courteous, so she ignored their "playing around."

"Trust me Vee! They know exactly where I'm coming from. I told them, if they're out there, they'd better take care of themselves. As long as they are under my roof, I want no babies before I attend a wedding, and I want no husbands or fathers knocking on my door."

Then she reminded Auntie Vera that the Daley brothers were no saints.

"Remember, Vee, I am married to the oldest one, the model for all the others."

She also indicated that she and Bern had informed their sons well about proper social behavior, they were happy they were grown men, according to the law, and nobody was complaining, so they left "well enough alone".

We heard that Vin and Jim had their fling that Christmas, but Auntie Vera left them to their mother.

Later I learned that James majored in accounting and received his degree. He worked for a private firm. Vincent quit college, became a chauffeur to a wealthy businessman and his family who adored him, bought some real estate around Montreal with his parents' help, and lived a leisurely life in one of his houses with his live-in girlfriend. James was not married. He still lived at home with his parents. Sometimes, on weekends, Vincent moonlighted, by driving a bus from Montreal to Quebec City, "just for the heck of it."

Once, Vincent had told his parents that he wanted to move across the border to the United States and drive an eighteen-wheeler from coast to coast. His parents were alarmed.

Uncle Bern told Dad, "Tunny, it put the fear of God in me. I beg you to pray for my Vincent Daley. Maamie is praying for him in Montserrat, and Becky's family is praying in St. Croix. May the Lord have mercy on Vincent Daley!"

Dad made us get on our knees, and we prayed for Vincent Daley. Evidently, prayers worked. We never heard about that situation again.

Chapter VIII

Weekends at the Daleys and Duberrys

A Different Kind of Marriage

Maamie Daley "settled her accounts" (paid her bills) on her trip to Town on Friday mornings. She did her general shopping, and went to the bank. She made sure she had enough change to serve her customers at the market on Saturday, cashed money gifts from her children abroad, made deposits to their savings account, and placed Percy's wages in a little leather pouch that Parpi had made for that purpose. No one at the Big House had a checking account. They were not yet popular among the ordinary folks in Montserrat.

If Maamie Daley did not get a ride home, she hired a car. The chauffer, a villager who knew her quite well, would help her place her purchases inside the house. He then dropped her at the farm to help "wrap up things."

There were several rippling brooks near Parpi Daley' farm, and on Fridays, we fished for crayfish under the rocks and placed them in large vats of brook water for the market the following day. Syd had become perceptive at knowing just where to find them. Sadie and I went to a separate brook. We screamed when they nipped our fingers and the boys made fun of us. One year I took one dozen pairs of light rubber gloves to Montserrat. Only Sadie and I used them to pull the crayfish from their hiding places. The boys wanted to prove their machismo, but I thought they proved their idiocy.

Parpi Daley grew everything on his farm, but that year, he had an abundance of corn, string beans, and carrots. Montserrat's fertile soil was especially kind to carrots. The sweet potatoes were sweeter and bigger than any we had seen in New York, but the carrots were bitter. Once again, I heard how the rich deposits of fertilizers from the volcano replenished the soil. Maamie Daley reminded us how fortunate we Daleys were to own that land.

On Fridays, we also harvested the vegetables and herbs that Maamie sold on Saturdays at the market in Town. Late on Friday afternoons, Parpi, Percy and the boys loaded the truck. Early on Saturday mornings, Percy drove the truck to the market accompanied by Maamie Daley. Parpi Daley and the boys loaded the surplus on his donkeys and left for the market. Sometimes, Sadie and I carried the baskets of thyme and scallions, "hubbs and chibble' in Montserrtian, because they were not heavy. We had helped Maamie Daley to tie them in a cone-shaped package made of cheyney bush, a large leaf banana-like plant that bore no fruit. I learned to tie "hubbs and chibble" as neatly as Maamie Daley and Sadie, using any of the vines that grew freely around the farm. The cheyney bush, nature's own foil, was widely used for baking breads in the stone oven, and for cooking ducknas, made of sweet potatoes or cornmeal with a host of other ingredients.

One Friday afternoon on the farm, one of Parpi's donkeys dropped dead. All of us helped to dig his grave. Parpi was sad. He actually kissed his old jackass good-bye, after he had whispered something in his ear.

Since they had surplus vegetables for Saturday's market, we had to get them down to the Big House before dusk. After they filled the truck and the bags that the other donkey would carry, Maamie Daley filled five trays with corn, and made five large buns from a vine called "whiney." Maamie placed a bun on Sadie's head and then the tray.

I said, "Maamie, what's that green bun?"

"It's a wad, Mags, Sweetie," she said.

"A wad? What's a wad?"

She placed a tray of corn on my head. It pressed hard on my scalp, in spite of my straw hat. I started to droop under the load. She removed the tray, placed a wad on my head, and then replaced the tray. The load seemed much lighter. The wad also leveled the tray, thus making it easier to carry. She then demonstrated it on Syd's head. That day, Syd and I took our trays of corn to the Big House, but whereas the natives were able to balance theirs while they swung their arms freely, we had to hold ours in place. Percy returned to the Big House with the truck for a second load that Saturday morning, and took the surplus to the market. Sadie and I rode with him.

Syd and I often saw other vendors balancing their trays of goods on their heads, but it had become a natural sight for us. After we had experienced carrying our trays of corn to the Big House, I respected Parpi Daley's donkeys. By the following Saturday, Parpi Daley had bought another donkey in St. Johns in the north. It was rumored that a certain Mr. Herman Sweeney, whom Parpi knew quite well, caught and tamed wild donkeys and goats in the rock island called Redonda located off the coast of Montserrat.

Saturday was Maamie Daley's market day. I liked her market outfit. She wore a full-length green farmer's dress with long side pockets, and a white pinafore with a large front pocket. She wore a red, green, and black bandana, tied in the African style. In spite of the large pockets in her pinafore and dress, she kept all her paper money in the fold of her bandana. I saw some of the other women turn, look around, and quickly slip their paper money in their bosoms. Sadie called them their "teats" banks, a term she said she had learned from her father.

"You say you want to write about your Caribbean experience and their sayings, some day, Maggie? Just listen to Dada when he tells stories like the one he told about the Montserrat shark, or when he is just joking around."

"Okay, Sadie," I said. "Thanks again. I'll do that."

"Sellers here in the market speak their own lingo, too. Listen carefully and learn," she added.

The market was a meeting place for folks from all the villages, east, west, north and south. It was there that they greeted old friends, gossiped, and made their purchases of fresh produce, before returning home. It resembled our farmers market, but with a Caribbean touch. I wondered if they had no home gardens, or if the soil were not as rich in all parts of the island. I did not understand why they had to come to the market to shop, when they could grow their own vegetables at home.

I noticed that while Maamie Daley was distracted, Sadie and Keith sneaked away. They walked to the Village of Cork Hill, about two miles north of Town, to visit their grandfather, Sebastian Duberry, "Duby," who was an alcoholic. Their parents did not want them to associate with him, because he spoke profanities and badmouthed them. Sadie said her parents got what they deserved. She and Keith loved their Grandpa Duby. They told me that they had never heard him curse anybody. When they returned, Maamie Daley pretended that they had never left. I heard her scold Auntie Vera once, telling her that she and Sym should not deny Duberry his right to see his grandchildren.

"You and Sym are wrong, Vee," she said adamantly. "Just you wait Vera Duberry! If you think your children are precious, you'll find out who your grandchildren are."

Auntie Vera pouted, but she did not respond. According to Maamie Daley, Duby was bad enough before, but when his wife died and his daughter, Lydia, left home, he gave his soul to the spirit in the rum bottle.

While Sadie and Keith were gone, Syd and I worked as spies for Maamie Daley. We went from stall to stall checking to see which vegetables were scarce and which were bountiful. Maamie practiced the marriage of vegetables, and she used the information we gathered to make her plans. That Saturday, only Maamie had string beans. She married the string beans to the carrots. Those who wanted string beans had to buy carrots. She parceled them out side by side on one of the four long tables that formed her cubicle.

The first client said, "Morning Mother Daley!" and reached for the beans.

Maamie Daley mumbled something while eyeing the customer. I thought that she was not at all courteous.

"They're married!" Maamie said in the Montserrat lingo, "Dem a married!" standing tall and looking the woman in her face.

"To what?" the customer asked indignantly.

"The carrots," Maamie replied defiantly.

"I don't need carrots," she responded in Montserratian. (Me no need carruts.)

She reached for the string beans again. Maamie Daley moved determinedly closer to her. I realized for the first time how tall she was. In a clear voice, she repeated that the two vegetables were married, saying, "Since you a play deef, lay me tell you oogain, dem a married.[14]" The

---

14   Since you are pretending to be deaf, let me tell you again, they are married.

woman backed off, muttering profanities, and Maamie returned to her seat, choopsing (sucking her teeth).

Parpi Daley was a quiet man. He observed the scene from nearby. After that incident, he walked about the market, talking to his friends. He left all negotiations to Maamie Daley. She said that if it were "up to Boy," he would give away all the fruits of his labor. "Damn fool!" she muttered, although she, also, was rather generous. Normally, by 4.00 p.m., Maamie had sold everything, the wedded veggies, and the unmarried ones.

Parpi Daley allowed Percy to use the truck for his personal business on Saturdays. However, he had to return to the market by 3:45. Maamie Daley did not interfere, although someone told her that he went as far as the Village of Rendezvous to see his grandmother, and then to his aunt in Salem. They never had to wait on Percy. He always returned the truck on time.

I liked the fruit that Montserratians called manciport. In some countries, they call them mammy apple. Percy often brought manciports from his aunt's property on Gun Hill Mountain, in Salem. As a reward, Syd and I took Percy T-shirts from New York. Dad also liked him, and sent him sneakers, and work boots.

"Maggie, tell Mr. Tunny I say thanks. All the Daleys are good to me. I have been with Parpi Daley since I was eighteen," he said. He wrote a brief note of thanks to Dad. I was surprised at his handwriting and the contents of the note. They were quite good. Even Percy spoke the King's English in Maamie Daley's presence. She demanded it.

Before we left the market on Saturdays, Parpi and Maamie Daley put their heads together and "reasoned." They spoke of the receipt of the day, and then she gave him his weekly stipend. It was a fascinating ritual, worthy of being filmed, and I never missed it. She counted his money and placed it in his outstretched palm. He counted it quietly along with her. He held his palm high in front of her nose, and she added a few more dollars. After the third count, she stood and eyed him. He placed the money in his age-old wallet, put it in his pocket, and walked away shaking his head. Sadie, Keith, Syd and I kept our eyes on him. He whistled, motioned "Come!" and we ran to him. He took us to the sweets shop. In Montserrat, they call candies, sweeties. Each of us could choose four dollars worth of sweeties. I liked the jawbreakers, those hard caramel-flavored candies and the "pull pulls," the sticky long sweets of all flavors. Syd liked the coconut

37

candies and pear drops. Sadie and Keith liked a mixture of all of them. Parpi then took us back to Maamie Daley.

Percy normally entered the shop after we had chosen our sweeties. By then the queue was long. He had preordered and paid for his chocolates, and went to collect them. He often left with a large lollypop, sporting a bubble jaw, and a stick hanging from his lips.

Percy, Parpi and the boys put the empty trays and bags on the truck at closing time. Percy returned them to the shed at the Big House right after he had counted his wages, thanked Maamie Daley, and pocketed the leather pouch in which Maamie had placed it. On weekdays, Percy often waited for his dinner that Maamie Daley had packed for him, took it home, and ate it; but never on Saturdays. He had told Maamie Daley that his girlfriend was waiting for him not far from our house, and after saying goodbye, he ran to meet her. They ate out on Saturdays.

"That's a smart modern young woman," Maamie Daley said. "She waits for her man when he has money in his pocket."

Upon hearing that, Auntie Vee placed her arms akimbo, stared at Maamie Daley, shook her head, and smiled.

When the weather was good, Sadie and I walked with Maamie Daley to visit some old friends who still lived in Town. When it rained, Maamie Daley, Sadie and I rode home with Percy in the truck. Maamie Daley often scolded him about his fast driving, so he practically crawled to the Big House when she was in the truck. Parpi Daley rode home on one donkey, and Syd and Keith rode the other. Keith said they normally got home before Parpi Daley, because he stopped along the way to greet his friends.

I liked to walk with Sadie and Maamie Daley in the cool of the early evening. The setting sun with its orange glow was on our right as we headed south. The sunsets in Montserrat were unlike any I had seen in New York. I learned later that it was partly because of their golden reflections on the silvery waters of the Caribbean Sea. One evening, I watched the sun as it made its descent into the horizon and literally dropped out of sight, leaving a dark shadow behind.

Auntie Vera fussed with Maamie Daley on Saturdays when we walked home.

"For God's sake Maamie, you work like a mule all week on the farm and in this house. You are not a pauper. Can't you hire a car or take a bus on Saturdays after you spend all day on your feet in the market? Why don't you spend some money? Don't save it for my children. I told them already that Sym and I will educate them, and then they will be on their own. You know that my brothers send me money often, thinking they should reward me for staying home with you and Parpi, and they are more generous to you. You have never, ever, received an empty letter from my brothers and sister. You're a miser, Maamie."

"Have I ever complained to you, Vera Duberry?" Maamie asked.

"No, Maamie."

"Have I ever asked you for a loan?"

"No, Maamie."

"Then, stay out of my business! I am not bothering with you. Let me stretch these two legs that the Lord gave me, as long as I can. I have some friends who will be happy if they could get out of bed."

Auntie Vera shrugged her shoulders and walked away.

Sadie said, "Maamie Daley, don't bother with Mama. Keep on using your **'M-11.'**"

"You're right, Sadie, Sweetie. My **M-11** was never in better shape."

Maamie Daley strutted around the room, raising her legs very high. I was still wondering what the heck the **M-11** was. Upon seeing my inquiring look, Sadie explained what "**M-11**" was. She said, the "M" stands for Montserrat, and the "11" stands for the two legs that hang parallel to one another.

When I finally understood, I said, "Oh, I see."

"In your case, Maggie, your "M" would mean "Maggie. You were not born in Montserrat."

"I get it. I like that. I'll tell Dad when I get home. Don't drop me to the store, Dad! I'll use my **M-11**. Wait a minute, Sadie," I reasoned. Shouldn't it be **M-one-one**? You make it sound like we have eleven legs."

"Go ahead, Maggie," she said. "You, Americans, like to change things, but don't mess with our patois. Accept it, or leave it alone. It is **M-11**, okay?"

"Okay, Sadie. **M-11** it is."

Getting back to what Auntie Vera had said, Maamie Daley was cheap. Parpi Daley told us so every Saturday after she had given him his allowance, but Syd and I already knew that. When we left New York, Mom and Dad gave us spending money, but Maamie Daley took it from us when we arrived at the Big House. She did not want us spending money too freely in the island. She said children should not spend what they had not earned.

Yet, when Mr. Piper, the ice cream man, rang the bell of his cart in the road near our house, she gave the four of us money to get ice cream. However, we had to return the change to her. She returned our money to us at the airport just before we boarded the plane. If Vin and Jim had come when they were younger, she would have taken every cent from them, too, and returned it when they were ready to board their flight.

Only Sadie defended Maamie Daley. She said that Maamie Daley had opened accounts for Keith and her, and deposited $500.00 or more after their midsummer holidays. That was their way of paying for their help on the farm. Syd and I got gifts of sweets, Montserrat T-shirts, and other island souvenirs as our gifts from Maamie Daley. Maamie and Parpi always sent Dad and Uncle Sol's corned pork, tea bush, and peeled and sliced dasheen.

Maamie Daley used to buy school shoes and socks for Sadie and Keith, but Mom and Dad began to send them from America, since Sadie and I, and Keith and Syd used the same sizes.

Keith and Sadie could not wait to open their packages when we arrived at the Big House. Their excitement matched ours on Christmas morning, when we ran to see what was under the Christmas tree for us. Their names were on their packages in our luggage. Mom was always sure to send Auntie Vera a dress or two, stockings, and fancy underwear. Dad sent shirts and slacks for Uncle Sym. They sent nightgowns and pajamas for Maamie and Parpi Daley, until they protested.

"Why do Tunny and Lisa send us so much sleepwear?" Maamie asked. "We are not bedridden."

I told them of Maamie's complaint, and Mom said, "Maamie is right. After all, they are still very spry."

Following their complaint, they sent Maamie church dresses, underwear and other clothing, and slacks and shirts for Parpi Daley. Occasionally, they sent them shoes. When Parpi saw Percy's boots, he asked for a pair, and got it. Dad also added a pair for Uncle Sym.

Normally, my parents joined with Uncle Sol, and sent the Daleys and the Duberrys a barrel of foodstuff at Christmas. They liked Virginia ham, so my parents were sure to pack at least two of them. They also received packages from Uncle Bern in Canada, and Uncle Paul in England. Maamie and Parpi Daley shared much of their gifts with their elderly friends and with poor families.

I found out later that Parpi Daley gave some of his pajamas and other clothing from America to Sebastian Duberry. Dad did not mind. He said he liked Duby. One year, he sent him a pair of shoes and a pair of sneakers, (soft walkers in Montserrat), and one dozen socks, in the Christmas barrel. He wrote to thank Dad. We read the letter. Duby Duberry was a very intelligent man.

I told Maamie Daley about his letter and of how intelligently Duby had expressed himself. She said, "Mags Sweetie, Duby is very crabbit."

"Crabbit? What's that?"

"Intelligent," she said.

One Saturday, Syd and I finally met Sebastian Duberry. He had entered the market at the far end. I wondered why Sadie and Keith had not left the market earlier. He beckoned them to come, and they ran to him. He was a tall man with a light complexion and the largest cat eyes I had ever seen. Sadie resembled him. Keith called us and introduced us to Grandpa Duby. We automatically called him Grandpa Duby.

"So you are Tunny's children," he said. "I am so pleased to meet you. Your father is very kind to me. God bless you all."

We shook hands. I noticed that his face was blotchy, but he did not seem drunk to me. I turned around and saw Maamie Daley gazing at us. She had seen us with Grandpa Duby.

"Sebastian Duberry, mind your manners and come and greet me, as you ought!" she shouted over the hubbub of the market place. Maamie Daley had a big mouth.

Keith and Sadie held his hand, and we walked back to Maamie's stall. Maamie hugged him, and smoothed his hair. Parpi joined us. Grandpa Duby said he was in Town on business. He seemed a little uncomfortable around Maamie Daley, so Parpi Daley led him away. They walked around the market together stopping now and then to make their point. I learned later that Maamie usually scolded him about his drinking, and he would cry.

I did not see when Grandpa Duby left the market. Keith and Sadie must have left with him. They returned to the market shortly afterwards.

Sadie and Keith drew Syd and me together. Sadie told us, "Please do not tell our parents that we visit our grandfather. I love Grandpa Duby. Mama and Dada were wrong to tell him to stay away from us, and Maamie Daley told them so. When they badmouth him, I get angry as hell," she concluded. "But they taught us to respect them. Grandpa Duby is Dada's father. Why doesn't he respect Grandpa Duby? Isn't that what the Americans call a double standard, Syd?"

"Yes, Sadie," he said.

"Grandpa Duby should visit Parpi Daley, but he doesn't want to confront Mama and Dada. Sometimes they meet secretly in Town on Saturdays. Other times, Parpi Daley visits him in Cork Hill. Montserrat people are damn fast (nosey), and someone told Mama that they saw Parpi Daley in Grandpa Duby's house. When she asked Parpi Daley about it, he said, 'Vee, mind your manners. Do not question your father!'"

"Good for Parpi Daley," I said.

I could not wait to tell my parents of my introduction to the wad. I had practiced patiently, until I, too, could balance loads on my head while swinging my arms freely. Dad was delighted that we had learned to carry loads on our heads. He claimed that it was an African tradition that became popular in Montserrat and the other islands. Syd had documented everything in colored photos.

Upon my return to New York, I made a wad with my bath towel, filled our largest pot with water, balanced it on my head, and walked into the living room. I circled the room, swinging my arms freely. Mom placed the photo of me with my load aside, and applauded me. Ejay clapped and laughed. Mom kissed him.

"Mags, you are a true Caribbean woman," Mom said. "Look Tunny! Maggie is wonderful!"

That was the first time Mom had called me "woman" and I was happy.

I said, "Thank you Mom, Sweetie."

Later, Mom had the photo enlarged and framed. One day, Ejay walked into the room balancing Syd's skateboard on his head, swinging his arms as I had done in my demonstration. We applauded him. He took his bow and left the room.

Chapter IX

Other Distractions of the Daleys

We played with the children in the village, in the afternoons, and especially on moonlit evenings. We gathered at the seashore to swim and have fun on Sundays after Sunday school and morning service. Sadie's friend, Virginia Charles and her brother, Craig, were their closest neighbors. Their father, Percival Charles, known as Legs, no doubt because he had very long legs, was the village tailor. Jamella Charles, their mother, was a quiet woman. She did not work, but helped her husband in his tailor shop. I learned later that she had had a stroke from which she had never fully recovered, after the birth of Craig.

When we went to the beach, our Montserratian friends used to leave us in the shallow waters at the shoreline, because they swam "like fishes". Syd was the first to feel confident to swim out with Sadie and Keith and the village kids. There was an estate called Broderick's that was near the mountains. They would swim out for miles. When a swimmer "leveled Broderick's," he earned his kudos. Syd received his slaps on the back when he did it. It took me a while, but I too "leveled Broderick's." They did not acknowledge my accomplishment. I was "only a girl." Boys were the same everywhere.

Uncle Sym was the one who really taught me how to swim. I was happy to join the children. Like Sadie, I liked to swim when it rained. The water was serene and warm then, and the raindrops formed ripples in the sea that added to its stillness.

The village children were our playmates on moonlit nights as well. They gathered in our yard at the Big House. Maamie Daley always had drinks for us, and sometimes served them sweet biscuits, (cookies) that we had brought her from America, which delighted our friends. She made them queue up to make sure that everyone got some goodies. One little girl rejoined the line. A newly arrived boy, seeing her munching, and fearing that Maamie Daley would run out of cookies, took exception. That day I learned one of the funniest sayings in Montserrat's patois.

The boy asked, "A way you tink you a go?"[15]

She promptly replied, "Up in a you nooaz hooal go spend one day."

I asked Sadie and Keith what she meant. Syd jumped in, and said, "Even I know that, Maggie. 'Up in a you nooaz hooal go spend one day', means 'Up in your nostril to spend a day.' In other words, 'Mind your damn business.'"

Sadie said, "Syd, keep on learning. You are a real Montserratian."

I repeated the patois, "Up in a you nooaz hooal to spend a day," and burst out laughing. Sadie tried to interrupt my laughter, but could not. She thought I was nuts. I wondered if Dad knew that one. The girl got her cookies again, and walked away still munching.

Maamie Daley and Auntie Vera gave Sadie a surprise birthday. They spread the tables from end to end in the shade of the Big House and the fruit trees. There was food everywhere. Neither Sadie nor I knew of the plan, except that Maamie Daley had told us that it was a little farewell party for Syd and me. They made goat water, fried fish, baked sweet potatoes, salads, vegetables, and all kinds of cakes, tarts, and sweet biscuits. I told Maamie Daley about our apple pie, and she was sorry that American apples, delicious and Granny Smith did not grow in Montserrat. They knew those apples because Dad peeled and sent them for them.

I went outside, and picked eight firm mangoes from my favorite mango tree, "Ladies' fingers." I washed, peeled and sliced them. I sprinkled a little brown sugar, ground cinnamon, nutmeg and lime juice on the slices. I threw in a few raisins, and made the cake-dough crust. I placed it in a large pie dish that Auntie Becky had sent for Maamie Daley. There was enough left to make a small sample. The family liked it so much, that Maamie Daley decided not to serve the pie at the party.

Maamie said, "Mags, Sweetie, this is very delicious. Thank you for teaching us another use for our mangoes."

Parpi Daley cut a large piece, and ate it slowly. He stood and kissed me on the forehead. "Mags, my little Shug, you are just like my Shug in the kitchen. This is delicious." I thanked him.

---

15   "Where do you think you are going?"

Maamie Daley said, "Mags, Sweetie, please make a mango tart for my Tunny when you get home. I would prepare a glass jar of sliced firm mangoes."

Auntie Vera said, "Maggie, the pie is wonderful. However, do you understand why all of us think that Tunny Daley is Maamie's favorite child? Maamie, I seldom hear you speak of 'my Vera,' 'my Bern, or 'my Ellie.'

Maamie Daley blushed and became huffy, but said nothing.

It seemed that every child from the village was at the party because they knew that the Daleys served a lot of food at their bashes.

We had live music. A neighbor strummed his guitar and sang. Later, when they pulled out the liquor, another musician joined in with his fiddle. Parpi Daley had a beautiful voice, and he belted out some of the old calypsos. Maamie Daley joined him. We danced, and laughed and sang.

Sadie was completely surprised when they rolled out her birthday cake, and the band played "Happy Birthday." She would turn fifteen in three days. She received gifts from all her uncles, aunts, and some cousins abroad. She received two envelopes from my parents, one from Maggie, Syd and Ejay for $100.00, U.S., and another from Uncle Tunny and Auntie Lisa in the same amount. Her parents gave her money, too, and Maamie and Parpi Daley made deposits in the account they had opened in her name. Sadie's bank account was growing.

It seemed that Auntie Vera had sent invitations to her brothers and sister and their families. She explained that she just felt like giving her daughter a party. Keith's birthday came at Christmas, and they often celebrated his then.

Sadie thought that I had known about her party and kept the secret. I reminded her that Maamie Daley had told us about her "little farewell party" for Syd and me in her presence.

"Sadie, just accept it. The adults completely surprised us." I told her. "You helped to cook for your own surprise. Ha! Ha! Ha!"

There were certain customs that I had to learn by observation. I noticed that every time they opened a new bottle of liquor, they poured some at the open front door. If they threw water outside after twilight, they say, "Who is there, please to move!"

On that occasion I asked Parpi Daley about it, and he explained it very well.

"Mags, we honor our departed loved ones by inviting them to drink with us at festive times. We know they are around. After all, they were with us in life. Why shouldn't we honor their memory after death? Since we know they are present in the spirit, and not everybody can see them, we ask them to move when we throw water out at night. You are from America. You do not know of the time when we threw more water out at night. We used bath pans to wash our children and ourselves, so we had a lot of dirty bath water to toss outside. Times have changed, but the custom remains."

"You know for sure that they are here, Parpi?" I asked nervously.

"Yes."

"Who are they? Can you see them?"

"They are my parents, Shug's parents, and other relatives, and some good neighbors. I've seen a few in my day, and I know when my Mummah is here," he said. "I smell fresh roses. They were her favorite flowers."

He looked at me and saw that I was getting scared.

"Don't be frightened," he said hugging me. "They are our guardian angels."

"Really?" I asked.

"Oh, yes. When you get older, you'll appreciate their presence. Remember they will never harm you. By the law of average, Maggie, one of these days, I'll be one of your guardian angels."

I stared at Parpi Daley, because I knew that he was right. He smiled and hugged me again. I was glad that I had that long chat with Parpi Daley. I kissed his cheek.

The adults were into their rum, as were the Dailey jumbies. The party was in full swing by then, and I joined the others on the floor. Keith was crazy on the dance floor, doing all kinds of wild moves. Syd decided that he was not going to let a Montserratian boy beat him, so they danced to the pleasure of all who were present. They clapped rhythmically. Sadie joined them, doing my wild moves. I joined in, and Maamie looked in wonderment at the representatives of the Daley clan of our generation.

The party ended past midnight. We slept well into the next day, Sunday, but everyone had to be up for church. We went to the 11:00 a.m. service instead of the 9:00 a.m., although some of us were still bleary-eyed.

Uncle Sym often went for days on deep-sea fishing trips. Auntie Vera worked at a bank in Town. Normally, she got a ride to and from work, or she hired a car. We did not eat until everyone was present. One afternoon, Auntie Vee was late getting home. Maamie grew impatient. She hated to reheat food.

Sadie had told me, secretly, that her parents had ordered a new car, and that it might arrive before we returned to America that year. That afternoon, when Auntie Vera was late coming home from work, I suspected that the car had arrived.

Maamie Daley fussed. "Vee knows I like to eat when my food is ready."

About thirty minutes later, Auntie Vera drove up in a shiny red Bentley, blew the horn and Sadie and Keith ran out to admire their new car. Syd and I went to examine it, too.

Maamie Daley shielded her eyes from the setting sun, and uttered, "Well my God! Vera, is this motor car yours?"

"Yes, Maamie. It is," she said proudly. "Surprise!"

Upon hearing the excitement, Parpi Daley came from the back verandah and ran towards the car. By then, we were all inside it, except Maamie Daley. Parpi Daley seemed to be quite satisfied with his old truck and his two donkeys. It was out of the question for him to own a car. Auntie Vera stepped out and Parpi sat behind the wheel.

"Vee, let me drive it one day," he said. "Come, Shug!"

"You want to kill yourself Gabriel Daley, you old fool? You won't take Magdalene Corbett Daley with you."

I knew she was upset. She did not call him "Boy".

"Now what kind of talk is that, Shug? Where do you think I go every Saturday when I leave you at the market? I meet with the fellows. They taught me how to drive these new automatic cars. I drove from St. John's to Salem and back many times," he said gloating. "Have I ever mash-up my truck?"

"Parpi, you drove a car?" Auntie Vera asked proudly.

"Of course, Vee! I drove like a champion up and down Fogarty Hill."

Maamie looked at him askance. Parpi Daley pulled out his driver's license and showed it to us. It seemed that he had never owned a drivers' license before, although he drove the truck. Uncle Sym had signed for it, so it was registered in his name. Parpi Daley just never bothered to get his license back then.

When he tried to show Maamie Daley his license, she turned her back on him and said, "Gabriel, move from me!"

At first, Maamie Daley was surprised. Then she got furious. She stopped speaking to Parpi Daley. She said he was deceitful and could not be trusted. She said that after so many years of marriage, there should be no secrets between them. Parpi tried to pet her face, but she pulled away and pointed a warning finger at him. At dinner, it seemed that Parpi Daley was riddled with guilt. He tried to smile at her, but she ignored him. That night she locked him out of their bedroom. I felt sorry for him. He slept in the spare bed in Syd's room. That went on for two days.

On the third night, just before midnight, we heard a loud scream. Everybody ran to the hallway. Auntie Vera turned on the light. Maamie Daley was walking around like a zombie with her hands raised high above her head.

"What have they done with my Boy? Where is he? Vee! Vee!"

Parpi Daley ran out of the room and said, "Here I am Shug." He hugged her. "Shug, I'm right here. You know that your Boy is always here." She opened her eyes, stared at him, and hugged him tightly, saying "Boy! Boy!'

"Maamie, what's the matter with you? Are you insane? First, you locked Parpi out of your bedroom, then you get up in the middle of the night and wake up the whole house." She turned to Parpi. "And you with your 'Shug.' Will the two of you stop it, get into your room and go back to sleep!"

Parpi led Maamie to their room. He tickled her just before they closed the door and she giggled and said, "Boy, behave yourself!"

Auntie Vera was furious. She turned the light off and told us to get back to bed. However, not before she insisted that her parents were insane as she retuned to her flat. The next day, Maamie and Parpi Daley acted as if nothing had happened, and so did everyone else.

Since Auntie Vera had the car, our travels to church on Sundays changed a bit. She took Maamie and Parpi Daley and two of the elderly friends to church, and returned for us. Uncle Sym went to church only on special religious holy days. There was none to celebrate while we were there, so we never saw him in church. When the Parson stopped by to visit Maamie and Parpi Daley, Uncle Sym hid. As far as the Parson was concerned, "Simeon Duberry was incorrigible." I heard him tell Auntie Vera so.

"I have enough religion in me to take me to heaven and back. I hear once you see Heaven you wouldn't want to come back. God knows my heart."

"What will you do if the good Lord comes for you today, Sym?" Maamie Daley asked him one day.

"Go willingly. Do I have a choice, Maamie Daley?"

"Well," she said pensively, "No, you don't."

One day at the farm, I had an incident in the latrine. I was inside sitting quietly over the open pit, when the longest snake I had ever seen crawled in under the door. I screamed. My need to use the toilet vanished. I stood over the pit, in full spread, holding tightly to my long dress. Parpi and Maamie Daley ran to my rescue. When they entered, the snake was crawling towards me. Maamie Daley drove the snake away, saying that it was just as frightened as I was. Parpi Daley opened his arms and I fell into his grasp. Keith killed the snake.

"Maggie, Sweetie," Maamie said, stroking my cheek, "our snakes are harmless. They won't bite you."

"Oh yeah!" I said, still agitated. She hugged me and led me away from the scene.

I suffered from constipation for the rest of the week. I knew Mrs. Dyer's castor oil was the main ingredient in the mid-summer purge. Sadie and Keith had their own tales to tell about that. I did not know that it was also the cure for constipation in children, too. Dad and Mom had never subjected us to such purges. Maamie Daley reached for the bottle of the thick, brown gooey liquid having the consistency of glue. She placed it on the table. She did not force me to drink it, as she had done to her children when they were small. She opened the bottle. Upon smelling the foul concoction, my body took care of its need.

Syd and I had heard our father speak of the annual ritual of doses of castor oil after their midsummer holiday. He did not eat chicken soup, because it reminded him of the castor oil ritual. Maamie Daley gave them chicken broth following the purge. It must have been a messy situation. They had no indoor plumbing at that time.

"What's a purge?" Syd had asked Dad.

"A cleansing," Dad said. "We were never sick. Every time we claimed that we were sick, Maamie touched our foreheads. If we didn't have a fever, she reached for the castor oil, and we galloped from the house like racing horses, and sprinted to school."

"Dad, I had the pleasure of seeing Miss Lizzie Dyer, the owner of the castor nut trees, and the producer of the insipid brew, at the bay. I found out that the village children still despised her, and that if it were not for her guard dogs, Grab and Bite, they would have cut her trees down."

"Grab and Bite, eh?" Dad asked. "Sol and Paul got a sound lashing from Parpi for trying to cut down those damn castor nut trees. Paul actually cut down several limbs from one of them. Paul was the lookout. Sol dropped one of his soft walkers (sneakers) in her fenced yard, when Miss Lizzie's fierce bulldog, Goliath, grabbed his foot. Parpi had to pay her for it. Maamie told them she wished she had a castor-nut tree to cure them of their night prowls."

I stood up to leave and whispered to Syd, "Ask me, a way you a go?"

"Maggie, gall, a way you a go?"

"Up in a you nooaz hooal to spend a day."

Dad laughed, and so did I. Mom and Ejay wanted to know what we had said, and why it was so funny.

Dad said, "Boy, did that take me back to my childhood." He burst out laughing again, and so did I, while Syd explained the saying to Mom and Ejay.

Chapter X

Montserrat Was Changing

Syd and I had returned to the Island year after year, but on our tenth visit, we found that the old house had gone through another transformation. Electricity! They had finally wired the villages. Maamie and Parpi Daley had added a new kitchen to the main house. She had a large four-burner stove with an oven. They had fastened a large gas canister to the kitchen wall outside, under one of the windows. Maamie Daley's cast iron skillets must have appeared incompatible with the ceramic tiles, so Uncle Sym and Keith built a cupboard (closet), especially for them. She displayed her stainless steel pots on hooks on the kitchen wall.

It was getting to look too much like America to me. I missed the old kitchen, with its dirt floor and quaint look. They had converted it into a large recreation room, with wood flooring and painted walls. The only thing left of the old kitchen was the curing room for the corned pork. Uncle Sym entertained his friends and relaxed there when he was not at sea. His hammock hung from the rafters. I never got into it, but Syd told me it was comfortable.

I managed to voice my displeasure with the changes, and Auntie Vera disputed with me. She asked me if I did not think it was time for Montserrat to enter into the twentieth century. I had to admit that she was right.

They had a refrigerator. I opened it, immediately, to see if Maamie Daley had given in to that modern contraption. Auntie Vera had one bottle of milk on the top shelf, a pitcher of lemonade and a bowl of homemade butter on the second shelf. She had written her name on them, although she knew that Maamie Daley would never touch them. The freezer was set at its lowest point with two ice trays of unwanted ice cubes. The vegetable containers were empty. Syd and I still preferred to drink the cool water from the calabash goblets.

I said, "Maamie Daley, there's no food in your refrigerator and freezer. People will think you're a penny pincher."

"People will talk, Mags Sweetie, but when friends drop in to see us, I give them fresh food."

"Maamie Daley, you have a freezer. It's a good place to keep ice cream."

"Then, you ask Boy to pull out our ice cream maker. Tell Keith I say to go and get me two ripe soursops and two dozen ripe mangoes."

I said, "Maamie Daley, we will pull out the ice cream machine and get it ready for tomorrow. Instead of buying ice, we can make our own." I placed several plastic bowls full of water in the freezer, and set it to its top freezing point.

Maamie Daley's homemade ice cream was another of her specialties, especially soursop and mango flavors. We made it regularly. I also helped Maamie Daley to churn butter. I convinced her to store it in the refrigerator. Before that, she kept it in a bowl in a container of cold water that she changed daily. It kept the butter from becoming rancid, and the ants could not get to it. The butter was always soft. However, she never bragged about her refrigerator. In her mind, it was just another of the modern contraptions that would ruin the world.

It suddenly dawned on me that if my parents could buy Maamie Daley a washing machine, I would not have to wash by hand any more. I thought, "When I return to New York, I will ask Dad to send her a washing machine. She would not need a dryer. I liked the fresh smell of laundry dried in the open air."

When I told Maamie Daley about the washing machine, she was horrified. Although she did not do large wash loads any more, she washed her panties every night.

"No machine can wash clothes clean enough for me, Mags, Sweetie. I hear that they have them in our hotels, and the only thing they do is save time. You see how bright your white clothes are when you wash them here? Now, tell me what is so wonderful about the washing machine."

"You're right, Maamie Daley," I admitted. "Sometimes, we do have to wash a load twice."

Mrs. Abby Neal Dear, Maamie Daley and Auntie Vera's washerwoman, was almost a family member. She was Parpi Daley's god-sister. My great-grandfather, Natty Daley, and Parpi Daley had built a cistern for Abby and her mother, Jozzie Neal, to enable them to run a little laundry after the death of Abby's father. When Abby's mother died, she kept her business. However, she went to the Big House twice a week, on Mondays and Wednesdays, to wash and iron for Auntie Vera and Uncle Sym, and Maamie and Parpi Daley. On the advice of Maamie Daley, Auntie Vera made Sadie take care of her laundry and Keith's. I told Sadie it was unfair, but she told me that Maamie Daley had explained to her that she had to be prepared to wash for her own family when she grew up. I had no idea then that my turn would come.

One afternoon, after she had ironed and folded the clothing, Abby pulled out a manila envelope containing recent photos of her sons, James, John, and Andrew. She had given each boy the double surnames "Neal Dear". She showed them to Maamie and Parpi Daley who looked approvingly at Abby's three sons. They were in Toronto, Canada. They had attended the wedding of one of their relatives, and looked handsome and elegant in their tuxedos. Abby Dear glowed when Maamie and Parpi Daley praised her sons. After she left, Maamie told us her story.

She said, "My darlings, especially you, Mags and Sadie, Sweeties, listen carefully to Abby's story. You are young women, and you are already spoiled by the damn modern contraptions. We have electricity, but sometimes, it doesn't work. It never hurts to learn the old way.

"Abby was very crabbit, or naturally clever. Everyone thought that she would have become a teacher, a nurse or even a physician. Then her father, Piper Neal, died. Poor Jozzie, who was completely dependent on Piper, had no means of supporting Abby and her two sisters.

"Thank God, Jozzie's grandmother had taught her how to wash and iron, and she taught her daughters, Abby, Jane, and Dorothy. Abby was the prettiest and most delicate of the three children, but she loved her mother, stayed close to her, and helped her with the business. When they became of age, Jane and Dorothy stole some money from Jozzie, and ran away from home. Jozzie never heard from them again. People said that they had seen Jane and Dorothy in Birmingham, England. However, poor Jozzie had to struggle with Abby to make a living.

"Boy and his father helped them when they could, but remember, we had a house full of children, too, and times were hard. Abby met and married a young sailor from somewhere up the islands, a term used by

53

Montserratians to speak of the islands lying to its south. His name was Emanuel Dear. Abby and Emanuel made a handsome couple. They had three sons, John, James and Andrew. Abby and her boys were always at the wharf to welcome Emanuel when the boat docked, but one afternoon they waited in vain. He was not on the boat. The other sailors told her that he had jumped ship in Nova Scotia, Canada, and he was 'a wanted man.'

"Abby had never made the acquaintance of Emanuel Dear's family, but he left her the names of his parents and their address in Roseau, Dominica. The letter returned stamped, "Addressee Unknown". Just about then, Jozzie died. Poor Abby had four mouths to feed. The boys were crabbit and very tractable, (helpful) and they helped her, as they grew older. She did all she could to educate them, and they passed the eleven plus and went to the Grammar school. They earned their certificates with honor. James and John left for Toronto with the help of their French teachers, a Canadian couple, at the Grammar school. They later moved to Montreal. Abby told us that they studied at a university there. They sent money and packages to their mother and brother, and later they sent for her and Andrew, but she could not tolerate the cold winters, and returned home. Andrew wanted to come back with her, but she insisted that he stay with his brothers, and pursue his education. He became a mathematics teacher in the secondary schools there, while John and James worked in business.

"Boy and I had asked Bern to add indoor plumbing to Abby's house. He did not hesitate. Abby provided the material. Vee and Sym lent her the money, and she paid them back little by little. She added two bedrooms and another bathroom using the money from the boys.

James and Andrew sent the money for Abby to remodel her little house, complete with two extra rooms and another bathroom. However, she did not change the original structure in deference to her mother and grandmother. They had gotten married, and each had a son, whom Abby longed to meet. .They planned to return home, when they could afford the trip.

They returned home last Christmas without their wives. The boys, Andre and Pierre, were almost five years old. The whole village had met them, because Abby paraded with them and introduced them to everyone. When she was little, she had won a number of swim meets. They, too, loved the sea, and she spent early mornings and late afternoons there with them, teaching them how to swim. They collected many conch shells, and took a number of them home to Canada.

"Since we are the closest to family that they have, we entertained James, Andrew, their sons, and Abby here at the Big House. Now, they correspond with us, too.

"The little boys raised hell when they had to return to Canada. They wanted to stay with 'Memée Abby'. Their fathers lied to them and told them that she had gone to Canada to visit their Uncle John. Actually, Abby had hidden here with us.

"Andrew's boy, Andre shouted, 'Bull shit! Andy, you're lying. Mémé didn't say good-bye to us.'

'That's right,' James boy, Pierre, said. 'I'm waiting right here for Mémé. Jimmy and Andy, you go back to Montreal.'

Abby heard every word. She cried bitterly. She wanted to see them.

"She told me, 'Maggie, everything with those little boys is 'Bull shit!' My sons just laugh. I hate when they call their fathers Jimmy and Andy. I tell them the boys lack training. I told Andre and Pierre that they should not say 'bull shit' in polite company. They said, 'Okay, Memé!' They are very bright. They speak English and French fluently. If I had them here for only a month, they would be normal little boys.'

"Andrew, James and the boys drove by to say good-bye on their way to the airport. Abby damn near ran out to see them. They called from the airport to thank us."

"Why does Miss Abby still do your laundry, Maamie Daley?" I asked.

"It's a force of habit, Sweetie. The boys asked her to stop, but people of our culture find it hard to stop working. When we stay busy, we feel alert. Abby works here at the Big House. She also has three customers in Town who will be very unhappy if she retires: the magistrate, a headmaster and a dentist. She is the best at what she does. I hate to admit it, Mags, Sweetie, but soon from now, your washing machines will replace all the washerwomen in Montserrat. Things are changing too fast for me."

"Did her sons run into their father in Canada?" I asked.

"No, but I never told Abby what Sym had told us regarding Emanuel Dear. He was really a fugitive running away from the law in his country. It seemed he had stolen a large sum of money from the business where he worked. He was a wanted man. His real name was Arthur Roberts. Emanuel, or Arthur, told someone that it was better that his sons never find out his real identity. He was actually from Guyana."

"Do you think he did the right thing, Maamie Daley?" Sadie asked.

"No Sadie, Sweetie! He wrecked Abby's young life. She and her boys did not deserve to be treated like that. She has never looked at another man since, although she had many offers of marriage. Besides, Emanuel Dear didn't have to go anywhere. Who would have found him here in little Montserrat? He was in church every Sunday with Abby and his sons, when he was not at sea. Sym and the other fishers who knew about it never spread her business around Montserrat, and this is the first time I'm speaking about it. I know it won't go further than here."

All of us pledged "Oh, no, Maamie Daley."

"I thought that there was a lesson in the Abby's story, so I said, "Thanks Maamie Daley. Therefore, that was why you taught me how to wash by hand when I was thirteen. Sometimes, we have blackouts in New York. At least, I will be able to wash my panties." She smiled.

After I learned to wash by hand like Sadie, I had to do my laundry and my brother's. Back home in New York, Mom made Syd help me, too, but it was simple enough. He loaded the washing machine after I had separated the white garments from the colored pieces, and added the detergents, and turned it on. Then he helped me to fold and distribute them.

There was a routine to hand washing at the big yard. There were four wash pans in a row under the calabash tree near the cistern. We separated the white from the colored clothing and soaked them overnight. After the wash, we spread the white clothes on the rocks and grass to bleach them in the sunlight. We had to wet them continually to keep them from scorching. No laundry bleach on earth could produce such bright clothing.

We poured boiling water on the cassava starch, and diluted it with cold water in the starching pan. We rinsed the garments thoroughly, and starched the outer cotton clothing. Maamie Daley helped me to use that starch which, when over done, left the clothing as stiff as cardboard. They always added "bluing" to the starching process.

Another of my Montserrat's lessons that I liked, was watching the production of starch. Parpi Daley grew cassava, "cussada" in Montserrat, on his farm. It was the bitter cassava, which meant that it was not a vegetable. It was a potent poison when ingested. Someone told me that no matter how long one cooked it, it remained too hard to chew. The difference between the bitter and sweet cassava was that the sweet one cooked rapidly. However, some folks did not tamper with that vegetable. We liked it at the Big House, because we trusted

56

Parpi Daley to know the difference. He only grew the sweet cassava in his home garden.

At harvest time, they peeled the bitter cassava, and grated "shacked" them on the largest grater I had ever seen. It was round, about four feet long. The grater was part of a contraption operated by pedals. Three men sat at the grater. It was a delicate operation. Two of them held the cassava on the grater as the third man pedaled at a limited speed. Sometimes, the man at the pedal also grated the cassava. They had to coordinate their actions, or they could damage their fingers. The grated cassava fell into a wide aluminum receptacle with a large fine-mesh strainer that separated the milky sap from the meal. They covered everything with burlap or crocus bags and left it overnight.

Upon seeing my fascination with the operation, Maamie Daley told me that they covered it to protect the stray animals. If any animal drank the cassava water, it would die instantly.

The following morning, they removed the burlap bags. They kept all the animals, including the chickens, away from the area when they spilled the water. The milky part had solidified into the whitest starch I had ever seen. They dug into it with large wooden forks, thereby separating it. Then they put it to dry in the sun. They emptied the meal from the huge sifter into a deep wood tub, washed their hands thoroughly, and rubbed it until the meal was thoroughly blended. Parpi Daley and Uncle Sym would salt the meal to their taste, and make cassava bread while the meal was moist. Later, they stored the rest as farina, or cassava meal, called moosha in Montserrat. Moosha dumplings were a favorite among the Daleys.

I liked cassava bread, especially with my coco tea. When left in liquid, it became porridge. I liked my coco tea cassava bread porridge. It was also good with avocado, and codfish. Syd did not like it, in any form.

Maamie Daley did not want to see any panties in the regular laundry. I had to wash my panties every night, and she accepted no compromise.

When I mentioned it at home, Dad said, "When I was little, the panty line was in the rear verandah, because we had no indoor plumbing."

In my day, Maamie Daley had a folding rack on which she dried hers and mine in her bathroom. I asked her why the men did not wash their underpants nightly.

"Maggie, Sweetie" she said, "a young woman must learn to keep herself clean. If you only have two pairs of panties, you should be wearing one while the other is drying or clean somewhere. Men would always find women to wash their dirty clothes."

"But Maamie Daley," I said, "I have dozens of panties. So at home, they go in the regular wash."

"That's the trouble with America," she said. "Abundance will be its downfall some day."

"Why?" I asked.

"Maggie Sweetie, do you really appreciate having dozens of panties? No, you do not. Isn't that something else that you take for granted?"

I pondered what Maamie Daley had said. She was probably right, but I still preferred to own lots of panties, especially when my village girlfriends told me that they only had two or three of them. That year, before I returned to New York, I gave my new panties to the girls with whom we played. They were ecstatic. They liked American panties. They told me the British knickers were not as stylish.

"Knickers?" I asked.

"Yes. That's what they call panties in England," one girl said.

Syd always left T-shirts and sneakers with some of his friends who had none. Sadie also had many panties, because she received underwear from our family abroad. However, like Auntie Vera, whom Maamie Daley had also trained, Sadie washed her panties every night.

Maamie Daley taught me how to fold Syd's pants so that the creases would be sharp and even, when pressed. My creases were so fine, that even Keith wanted me to iron his pants. I declined when I saw Sadie's displeasure. She told Keith that it was time for him to learn to wash and iron his own clothes. He hugged her and told her he was only joking.

Before they got the electricity, we used flatirons heated on a charcoal stove, called a coal pot. We had to wipe them with a rag each time before using them. They had three gooses. I believe that they were the precursors to steam irons, except that they were made of cast iron and filled with live charcoal or cow dung, according to Tunny Daley, my dad.

I did not say anything, but I thought that bull dung was decidedly more famous than cow dung. I never heard, "Cow shit!" It was funny, but I did not think my grandparents would have appreciated hearing it.

Montserrat was fast becoming a tourist attraction, and Maamie decided to take full advantage of it. She made native beverages: sorrel, ginger beer, and a tamarindade. She had invented a mango drink that was awesome. She sold them on the beach in the shade of the seaside grape trees on

Sunday afternoons after church and Sunday school. The refrigerator served a purpose, after all. She made blocks of ice in the freezer, and combined it with what she bought at the ice factory. She kept the drinks cold overnight in the refrigerator. Auntie Vee finally bought her own refrigerator that she kept in her own flat.

Maamie was a good businesswoman in the market place and on the beach. "Come, good people! Get a taste of Paradise! Have a drink made of pure spring water and fresh fruits!" she announced.

The tourists believed her. It was spring water. Right! Maybe it was better than any water they had back home, but it sprang from the cistern above the kitchen in the shade of the largest calabash tree on our property. Parpi Daley, Uncle Sym and Keith built the rolling cart in which she kept her containers of drinks. It was reinforced with cork, and aluminum sheets. They also sprinkled sawdust on the ice to keep it from melting rapidly.

She showed me a handful of dollars one Sunday afternoon, and said, "Mags Sweetie, this is what we call 'turning our hand.'"

She asked me to separate the American, Canadian, and other dollars from their local money. In that short time, she had made over $250.00, Eastern Caribbean (EC) clear profit. Americans and Canadians gave her their dollars without considering the exchange rate. There were a few British pounds among the dollars.

"Maamie, what is 'turning your hand?'" I asked.

"We buy things and peddle them at a profit. I buy sugar. Boy produces ginger and sorrel. Tamarinds grow abundantly on our property and along the roadside. I pick ripe mangoes, soursops and other fruits, and make my drinks and sell them. You counted it, so you know how much I made today."

"That's good, Maamie Daley. You are so crabbit! I love you."

"I love you too my Sweetie, namesake." She bent and kissed me on the forehead.

I wondered why Maamie Daley had asked Mom to send her two hundred plastic cups. Mom caught a sale, and sent her five hundred 9 ounce cups. They did not sell them commercially in the island, as yet. It gave Maamie an advantage over her competitors, who were still washing glasses. Every Sunday, she sold all of her drinks and wished she had made more. We, children, went along the beach picking up the used paper cups. Maamie Daley was the neatest woman I ever knew. However, she had to lecture the children who collected them for use in building their sand castles, and then abandoned them on the sand.

Maamie Daley called the children together, and gave them American hard candies. "Now you listen to me, my little ones," she said. "You know my grandchildren, Sadie, Keith, Maggie, and Syd. You see them going along the seashore picking up these used paper cups." She held one high above her head. "Some of you have been collecting them, and leaving them where you use them. Not good! We have tourists who will speak badly of us if we leave our beaches dirty. Do I make myself clear?"

"Yes, Maamie Daley," they said, because they knew her well.

She gave them Tootsie Rolls, and they returned happily to their tasks. When we were ready to leave the beach, they brought their paper cups and deposited them in a crocus bag that we took back to the house.

"Thank you, little ones. Now you do this every week, you hear me?"

"Yes, Maamie Daley!" they replied, said goodbye, and left, still sucking their candies.

Sometimes, Auntie Vera cooked on Sundays. She was just as fine a cook as Maamie Daley. She was not the vendor type. She said she left that to "Sym and Maamie." We had dinner buffet style on the back verandah just off the kitchen, when Auntie Vera cooked. She opened two folding tables, and set them up in a party style. She tended not to cook as much as Maamie Daley did. Visitors on Sundays had to eat cake.

"Vera Duberry, you tell me I am cheap," Maamie said when we had emptied all the serving bowls. "Not a scrap is left."

"Maamie, I am not bothering with you," Auntie Vera said. "I already whipped up something for Friend and Foe."

Parpi, Syd and the boys returned to the animal pens on Sundays to deliver their food, and filled the troughs with water. I was surprised when Keith drove the truck back to the Big House one Sunday, because he had. no driver's license.

New hotels and restaurants sprang up all over the island. The number of taxi drivers increased. They rivaled each other by driving like maniacs through the villages. The island planners seemed to have forgotten to build sidewalks, so we had to walk on the edge of the roads. The speedsters raised clouds of dust on the unpaved roads, especially when they took tourists to the springs in the mountains. Eventually, they paved all the roads, but there were still no sidewalks.

How the time had passed. Syd and I had been going to Montserrat for eleven years. In the fall, I would enter my senior year in high school. My parents said they would not be able to send us to Montserrat every year, because Ejay was getting older, and they wanted him to know Montserrat and his grandparents.

However, Ejay never went to Montserrat until Syd graduated from college. Our roof had sprung a leak, and Mom and Dad decided to replace it instead of patching it. They also decided to replace the old pipes that they had fixed from time to time. They installed copper pipes. Uncle Bern promised Dad that he would spend a week with us that fall, and help with the major repairs. He asked Dad to take the measurements, and order the materials as he had instructed him. Then, too, my parents had to plan for my going to college.

With that forewarning, Syd and I decided to take to the road, get to really know Montserrat, and enjoy ourselves that summer. We chose only to go to the farm on Friday afternoons, to help with the harvesting. We toured the Island a few times on Vincent and James' bicycles that Uncle Sym and Keith had kept in excellent repair. Syd took hundreds of photos. Syd confessed to me later that he and Keith "escaped from the fortress" sometimes at night, and rode through the villages.

"Why?" I asked him.

"That's what young men do, Maggie," he said. "You wouldn't understand."

"I'll ask Dad when I get home," I said.

"No, Maggie! Please don't go there."

"Okay, I won't. I promise."

I felt like a native becoming reacquainted with my homeland. We rode freely from village to village, speaking patois. We must have sounded authentic because no one criticized us. However, one of the vendors of the market recognized us, and asked why we had abandoned our American accent.

Syd said, "A one Monstrshan me be. A ya me barn, and a ya me reah, no true Maggie?" ("I am a Montserratian. I was born and raised here. Right, Maggie? ")

"Yes, A true, Syd." I said laughing hysterically. ("Right, Syd!")

There was new construction everywhere. Montserratians abroad had continued to build new homes and renovate their old ones in preparation for their retirement. No one from the family had built in Montserrat. They knew they had the Big House and acres of land.

Some tourists went to Montserrat out of curiosity, and returned for its beauty and congeniality. Some bought property, and settled there. Radio Antilles had chosen Montserrat as the location for its broadcasting station in the Village of O'Garro's in the south. Its broadcasts were heard throughout the Caribbean.

Others built a large recording studio somewhere in one of the hills. The Beatles and other top recording artists chose it as the location for their recordings. They walked freely around Town. Only tourists, who recognized them, pursued them. Montserratians did not encroach on the privacy of celebrities. I heard that a well-known musician stopped a Montserratian one day, after the man had greeted him casually, and kept on walking.

"Excuse me, sir. Do you know who I am?"

"Of course," he said in real Montserratian. "Me know who you be, Sa. You one oo dem musishans who come ya a recard you music. (I know who you are, sir. You are one of those musicians who came here to record your music). You want you privacy, me want mine, so you have one good day, Sa."

Soon after he had said that, he was on his way again, leaving the well-known musician somewhat surprised.

The musician was dressed in khaki shorts and sandals. He wore no shirt. He held the hand of his little son who walked slowly at his side. He must have thought to himself, 'They really know who we are. They do respect our privacy."

I could sense a feeling of sadness as our departure drew nearer. I would miss our annual trips to Montserrat. I would miss Maamie and Parpi Daley, Keith, Sadie, Auntie Vera and Uncle Sym, and of course, Grandpa Duby. I would miss the Big House, the yard, Friend and Foe, the farm, the "Mighty Watchman," and Montserrat. I would miss the village kids with whom we played in our spare time. I sensed that Syd would miss going there, too. I mentioned it to Maamie Daley about four days before our return to New York, and she hugged me. Syd was lurking nearby, and she hugged him too. Then, Maamie Daley prayed for us.

She took us to her bedroom, knelt at her bed, and we knelt beside her, Syd on her right and I on her left. She asked us to close our eyes, and we did. She placed her arms on our shoulders.

"Dear Lord," she began, "please bend your ears and listen to the trembling voice of this grandmother. Please, protect my little darlings.

They are not little any more, but I still see them, running around the house, calling for their father the first time they came here. My little Syd is now a tall young man, bigger than my Tunny, his father. I have watched my little Mags, Sweetie, grow into a charming young woman. Dear Lord, they will not be coming here every year any more. I know that America is a big place, and the streets are not as safe as our roads here, and my little Syd has started his night roving. So, Lord, please look with favor on them. I will miss them, dear Father. They are as much a part of the Big House as all my baby Daleys who were born here. Please cover them with your wings and let them feel your presence every day."

As I listened to my grandmother praying for us, unchecked tears flowed down my cheeks. I opened my eyes and looked quickly at Syd. He, too, had tears on his cheeks. At that moment, we heard footsteps. Maamie Daley said, "Boy, is that you? Come and pray with us. Ask the Lord to bless our little ones. They won't be coming here on holiday every year any more."

Syd and I opened our eyes. By then, Parpi Daley had knelt behind Maamie, and rested one palm on Syd's shoulder, and the other on mine. Then my grandfather prayed for us.

"Lord, I am not a great speaker, but I speak from the heart. You are a great God, and You know all our needs. I ask You to protect our Syd and Maggie every moment for the rest of their lives. Each year, when they leave us, my heart feels heavy. Syd once told me of fights in their schools over there in that big country. Here in Montserrat, we respect our schools. Lord please strengthen my son, Tunny, that he will be strong for his children. All of us need Your care, oh Lord. Amen!"

Maamie Daley said, "Thank you, Boy. Now children, let us say the prayer that our Lord taught His disciples. We are sinners, but as long as we try to do God's will, we'll be His modern-day disciples."

We recited the Lord's Prayer. I wished someone's camera were rolling. But, then, as I reflected, I thought, "That was a private moment for Syd, Maamie and Parpi Daley, and for me." A camera would have been most intrusive. I vowed that I would remember that moment for the rest of my life.

I hugged Maamie Daley and said, "Thank you, Grandma. Thank you for everything you have taught us. I love you. Don't worry! I'll come back when I can. I held on to Parpi Daley, kissed his cheek and said, "Thank you Parpi Daley, Grandpa! Thanks for being the father of my Dad, your Tunny. I am so happy I have spent all these summers with you. I tell you, now, that you are the best grandfather in the whole wide world. I adore you. But, most of all, Maamie and Parpi Daley, thank you for praying for us. I'll remember this moment for the rest of my life."

I saw Parpi Daley wipe the tears from his eyes, as he planted a kiss on my cheek.

Syd said, "Parpi Daley, if I become a farmer, it will be your fault. You will never know what being with you on the farm means to me. First, I brag to my friends back home. Then, I show them photos of you, the Big House, the farm, and The Mighty Watchman, and watch them get jealous. Because of you, I have walked where my father walked, played where he played, worked where he worked, and slept where he slept. That means more than gold to me.

"Mom loves you, and wanted us to know you, because she did not know her grandparents, or her parents, for that matter. I feel so sorry for her, because as an orphan, she was raised in foster homes. She told me she named me Syd Murray hoping that sometime, somewhere, somebody would recognize the name and tell me about my grandfather. One of her foster mothers told her that her father's name was Syd Murray, and that he had dropped her and her sister off and promised to return for them. He did return, but Mom was in the hospital, and he took her sister and never looked back. I feel proud that I know you."

Syd was a man of few words, so his monologue really surprised me. He hugged Parpi Daley. I did not realize how tall Syd had grown, until he approached Maamie Daley and soared above her head.

"Maamie Daley," he said, kissing her, 'you will never know what coming to Montserrat all these years has done for me. Do you know that Maggie and I do not watch television much at home in New York? Television is already here in this island. I hope that you will never get used to watching it the way we do in America. You are my favorite grandmother, my favorite cook and my superwoman. Thanks for taking care of all of us little Daleys. The girls are running me down, now. However, if they don't have a lot of your qualities, it will be later for them. Thanks to you, I'll know a good woman when I meet her."

"Syd, don't bother with those girls," Parpi Daley said. "Woman has been woe to man since Adam's time."

"Is that so, Gabriel Emanuel Daley?" Maamie Daley asked.

"Not you, Shug," he said. "I am just giving the boy some advice on women in general."

He hugged his Shug and kissed her.

Syd said, "Parpi Daley, you don't know those girls in America. They are bold."

"Be strong, boy! Be strong! That is, unless you run into one like my Shug."

We laughed. They hugged us, and we left their room happy, because our grandparents had prayed for us.

Later, I said, "Maamie Daley, guess what gift I want to take home to New York?"

"What, Mags, Sweetie?" she asked.

"I want four calabashes; one for me, one for Mom, one for Dad, and one for Ejay."

"Who am I, Maggie?" Syd asked. "I am Syd Murray, named for my Mom's dad. Tunny and Lisa Daley are my parents, aren't they?"

"Do you want a calabash too, Syd? I asked.

"Thanks for recognizing me, Maggie. I'll ask Keith to engrave my name on mine. He's good at calligraphy."

Parpi Daley called Keith and Uncle Sym. We went to the calabash tree. They chose ten large calabashes. I had never seen the inside of a calabash until that day. It did not have a pleasant smell. They asked Sadie and me to pick some limes, and we ran to get them.

The calabashes were oval. Parpi Daley and Uncle Sym got two saws. They sawed five of them in the oblong shape, and five in the round. Maamie said that she wanted us to have two each. Suddenly, I saw her snap her fingers. She thought for a moment, and said, "What about my Sol? When you get home, he'll be around looking for corned pork, yes?"

"Yes, Maamie Daley," Syd said.

"Then, he must have his calabashes, too," she said. "If my Sol ever shows that little jealous streak he has in him, you tell him Boy and I want to see him before our eyelids close in death."

She went to the tree, and chose two calabashes for her Solomon.

After they had removed all the calabash "stuff," they scrubbed the interior with steel wool that Uncle Bern had sent them from Canada. Then, we helped to wash them with limejuice and the lime rind. When they were clean, the interiors were smooth and white. Keith sat with a penknife and an ice pick and skillfully etched our nicknames on the calabashes. Syd had no nickname. They put the calabashes in the sun to start the drying process. I knew Dad would know what to do when we get home.

Maamie treated the calabashes as if they were precious jewels. She wrapped them well in tissue paper from two of her many hatboxes, and placed half of them in the middle of Syd's luggage and the rest in mine.

When we were alone, I said to Syd, "So your night roaming is a secret, eh, phantom man? I think Maamie Daley even sees jumbies."

Syd said, "Maggie, I was stunned when Maamie Daley mentioned my night roving. I am sure Parpi knows too. You know, they raised Bern, Sol, Paul and Tunny." He burst out laughing.

"Wow!" I blurted out. My New York born brother is a Montserrat saga-boy.[16]"

One day, I stood on the plateau of the yard at the Big House, stared at the Caribbean Sea in the distance, with my arms akimbo, and asked myself, "Where Have All the Years Gone?"

It was not easy for us to say good-bye that year. Keith and Sadie said they would see us in America. Sadie said she was no Vera. She maintained that her mother was young and healthy, and that Auntie Vera did not need her waiting around to take care of her.

"Wasn't Auntie Vera a young woman when she decided to stay with her parents?" I asked.

"We have our choices, and Mama made hers. Would you stay home watching your parents get older so that you'll be there to take care of them, Maggie?" she countered. "I don't think so."

"Of course not," I said. "My parents already told us they don't want us hanging around when we grow up. 'Come to visit and leave.' Mom said. Then Dad sealed it by saying, "It will be welcome come, and welcome go, kids.'"

"That's one part of Montserrat's culture that is dying, Maggie," Sadie said. "People stay home or leave, now, if they want to.

"Maamie Daley's generation is the last to expect that. The boats were slow back then" Sadie explained. "Montserrat did not have an airport. Communication was bad. Cablegrams and the post were the only means of communicating with relatives abroad. Now, you could have breakfast in America and dinner in Montserrat. We have telephones. I cannot see me staying home to take care of your Auntie Vera. Besides, I don't think she'll want me to do it. If Mama were sick, I would be the first person at her side. I must ask her one of these days. In the first place, she insists

---

16   dude

that I must go away to the university. She did not tell me I must return home."

"Yes, Sadie. Times have changed," I said.

Before we boarded the plane, Maamie gathered us together, and she prayed for our safe arrival at our destination. It shocked us when Uncle Sym also prayed for us. He sounded like a pastor.

Syd and I cried openly when we said good-bye. I hoped, then, that my little brother, Ejay, would grow to appreciate the times he would spend in Montserrat with Parpi and Maamie Daley.

We took the inter-Island airline to Antigua to connect with our flight to New York. Syd and I were among the first to board the aircraft. He had the window seat and I sat beside him. A teenager, about my age, entered fussing, and took the aisle seat. I was speaking to Syd. She smiled, buckled up, and began to read the in-flight magazine.

About fifteen minutes into the flight, she introduced herself to me.

"Hello, my name is Caroline Donoghue. I saw you in the market in Montserrat one Saturday."

"Yes," I said. "I am Maggie Daley. My brother, Syd, and I have been going to Montserrat for many years. We love it." Syd nodded to her and continued to gaze at the Islands below.

"I hate Montserrat," she said. "This was my first and last summer there. My grandparents, Ben and Penelope Donoghue, sold their home in the Bronx and moved back to what they call 'their Paradise'. It's theirs, not mine. My father left the island when he was three, and his brother and sister were born in New York. He hasn't been back there. My mother is from St. Thomas. I can't stand it either. Maybe I just don't like the islands."

"What did you hate about Montserrat?" I asked.

"Everything," she said sarcastically. "I don't like the island, period. Above all, I don't like anything that crawls. I hate snakes, lizards, iguanas, crapauds, (frogs), and flies." She cringed, as she added, "Besides, their roaches fly. I saw one at my uncle's house, and when I reached to kill it, it took off like a baby jet. I screamed. My grandmother, who had witnessed the whole thing, said, 'Caroline, don't be so damn dramatic. Maybe it won't kill you to smile more often.' I said, 'But Grandma, it flew.'

"Now, do you see why I don't like Montserrat? Those crawling creatures give me the creeps. I can't stand the food, either. When my grandparents lived in New York, Grandma cooked normal, but when they returned to Montserrat, it's fresh fish, fresh meat, fresh this and fresh that. I said I wanted a hamburger. Grandma grounded the beef and made me a 'juicy burger'. But, it wasn't the same. She had no ketchup. How could she have forgotten to pack ketchup? Everything with her is 'healthy this and healthy that.' When it comes to food, I eat what I like. Grandma has high blood pressure, and Grandpa has high cholesterol. They need to eat healthy. I need to eat tasty. The trip was my graduation gift. I will be attending Hunter in September. I'm going to turn eighteen in December. I'll have a ball."

I didn't say anything. I did not like Caroline. She hated everything I cherished, anyway. I would not care to see her again. After I had listened to Caroline for a while, I found her to be annoying. I tried to shut her out. The flight attendant came by with drinks. She ordered Scotch on the rocks. The flight attendant asked for her identification, and she ordered cranberry juice. Syd and I laughed as we ordered apple juice. They served a meal that was substandard. Syd and I did not eat it, but Caroline ate hers fast, because they had served ketchup. It was some kind of chopped beef mess.

I was surprised when she asked, "Are you going to eat that, Maggie?"

"No, I said. It's too salty."

She asked for it, and I gave it to her. She emptied the packet of ketchup on it, and ate it as quickly as she had guzzled hers. She did not ask for Syd's beef mess. He and I ate the stewed fruits, and we asked for another drink.

I said, "Caroline, our grandmother gave us a lot of fresh fish and we liked it. I love my grandparents and my island family, and I love Montserrat. I liked the Big House where the whole family lived together. What's your grandparents' house like?"

"Nice. I don't know why they built such a fancy house in Montserrat. They should have built it in the Bronx. It's actually pretty. I am sure my father and his brother and sister will sell it if anything happens to them. They're not into Montserrat, either."

"So you like the house," I said. "You do like something about Montserrat."

I was surprised when Syd asked, "Where is the house?"

"In Richmond Hill," she said. "They do have some fine houses there."

Syd said, "My grandparents' home is not shabby, either. It was built by Daleys for Daleys."

She smiled at him, and asked, "Do you like Montserrat?"

Syd said, "I love Montserrat, unconditionally, and I'll shout it from The Mighty Watchman. My mother is from the South Bronx, with its paved-streets and tenement jungle, and she loves Montserrat."

Caroline protested, "I'm not from the South Bronx. My parents are professionals. They own their own home near the border of Mt. Vernon."

Syd did not reply. Caroline stared at him. She called the flight attendant, got a headset, and paid for the movie. I sighed deeply. I thought that Caroline was a spoiled brat. She disembarked quickly when we landed at Kennedy Airport. She was among the first on line to clear customs. Syd and I did not rush. She waved good-bye to us as she rolled her one-piece luggage to the exit. We waved back. I'd bet anyone that she had no calabashes.

Dad got excited when he saw the engraved calabashes. He stared at his name engraved in his oval and round calabashes. Mom took hers, and traced her index finger along her name. She gave Ejay his. He placed the round one on his head, and it fitted him like a glove. Keith took a picture of him.

Of course, Maamie Daley had sent Dad's and Uncle Sol's corned pork, cassava meal, and two large sacks of fresh pigeon peas, about ten pounds each. The new gift was the large jar of sliced mangoes. Dad chose the largest pot in the kitchen, measured four cups of pigeon peas, cut three large pieces of pork from his loin, and put it to soak. He went to the green grocers, and bought dasheen, sweet potatoes, and onions. Maamie had sent some "hubbs and chibble." When he returned with all his produce, Mom declared that if he were cooking, she would not cook that night.

"Leave the kitchen to the Daley men today, Lisa," Dad said. "Syd and Ejay, come with me."

Dad closed the kitchen door. We spied on them through the window in the door. He had Ejay removing all the pigeon peas that had floated to the top of the bowl. Syd was peeling the dasheen and sweet potatoes. Dad was kneading the cassava dumplings. Dad looked up, and I drew away from the door.

While the men cooked, Mom and I went to her room to chat. I told her about Caroline Donoghue, and she thought exactly as I had. Caroline was a spoiled brat. I told her that I had never tasted pigeon peas soup as good as Maamie Daley's, and it tasted far better in the calabash bowl.

"I'll tell you if I agree with you, Maggie," she said. "But Tunny's soup smells damn good."

"It's going to take a while, Mom. It must simmer. Maamie Daley said that simmering is the fundamental difference between good cooking and bad cooking. Her baby boy Tunny knows it."

Dad had telephoned Uncle Sol to come and get his corned pork and something special that his parents had sent for him. Uncle Sol and his girlfriend had a way of arriving just on time to eat, but she had gone out with some friends, and she would miss the pigeon peas soup, served for the first time at our home in calabashes.

Uncle Sol was quite happy to see his name engraved on two calabashes. He stared at them. I thought he valued the utensils more that year than he did the soup, though my father and brothers had made a soup that was every bit as good as Maamie Daley and Auntie Vera's soup.

I said, "Uncle Sol, Maamie Daley said she wants to see you before her eyelids close in death."

He said, "Okay Maggie. I'll talk to Maamie."

Mom had made a salad before Dad started to cook. As health conscious as she was, she could not see us eating all of those starches without something green. We ate seconds. I thought my little brother would burst. He just liked Dad's dumplings.

Mom said, "Tunny, Maggie had told me, but I could not believe that the soup would taste better in the calabash. Why?"

"No matter how fine our bowls are, there's a certain amount of lead in them. Calabashes grow on trees, dear. I wouldn't be surprised if they grew them in the Garden of Eden. Let's dub the calabash 'the organic utensil.'"

His explanation made Mom like her calabashes more. I suppose she believed that they were truly "organic."

Uncle Sol had several servings of soup, and returned to New Jersey a happy man with his corned pork and calabash bowls. In our house, Ejay got the most service out of his. He used the round one for his cornmeal porridge in the morning, and the oval one for his regular meals. I had created a calabash monster. If Mom dared to put them beyond his reach in the closet, he climbed on the table, got them, and left them within his reach.

Mom placed the other calabashes in our China closet with her sets of "fine" chinaware. She said they were every bit as elegant as any pattern of China, and she wanted them there. They were the source of many conversations when her friends came to visit. Keith had taken several photos of the calabash tree in bloom, and he had made a number of postcards from his photos.

One day, we got a call from Maamie Daley. I spoke to her for a while. She said that a good friend wanted to speak to Tunny. Dad picked up the phone.

"Sol," he yelled. "Solomon Daley, what the hell are you doing in Montserrat, boy? He paused. "I know your parents live there, but why didn't you say you were going? He paused. "Well, I'm glad the travel bug bit you."

He handed the receiver to me. "Thanks, Mags, Sweetie, for delivering my message," Maamie Daley told me. "I cried when my Sol walked into the Big House, as large as the daylight, unannounced. My back was turned to the door, when I heard Vee scream, 'Sol!' He picked me up, and spun me around. Then I cried in his arms. Boy is in his glory. If Paul comes home now, Boy will be dumbfounded. Sometimes a voice on the telephone is not enough."

Uncle Sol returned home with calabash utensils for all his friends. He bragged so much about his fine time down in Montserrat, that his girlfriend got jealous. He reminded her that she had chosen not to go with him.

We invited Maamie and Parpi Daley to New York for my high school graduation the following June. In the fall, I would attend Hunter College. Maamie wrote to say that if God had meant her and Boy to soar like black doves, He would have given them wings. No, they would never fly in an airplane, but they would send round trip tickets for Syd and me. We did not accept their offer. I asked my parents to tell Maamie Daley to buy the tickets for Sadie and Keith, instead, so that they could come to America on holiday. I wrote to Auntie Vera and Uncle Sym, to get their permission. Maamie Daley approved, and so did Uncle Sym and Auntie Vera. We applied for visitors' visas for Sadie and Keith, and got them. Keith and Sadie were excited. They had traveled to most of the Leeward Islands with their parents, but they were thrilled about coming to America. I knew that most Montserratians thought that New York was America. .

Syd had grown steadfastly, and actually looked older than his years. Since no one had invited me to my prom, my little brother escorted me. He looked smart in his new navy suit, white shirt, and light blue tie. He and

I did not attend the same high school, so my school friends did not know him. They told me that my date was the "cutest" of all the guys there. We had a ball, and wished that Sadie and Keith were there to enjoy that part of the American teen culture.

Chapter XI

Sadie and Keith in America

Syd and I were just as excited as Sadie and Keith were, when they landed at John F. Kennedy International Airport. Compared to the airstrip in Montserrat and the small airport in Antigua where they boarded the international jet plane, Kennedy was awesome. It was not far from our home in St. Albans, Queens. Keith and Sadie had grown also. He was every bit as tall as Syd. They were happy to see their Uncle Tunny and their Auntie Lisa, and to meet Ejay.

Sadie said, "Kennedy airport is bigger than Montserrat, Uncle Tunny."

"Girl, watch your mouth," he said laughing. "You are talking about my homeland."

Mom laughed hysterically, although she liked Montserrat. The first time she went there, Dad asked her what she thought of the Island. "It's a two by four, Tunny," she said. "However, I like it because it is green, beautiful, and intimate."

Ejay seemed miffed that no one had introduced him to his cousins.

"My name is Ejay Daley," he told Keith. "Daddy said I am the youngest Daley."

Sadie said, "I am glad to meet you, Ejay."

"You are the youngest Daley," Keith said. "We are your Auntie Vera's children. We are the Duberrys."

"Duberrys? What color are they?"

"That's their last name, Ejay," Mom said.

"Okay, Mommy," he said.

My graduation day and party were near. Maamie Daley and Auntie

Vera had made the largest fruit cake I had ever seen. Instead of using wine, however, they used Montserrat's famous white rum, Plastic, to keep it moist. When Mom opened the pan out of curiosity, she shouted, "Wooah!" and backed off. Although Dad did not drink, he wanted to cut it immediately.

"No, Tunny!" Mom said sternly. "This is not the corned pork. This belongs to Maggie. We will all enjoy it at her party on her graduation day."

Finally, my graduation day arrived. Mom's pancakes were among the best I had ever eaten. Sadie and Keith knew about the surprise breakfast she was preparing for me. I knew that Mom preferred to use the larger kitchen that Dad had built in our basement, so I suspected nothing when I got the whiff of good stuff coming from the basement. I showered, put on my underclothes and my robe, and went downstairs.

Keith stood at the bottom of the steps, dressed in a waiter's uniform, including the chef's cap. He said, "Good morning, Miss Daley, this way please."

When I entered, I saw the large round table beautifully set. A crystal vase with one dozen red roses were placed in the center. The players in my breakfast drama came forward bearing platters of my breakfast favorites. Everyone was wearing chefs' hats, including Ejay. He looked real cute. Keith seated me, but they remained standing. Surprisingly, Dad said the grace before meal.

"Family let us pray. Maggie, my favorite daughter," he said "I love you so much that I named you for my dear mother. Today, you will receive your high school diploma. I am so happy that you have invited Vera's children to share your special day with us. I have always prayed for you, and will continue to do so as long as God gives me breath. Dear Lord, please bless the food that we are about to eat. Bless those who provided it and those who prepared it. May it nourish our bodies!" Amen!

"Daddy, what took you so long?" Ejay asked, standing to fill his plate. "Next time, I'll say the grace. I like what Uncle Sol says, 'Thank God! Let's eat.'"

Keith and Sadie laughed, because they did not know how outspoken my little brother was.

Mom and her helpers had truly outdone themselves. We started with fresh squeezed orange juice and mango juice that Maamie Daley had made for me, and Dad's famous fruit salad made of all the fresh fruits of the season, topped with Kiwis. Sadie and Keith had never tasted Kiwis. They liked them. We had four different types of pancakes, bacon, sausages, ham, and scrambled eggs.

My parents did not permit us to drink coffee. It was Dad's idea, based on the Montserratian myth, that it dulled the brains of children and young people. Sadie made hot coco tea made from the homegrown coco beans from the big yard. Its natural topping of coco oil floated generously on its top. She prepared it as they did in Montserrat with cinnamon stick and bay leaf. We had gotten to appreciate its rich flavor.

After breakfast, I spoke. "Mom, Dad, my little brothers, and Keith and Sadie, thank you very much for this surprise breakfast. I think it is a wonderful way to start my graduation day. I wish Maamie and Parpi Daley were here, but Sadie and Keith, you are here, and I want to tell you how happy we are to have you.

"I thank God for all of you. I love you, dearly. Dad, I appreciate all the good things you said about me, but I thought I was your only daughter."

"Your mother and I are still young. You can have a little sister some day, Maggie."

"Say what, Tunny Daley? I know you've lost your mind," Mom said.

"I'd like a sister, Mommy, please," Ejay said hugging her. "Syd does not like me. He says, 'Get lost, Ejay! Can't you see I'm busy, Ejay? Don't touch my things, Ejay.' I love Maggie," he concluded.

"Ejay," Mom said, "I'll buy you a puppy. When they put sisters on sale, your Daddy will buy you one."

"Sisters are people. Mommy, if they can sell people, sell Syd, please!"

"You little twerp," Syd said. "You talk too much."

Sadie and Keith were hysterical. Since their arrival, Syd slept with Keith in a bedroom in the basement, and Ejay had their room to himself. I knew the two of them liked that arrangement very much.

I had managed to get three extra tickets, and Mom, Dad, Syd, Sadie, Keith, and little Ejay attended my graduation at the Avery Fischer Hall in Lincoln Center for the Performing Arts. I got three awards, one in History, one in Spanish, and my big surprise, one in English. I swore I could discern my father's voice in that huge auditorium. I spotted them and waved. All of them stood to applaud me when I walked across the stage to accept my awards from the chairpersons of the departments.

We met in the courtyard to socialize with our fellow graduates, teachers, relatives and friends, to receive the congratulations of our family and friends, and participate in the photo shooting. Syd seized the photo-taking opportunities. Sadie and Keith looked at the "mighty skyscrapers," and marveled at their proximity. Syd took them downstairs to see the subway station. We had driven into Manhattan with Dad in a rented van.

"I want Maamie and Parpi Daley to see New York before they die," Sadie said. "From what I have seen thus far, it is fascinating."

"Some run to New York, and some run away from it," Mom said. "However, if you hang around too long, it grows on you, and then leaving it will be harder to do."

My graduation party was a blast. Uncle Sol and Nancy Paulding, his significant other, were there. They liked to party. Ejay was no exception. Nobody could keep him off the floor. Dad just shook his head. When he did his twirls and his winding, they circled him. They shouted "Go Ejay! Go Ejay!" The shouts and applause fuelled him. He was not at all shy.

Uncle Sol said, "Tunny, when did you get so damn stiff. Shake your bodyline, boy. Where is the Daley spirit? Ejay got it, baby. Go Ejay! Go Ejay!"

He asked Sadie to dance, and showed Dad how he should be dancing. Just before a break in the action, Dad nodded to the musicians, and touched me on the shoulders. He bowed to me, and we danced the Viennese waltz we had practiced. They applauded us. I looked quite elegant with my Dad in my four-inch heels. I was so proud that I felt I was six feet tall. A hot calypso followed. Dad did not abandon me. He shook his bodyline. Uncle Sol and Mom, who were on the floor, exchanged partners. We had a fun time.

I saw Syd and Keith pour rum on the rocks and mixed it with Coca Cola.

"Take it easy, guys," I said. "Keith, remember Grandpa Duby."

"I'm cool, Maggie Sweetie," he said.

Sadie said, "If Keith spends two months here, he will think he's a damn Yankee."

That Saturday, a black German shepherd puppy entered into our family. Dad tried to name him, but Ejay objected saying it was his dog, and he named him Lucky. Of course, Dad had named him Friend. I supposed that if he had gotten two dogs, their names would have been Friend and Foe, but Ejay did not back down.

"Why Lucky, Ejay?" Mom asked.

"He is lucky to be with me in my house, Mommy," Ejay said.

Dad said that Ejay was almost five going on forty, and added, "He was here before. Okay, Ejay. Lucky it is."

Mom said, "Honey, he was the only one of our children who spoke in full sentences at eight months."

"Yes, and he hasn't shut up since," Syd said.

"Syd, please respect your little brother," Mom said.

"Sorry Mom! Sorry Emanuel Jay," Syd said.

"Emanuel Jay?" Ejay asked. "That's my name in school."

The following days, Syd, Sadie, Keith and I went to Manhattan. We traveled by subway. We took them to the Empire State Building, Macy's, the Word Trade Center, the Staten Island Ferry, the Statue of Liberty, and the Museum of Natural History. They were awed by the expanse of the Hudson River. They spoke of Tar River in Montserrat. Keith said that it would only be a drop in the Hudson. We normally returned home at dinnertime. We went to Harlem. We walked all over Harlem, and ate hot dogs from street vendors. Syd and I showed Keith and Sadie our old neighborhood, the Dunbar apartments on 149th Street between Seventh and Eighth Avenues, and returned to Queens via the subway. Keith liked the subway. Sadie thought it was scary since it was underground. She made the same comment when we went to New Jersey via the Lincoln Tunnel.

One Saturday afternoon, Dad and Mom took the whole family to Radio City Music Hall. Keith and Sadie liked it. Ejay got by the ushers, but he knew how to behave when he was dressed to impress, or Mom would "have dealt with him."

We spent six hours at the United Nations. We ate lunch in the delegates dining hall, courtesy of Uncle Sol, and joined the tour. Keith was very impressed.

At one point, Keith asked one of the lecturers if Montserrat would ever get its independence. He was thrilled to hear that it was being considered. When the tour ended, Sadie laughed.

"Keith, Montserrat will never meet the population requirement. Have you forgotten that we need twenty thousand inhabitants to qualify?"

"I know that, but I can still dream, Sadie," he said.

After the tour, we went down to the bookstore, bought a few books, and collected free pamphlets of the Caribbean, Africa, Europe, and the United States. We toured the grounds when we exited the building, and admired the East River.

Sadie and Keith, Syd and I spent three days with Uncle Sol and Nancy Paulding in South Orange, New Jersey. He drove us to Atlantic City on the first day. We did not enter the Casino. We enjoyed being on the boardwalk, and shopping in the boutiques. We went to the Jersey Shores on the second day. He took us to the shopping malls and bought us gifts. We dined in a fancy steak restaurant. Later, Sadie asked Uncle Sol why they had served such big portions of meat. He told her that America is the land of "big and plenty." They use plenty, but that they also waste plenty. Uncle Sol slept over the night he drove us home, because Nancy had left to visit her parents in South Carolina.

Sadie, Keith, Syd and I took Amtrak to Montreal, and spent a week there with Uncle Bern, Auntie Becky and our dear cousins, Vincent and James Daley. Neither of them had married. We had a ball. We met their girlfriends, briefly. They said they would rather show us a good time. Vincent drove us to Niagara Falls, and Auntie Becky went for the ride. It was my first time there, too, and we cruised into the Falls on a boat called The Maid of the Mist. We spent some time visiting distant relatives who had settled in Montreal. They took us to the theater, the movies, and to discos. It was not easy for us to leave our cousins, Vin and Jim, but we were exhausted. They knew how to party.

On the trip back home, Sadie said, "Mags, I think I like Montreal better than New York. The pace is slower. I have never seen people rush so fast to go nowhere, in my life. It's fascinating to watch them run for the trains, miss them, agonize, and then spend an hour fussing and hanging over the platform to see if another train was coming. The Canadians rush less."

"You do exaggerate, Sadie," I said. "The trains arrive only minutes apart."

We went to the movies a number of times in Manhattan and in Queens. Maamie Daley had said, "The cinema is an evil distraction." We never went to the "pictures" while we were in Montserrat, and neither did Sadie. Keith said he had gone with his friends, but only Uncle Sym knew about it. I wondered if Maamie Daley had heard of some of those porno films on the market.

"Mama thinks she's modern, Maggie," Keith said, "but your Auntie Vera still thinks exactly like Maamie Daley. When I told her I wanted to discuss sex with her, she froze. She stared at me and then called, 'Sym! Simeon, come quick!' When he rushed to us, she told him, 'Talk to your son.'

"I suddenly became a one-parent son. Maamie Daley was tightlipped, too. Dada told us everything, didn't he, Sadie?"

"Yep," Sadie said. "Good old Sym!"

One afternoon, Ejay told Keith, "I hear you are a good carpenter. Lucky needs a doghouse. Can you please help me build one?"

"Of course, Ejay! Uncle Tunny will help us."

Sadie and I spent some hours with friends at the Aqueduct Flea Market. When I saw the doghouse, I realized how truly fortunate Lucky was. Everyone congratulated Keith. Ejay took good care of his dog.

We took Sadie and Keith shopping during their last days in New York. Their trip was memorable, according to them. They were grateful. They had seen New York, parts of New Jersey, and visited Canada. However, Keith was sure that he would never leave Montserrat. He would visit North America, Europe, Africa, and maybe the Orient, but he would reside permanently in the Emerald Isle.

Soon after they returned home, Sadie joined Auntie Ellie and her family in Barbados, where she would attend the university.

During my four years at Hunter, I did not go to Montserrat. The telephone made it easy for us to communicate with Maamie and Parpi Daley and the occupants of the Big House. We spoke to them often. Things were not the same there, what with Sadie in Barbados. Keith had decided to become a carpenter, and started his apprenticeship with a very stern master carpenter, Mr. Aubrey Samuels of Gingoes. He and Uncle Sym had been friends since childhood. However, Keith was no novice. Parpi Daley and Uncle Sym had trained him well.

I had majored in Education, but it did not take me long to find out that it was not "my calling". I worked for Social Services, got my MA, and moved up the ladder.

Chapter XII

Ejay Daley's Magic

One year after Syd graduated college, he and I decided to treat our parents and little brother on a round trip to Montserrat. We yearned to see Parpi and Maamie Daley. The trip was good for Ejay, too. He had not long lost his dog, Lucky, to an accident. My parents did not replace Lucky, explaining that losing a pet was just as painful as losing a member of the family. They were right. Our whole family mourned Lucky.

Ejay declared, "Lucky was a member of the family, Mommy. He was a good watchdog."

Everyone agreed that Lucky was a member of the Daley family. The veterinarian knew him as Lucky Daley. Ejay said he would buy his own dog when he returned from Montserrat. By Maamie Daley's standards Ejay was crabbit. He always had some little job. He even had a small bank account that he cherished. He kept his bank book in a "secret place".

We landed in Montserrat on a bright, sunny day. The island, highlighted by its emerald halo, glistened in the afternoon sunlight. Dad told me that he did not realize that Montserrat was so beautiful in spite of Syd's photographs, that all of us cherished.

It seemed that our long absence had taught us to appreciate Montserrat's natural beauty, more. Syd snapped pictures so fast that I wondered if he were really focusing the camera. Mom and Dad looked at the rough waters on the eastern shores of the island. Occasionally, a school of multi-colored fish swam by, gliding through feisty waves. Moments later, I saw my parents staring at the green mountains that stood like guards over the land.

Auntie Vera was at work. Keith picked us up at the airport. He had gotten stouter and very handsome. He shared the Duberry's bronze complexion, and the large Daley's sexy eyes. He wore a neatly trimmed mustache and actually resembled Parpi Daley more than I had remembered. There were hugs and kisses all around. Ejay did not let Keith hug him.

"Daddy said I shouldn't hug men," he said.

They shook hands instead. Everybody laughed while Dad stared at him.

"You're right Ejay," Keith said, smiling. "But remember I am your cousin. Do you remember me?"

"Yes. You came to New York when I was little, and I still have the doghouse you built for Lucky. You know he died, right?"

"Yes, Ejay. I liked Lucky. I was sorry to hear about his accident. He was a nice dog."

Dad, Keith and Syd collected our luggage and loaded the van.

Someone shouted, "Eey, look Tunny Daley!"

Dad said, "A who dat know me so well?" He looked at the man, "A you dat, Nick Sergeant.[17]"

"Yes, a me.[18]"

Mom stared at Dad and Nick, as they embraced.

Dad turned and said, "Nick, meet my wife, Lisa, and my children, Maggie, Syd, and Ejay. Family, this is Nick Sergeant, a childhood friend."

"Glad to meet you," we said in chorus.

"The pleasure is mine," he said shaking hands with each of us.

"Drop by the house one day, Nick."

"I will, Tunny," he said. "Good to see you, boy!"

Keith announced the villages as we meandered our way down the winding road. We passed through Town on our way to the Big House. We arrived there to the open arms of Maamie and Parpi Daley.

Ejay greeted our grandparents. "Hello Maamie and Parpi Daley," he said. "I know you from your photos. I am your grandson, Ejay."

Maamie said, "You are wonderful, Ejay!" She gave him a long hug. Parpi hugged him, too. He did not object.

Maamie told Mom, "Lisa, every time I see you, you look prettier and prettier."

"It's the glow from you, Maamie," she said, hugging her.

---

17   Who is that who knows me so well? Is it you, Nick Sergeant?

18   Yes, it's me.

Maamie Daley turned to Syd and me, "My beautiful young adults, did you bring your college certificates to show your proud grandparents?"

"No, Maamie Daley," I said. "For that, you will have to come to New York." Syd and I received our long and loving hugs from our grandparents.

After all the greetings, we entered the parlor. Maamie had the table set and the aroma of stewed fish filled the whole house. We could not wait to take our places at the dining room table.

I must say that Maamie Daley had prepared all of our favorite foods. It was a feast, and we grateful Americans emptied all the serving dishes. Ejay hung on to Parpi Daley, exhausting him with questions, and laughing. Parpi did not seem to mind.

Uncle Sym and Auntie Vera arrived together. Ejay greeted them in the same manner as he had greeted our grandparents, saying, "Uncle Sym and Auntie Vera, I am your nephew, Ejay; the youngest Daley."

He shook hands with Uncle Sym, but accepted Auntie Vera's hug.

Maamie Daley had aged more than Parpi since our last visit to the island. Her hair was completely white. Parpi had a little hair at the base of his head. His bald crown shone like a looking glass.

I told myself, "Dundoo, you have aged too." The word "dundoo" reminded me of my cousin, Sadie, the missing link. Sadie had married during her third year in college, and although she stayed in school and got her degree, Auntie Vera and Uncle Sym were not pleased. She and her husband visited the family, and left for London. They lost contact with her.

On our first weekend, they had a party for us at the Big House. Many of the neighbors and relatives were there. Nick Sergeant and his wife Bella were there. Miss Abby looked well. She had just returned from a trip to Canada. Dad told her the next time she is in North America she should come to New York to see us.

"That would be nice, Tunny," she said.

They hired the village band made up of a banjo, a guitar, a goatskin drum, two graters and a fiddle. They played the kind of music that forced one to dance, tap one's feet, and snap one's fingers. Maamie and Parpi Daley danced a lot that evening.

Mom told me, "Maggie, I see where the Daleys got their party spirit. My Lord, it's wonderful."

"Mom, this is for you," I said. "Just have a good time. You are the only true American here."

"Don't you think I am an honorary Montserratian by now, after all these years with my Tunny Daley, Maggie?" she asked.

"Of course you are, Sweetheart," Dad interrupted, kissing her. He seemed tipsy to me, although I knew that he did not like hard liquor.

Ejay was fascinated with Parpi Daley. He just kept staring at him on the dance floor, and then copied all his moves. The party ended well into the night. We collapsed, and slept until past eleven o'clock the following morning.

Ejay loved Friend and Foe. He ignored Maamie Daley's warning that they were not pets. There seemed to be a mutual understanding among them. He went everywhere with Parpi Daley. In a number of days, he was riding the donkey and doing all the things that Parpi did. He learned how to swim very fast, and every morning, at sunrise, he, Maamie, Parpi, Mom and Dad went for an early swim. I joined them one morning, and found out what I had missed all those years. The water was invigorating.

One day, everyone went sightseeing, except Maamie Daley and me. We had a long talk. I asked her if they were sure that they would never visit New York.

"Not if we have to fly, Mags, Sweetie. Thank you very much for bringing my son Tunny and my daughter, Lisa, to me. Ejay is adorable. He is right. He is the youngest Daley of your generation, as far as I know."

"You are welcome, Maamie Daley. You say you will not take a plane, but suppose I get married."

"Your Parpi Daley is afraid. I'm afraid. You will have to send us many photos, and then bring your young man to meet us. Don't be like Sadie. She sure shocked Vera and Sym. Her husband is much older than she is. She's not happy. Her man is not right for her. Ellie and Chris counseled her, but she did not listen. She married so fast that they thought she was with child."

"Why do you say that, Maamie Daley? Did she shock you, too?"

"No. I do not mind the age difference so much, but he's a rough and unpleasant type, if you know what I mean. For the first time, my Sadie, Sweetie, was uncomfortable around us. O my Sweetie, Sadie! She thinks she's fine now, but this is only the wad."

"The wad, Maamie?" I asked.

"Yes. Don't you remember...?"

"Yes. How can I forget the tray of corn? The day I learned to balance loads on my head!"

"That was the real wad. The wad I'm talking about won't lighten the cross she has to bear. You see, Sadie is in a troubled marriage. Besides, no Daley or Duberry woman has ever divorced. She wouldn't want to be the first."

"Why not, Maamie Daley?" I asked. "She lives in London. Everybody is anonymous there. It's not like Montserrat where everybody knows everybody's business."

"Her mother is a Daley and her father is a Duberry. She cannot change our values. Even her Grandpa Duby is concerned about her. He told me so."

"When I get married, if I have to divorce, I will, Daley or no Daley. You and Parpi Daley are more like brother and sister. You are mad about your 'Boy,' and he adores you. My parents are happy. They love and like each other. If I can't live like you, when I get married, it's good-bye Charlie. We are not in touch with Mom's family. My grandfather, Murray, left Mom with her foster parents, and disappeared. What kind of a father was he? Mom is not concerned about him, any more. I want to be like Parpi Daley and you. We must keep our family together. I have not seen Uncle Sol's children since we were little. I stopped asking him for them, because he fumbles for an answer. I don't believe he knows where they are. Maamie Daley, please give me Sadie's address."

"We don't have it, Mags, Sweetie."

"Didn't she write to her parents and to you when she got to London?"

"No. You should know your Auntie Vera by now. She told Sadie of her displeasure with her husband, and they had some harsh words. Boy and Sym were not at all pleased."

"Maamie Daley, parents do not own their children, you know. You let your children go, Maamie Daley. Parents are their guardians while they are little, but when they grow up, they should leave them alone. That is, if they trained them well. That's what Pastor Bartholomew tells the parents at family meetings. 'Train them well, see them grow, then let them go. Their time is not our time. Do not set them up for a big fall!' Although Auntie Vera is with you, I am sure you will wish her well if she leaves you. Thank you, Pastor 'B'," I shouted.

"Your Parson is perfectly right, Mags, Sweetie. Do you think we don't know that? Let's have this conversation again when your children grow up."

"Did you say, 'my children?' Maamie Daley, I don't have any children."

"But you will some day, Mags, Sweetie. You will."

Maamie Daley hugged me, and I kissed her cheeks.

"Will you attend Syd's wedding, Maamie Daley? I think he'll get married soon."

"No, he will have to forgive us."

Maamie Daley and I fell asleep in the cool breeze. The family woke us upon their return home.

Ejay did not return to New York with us. He asked my parents' permission to stay with Maamie and Parpi Daley to attend school in Montserrat. He got it. He did not cry when we said good-bye at the airport. Mom had trouble waking him for school, especially in winter. He also had the bad habit of cutting classes. Dad whipped his butt. He threatened to call the authorities if Dad beat him again. Dad stopped his allowance, packed his belongings, put him outside, and tried to lock the door. He apologized and held on to Dad's legs. Mom cried like a little child.

Mom sat with Dad on the airplane. She looked sad. When we landed in New York, I spoke to her, and she said she wondered if she had done the right thing.

"Ejay is a trip," she said. "Why did I leave him with poor Maamie and Parpi Daley? What if he cuts classes? What if he is defiant?"

"Mom, trust me," I said. "Maamie Daley will take care of Ejay, if he steps out of line, and Uncle Sym will drown him." She glared at me.

They forwarded Ejay's scholastic records to Montserrat. He attended a small private school in Town. He liked his school. He accepted the harsh discipline. Mom and Dad paid for private tutors, especially in math and science. They were pleased with his grades. Four years went by quickly. Mom said she wanted to be sure that he would be ready for college, and she would go for him in late summer. Ejay wanted to finish his secondary education in Montserrat. He did not win that battle. She told Ejay she would come and get him.

After she hung up the telephone, she said, "Tunny, do you know what your son, Ejay told me?"

Dad did not reply. Her "your son" was his warning. He knew he would hear it anyway.

"'You don't have to come for me, Mom. I am a fifteen-year old man. I'm bigger than you.' I'll show him who is bigger."

Ejay said he would not cut classes upon his return to school in New York. He often marveled at how much they were able to accomplish with such limited materials and teaching resources, in Montserrat. He told us the reason was their strict discipline.

Then he added, "You mess with them, they'll mess you up."

We could not get Maamie Daley early on Christmas Day of Ejay's last year in Montserrat. There was a heavy volume of calls to the Island. I called early on December 26. She was excited.

"Mags, Sweetie," she said, "I tried to telephone New York, but our circuit was overloaded. Ejay gave us the shock of our life. The boy is a masquerade dancer. He said he wanted to surprise Boy and me. Only Keith knew his secret. I wondered why he was spending so much time with Keith. It turned out that Keith was taking him to rehearsals in Ryner's Village.

"On Christmas Eve, he told us, 'Maamie and Parpi Daley, you have to come to Town tomorrow.' We said our jump-up days are over. 'You come and have fun.' He added, 'Maamie Daley, you may be old, but you ain't cold.' Boy laughed loudly. We went to sunrise service at church. We had a fine Christmas breakfast, liver, lights, cassava bread, and rich coco tea. Ejay is a fine eater, and he appreciates good food. He can cook, too. He is the cook now on the farm. After eating, he said he had to leave, because he was going to meet his friends in Town. He was decked out in his new pants and shirt, and his new soft walkers, (sneakers). He explained it to us in this way.

'Maamie Daley, this is my last Christmas in Montserrat. Christmas in New York is dead. People run from store to store and buy their families gifts they don't need. They put them under the Christmas tree. They open their gifts on Christmas Day, and pretend they like them. Then, they sit at the dining room table and stuff themselves. If they are religious, they listen to Christmas Carols. But, take a look at the garbage bins for about a week after Christmas. Some kids already broke the cheap toys they got for Christmas. For us Daleys, it's a family reunion. Uncle Sol comes over or we go to him, but since his girlfriend can't cook, Mom said it was not fair to Sol, so they come to us. Christmas is alive here.'

"We made sure he had money in his pocket. Keith picked us up early. He had asked his friends to hold good seats for us at the Clock stand. Vera and Sym encouraged us, and we went to Town. It was very colorful.

"To tell you the truth, I was glad Ejay insisted. First, the steel bands played. They were good. The young pan men brought tears to my eyes, when they played 'Silent Night,' and 'Hark the Herald Angels Sing.' The mocco jumbies[19] were excellent, too. Their stilts were taller than most I had seen. People threw money in the ring.

"Then the masqueraders entered lashing their whips around the circle. The ring guards made sure that everyone stayed behind the rope. There were three dancers in the troupe. Everybody's eyes were on the one in the middle. He stomped rhythmically. His feet sounded like the beat of the goatskin drum. Then he raised his left foot, and spun like a top on his right foot. He somersaulted, leaped, split, and did his rhythmic foot dance again. He ended his spotlight by wining and doing a wild belly dance. The spectators, many of them tourists, threw money in the ring, American dollars, English pounds, Canadian and local dollars, etc.

"Boy said, 'I wonder where Little Boy is.' That's what he calls Ejay now. 'He should be watching this.'

"They applauded loudly when the middle dancer took his bow. He picked up a basket and walked among the spectators on the stand, collecting money. The people filled his basket. The cameras were clicking wildly. When he got to us, he whispered, 'I'm the best, right Maamie and Parpi Daley?' I was speechless.

"Boy whispered, 'Shug, it's Little Boy! It's Little Boy,' and he laughed until his eyes watered. He raised his mask and kissed us. We had a ball in Town. Little Boy is right. I may be old, but I am not cold."

"Later, he did the belly dance for us at the Big House. Vera, Sym, Boy and I sang and clapped. Then he went into his foot dance. He split, and spun on one leg, then on the other. Vera's mouth fell open."

'Little Boy, where did you learn all these moves?' she asked.

"He pointed to his head, leaped like a leopard, and stopped abruptly. We applauded him again.

"'Eastern Parkway, here I come! Maamie Daley, I'll be on the Parkway on Labor Day, next year.'

"Eastern Parkway?" I asked.

'Yes, every year, we celebrate Caribbean Day on Labor Day on Eastern Parkway in Brooklyn, New York. They have masqueraders, steel pan bands, all kinds of costumes, and food.'"

"Boy and I had decided to stay away from Town for the rest of the festivities. Three hundred Montserratians had returned from England, Canada, America, and other countries for the Christmas festivities. Other tourists joined them. They gave Little Boy $200.00 when the celebrations

---

19   Men on stilts who performed by dancing and performing all kinds of antics.

ended on New Years Day. I took it from him, and matched it in American money. He was elated."

I said, "Maamie Daley, I believe Mom is going to have a hard time bringing Ejay home to New York next summer."

"I will miss him," she said. "Boy will not mind if he can stay here forever. You said it best, Mags, Sweetie, we old folks must learn to let our young ones go."

In July, Mom and Dad went to Montserrat to bring Ejay home. They spent more than a month there. They told us that it broke Parpi Daley's heart. Maamie Daley was sad, also. Ejay swore that when he finished college, he would settle in Montserrat.

The first thing he showed us was his masquerade outfit. Ejay left, got dressed, put a disk in the boom box and went into his act. It was Dad's turn to laugh. Ejay entertained us until he fell exhausted on the floor. We went to the Parkway on Labor Day, but we jumped up with the crowd. Ejay had not arranged to join a troupe.

Ejay's years in school in Montserrat had served him well. He learned a lot in their more structured setting. Maamie Daley had indeed performed a miracle. Ejay's handwriting had improved considerably. He brought that discipline with him, and read avidly. He advanced rapidly in school, with high grades.

Unlike Syd and me, Ejay did odd jobs after school and on Saturdays. In the summer, he went back to Montserrat to be with Maamie and Parpi Daley. He helped Maamie Daley in her "turn hand" business at the Bay, by walking among the tourists, selling them drinks with his spicy sales pitch. Maamie Daley added coconut candies, "sugar cakes,"[20] to her supply at Ejay's suggestion.

Ejay told me that she made about a dozen mango tarts per week for one of the hotels, and sold others among the villagers. Maamie said Ejay told his clients that he would gratefully accept tips. They agreed, and he pocketed his tips with joy. Each week, Maamie Daley increased her supply, and sold out. Some tourists liked exotic Island snacks, and Ejay spoke glowingly of them. Ejay was quite comfortable with the "turn- hand business." He returned to New York with his head full of ideas for making money. He had his pocket full of dollars, because

20   Coconut candies made with grated coconut, sugar, spices and essence.

Maamie Daley had given him all the American money she had received on the Bay.

It shocked Syd and me, because she did not let us spend money when we were with her. She must have noticed that Ejay was not a spendthrift. I think he was downright cheap.

Syd had gotten a job in Georgia and moved there one year after Ejay returned home. He got engaged to his live-in girlfriend, Tabitha Baines. They dropped by briefly on their way to Massachusetts to a friend's wedding. They planned a December wedding. Syd said they would reside permanently in Georgia. Tabitha was not the friendly type, so we didn't get to know her too well.

Ejay told me that he really did not get to know Syd too well. "Do you notice, Maggie, that we're not close; you know, like brothers."

"No. You are mistaken," I said. "Syd is not very talkative."

"No, I am not. Keith is a cool guy. He respects me."

"Keith is more outgoing than Syd, Ejay."

When I considered what Ejay had said, I thought, "Syd, Keith, Sadie and I were together in Montserrat, but Ejay had no one of his age. He, alone, fetched the vegetables that Maamie cooked for dinner. He was Maamie Daley's sole spy at the market place, but according to her, he made no secret of it. I asked him about his chores at the Big House and on the farm, one day.

"I didn't mind," he said. "Parpi Daley calls me Little Boy. He is my Buddy. I spent more time with him than with my school friends. Sometimes, Grandpa Duby joined us after he had preached his wayside sermons. I spent a lot of time with Keith also."

Yes, Grandpa Duby had become a roadside preacher. He thought that Sadie had abandoned him, and he was not happy that everyone had lost touch with her. Ejay said that he had a good following, because he had stopped drinking.

Just before his graduation, Ejay told me "Maggie, I'm not going to Montserrat this year."

"Why, you've found a job?"

"Yes. I'll be working at the library. A friend of mine got me in."

"The library? I thought you would get something in retail," I said, "Macy's, Pathmark…"

"I take what comes. I'm an all around man."

Yes, Ejay was a man. He was the tallest in the house, and he was robust, too. He liked to measure himself with Syd when he visited us, and then call him "Short big brother."

"Parpi and Maamie Daley are going to miss you, Ejay," I said.

"I wrote to them and explained that I'd have to get into more books to start college in the fall. They are happy that I got the job in the library."

My parents expected Ejay to follow in Syd's and my footsteps, and attend a four-year college. Everyone thought that he would major in business. He said two years of college would be enough for him, so he decided he would attend the Queens Borough Community College. He would get an associate degree. Mom and Dad were not pleased, but they were happy that he had decided to get any kind of degree.

Mom said, "Emanuel Jay Daley, you disappoint me, because you are not stupid. Why not get your four year college, Son?"

"Mom, I can always build on an associate degree. What if I go to a four-year college, and drop out?"

"We Daleys are not quitters, Ejay," Dad said. "We finish what we start."

"Exactly, Dad! That's why I'll get my associate degree."

In spite of their disappointment, Mom planned a graduation party for Ejay. She sent invitations to all the Daleys. Mom's separation from her biological family was quite painful to her. That was the main reason she wanted us to know our grandparents and all of our father's people.

Mom told me, "I fell in love with your father because he loved his family, and he was handsome, athletic and faithful. 'Lisa,' he said, 'my parents live in Montserrat in the Caribbean. I know you have never heard of it, but I want to tell you that my brothers and I send money for them every month. You see, Parpi was a farmer, a butcher, a carpenter, and all the things he had to be to raise us. He and Maamie raised six of us, and sent my youngest sister, Vera, to the university in Trinidad. They sent my brother Paul to the university in England, and helped Solomon and me to earn our certificates in machinery here in America. I love my father. My mother taught us how to speak the "King's English." She taught us basic arithmetic and some advanced mathematics, and tested us verbally every night. She has a head like a calculator. We had some interesting geography lessons. She was our in-house teacher. Parpi sat in on all our lessons. You have admired my handwriting. Maamie Daley taught us how to hold our pencils, first, then our pens. She actually guided our fingers until we learned to form the letters by ourselves.

"Lisa, if I can only afford five dollars a month, I'll send it to my parents. You'll love my mother. We call her Maamie, but most folks call our parents Maamie and Parpi Daley.' I think they were a little disappointed when Sol and I didn't get our college degrees, but we were fascinated with machinery since we were little. We have finally convinced them that machinists make decent salaries."

I said, "Mom, you are a great mother. We love you as much as Dad loves his parents. We love Dad, too, because he is always there for us."

Dad, Mom, Uncle Sol and I attended Ejay's graduation. He got one award in history. Dad and Mom were shocked. He said that his tutor, a retiree in Montserrat who had taught history in New Jersey, made sure that he kept up with his American history. Uncle Sol and Dad took us to dinner at a popular restaurant in Long Island.

I asked Mom why she had scheduled Ejay's party for one week after his graduation. She said she had to plan it around her schedule at work. Ejay's party turned out to be more like a family reunion. Many of the Daleys decided to come to New York that year. Uncle Paul and Auntie Alexandra flew in from London. Uncle Bern and his family came from Canada. Dad was happy. I lamented that Maamie and Parpi Daley would not be there. It was prearranged that we would house Uncle Paul and Auntie Alexandra, and Uncle Bern and his family.

I heard my Dad's rowdy laughter rising above all others in the room. I had heard Maamie Daley say on many occasions, "My son, Tunny, your father, was always the mischief-maker."

Vincent, James, and Ejay were true chips off the Daley block.

When the Daley men got together, they relived their childhood antics. Mom eavesdropped on one of their man talks that morning.

As she prepared food for them, Mom whispered in my ear, "Mags, I got the best Daley. Those Daley men are terrible," she laughed. "But," she mused, "I love them. They are my brothers."

The food for the party was already in place. Maamie Daley had taught me how to make ginger beer, Dad said it was excellent, so I made gallons of it, and stored it in the large earthen jugs that Dad had brought home from a flea market. Uncle Sol and Dad made goat water, following Maamie Daley's recipe to the letter. Although she did not use a recipe, Maamie Daley had carefully written down all the steps she took in making Montserrat's national dish. She assured her sons that it could never taste the same, because their frozen meat was "twice dead". Maamie Daley was wrong. They bought the fresh *kiddy* meat somewhere in a village upstate, New York, on a farm run by Jamaicans. Dad told us that they had chosen the goat themselves.

Maamie Daley and Auntie Vera had sent Ejay's fruitcake with a friend who was returning to New York. The woman called to ask Dad to pick it up at her house in Roosevelt, Long Island. I saw the cake on our dining room table addressed to Mr. Emanuel Jay Daley, Little Boy. I recognized Maamie Daley's handwriting. Other cakes, coconut plate tarts, apple pies, and cookies covered with cellophane wrap were also there. If I had looked closer, I would have seen the three large mango pies.

The grill was clean and ready for the barbecue. Syd would man the grill. Ejay was elated that Syd had come to his party. Syd took him to the store to buy him something he really needed. He did not find what he was looking for, so Syd wrote him a check. Ejay was happy to spend quality time alone with his brother, at last. Tabitha did not come with Syd. Mom was not pleased.

"I don't know about Tabitha Baynes," she said. "She is really a strange creature. Sometimes, I want to tell Syd about her, but my better judgment…"

"Mom, please use your better judgment," I advised her. "Remember what Pastor Bartholomew said."

She hugged me, and said, "Maggie, you're right. However, Syd told me that Tabitha doesn't want any children, and neither does he. You know that's a lie."

"Mom, let Syd figure it out. He is grown," I said.

She agreed with me, tacitly.

Dad had rented six large round tables, and we borrowed chairs from our church. I had offered to decorate our basement for the party. Dad and Uncle Sol had painted it in high gloss white, and it sparkled. They painted the patio, and opened their patio umbrellas. Everybody including the party man, Ejay, had pitched in to spruce up the yard. Everything was done except my part. I had a snack, grabbed the ribbons, scissors, tapes, and the tablecloths, and headed for the basement.

Mom said, "Maggie, the balloons are on my bed. Please take them downstairs. Ejay and his friends will inflate them there."

We had decided to use the colors of Montserrat, emerald green, white, and gold.

When I approached the door, I heard voices, so I knocked. Someone opened the door from within. I screamed, "Maamie Daley! Parpi Daley! Auntie Vera! Uncle Sym! Keith!" I heard footsteps behind me. Ejay, Mom and Dad laughed loudly. It was not the Big House, but my parents' bedroom was the scene of great joy for me. They had planned a surprise for me, and it worked. I wondered why they surprised me, and not Ejay.

After all the hugs and kisses, I took Maamie Daley aside and asked, "Maamie Daley, how come you are here?" She understood me perfectly.

"Little Boy said if we didn't come to his graduation, we would never see him again. Boy was not very happy to hear that. The next thing I knew, Vee, Sym and Keith decided to join Boy and me, if we would come. I told my children that we were considering a trip to New York, and they said they would meet us here. Ellie could not make it, because she's saving for the wedding of her twin girls. After New York, we'll head for Canada and then to Barbados."

"I'm sorry Auntie Ellie and Uncle Chris could not be here. But, tell me quickly, how was the flight?"

"Wonderful!" she said, her large eyes beaming. "Boy and I are as happy as black doves. Mags, Sweetie, we like to fly."

"That's great! Maamie Daley, I hope you didn't empty your pinafore pocket. I'll help you pay for this trip."

"You didn't hear the best part, Mags, Sweetie. Our sons are paying for everything," she said beaming.

"So, Maamie Daley, it took your Little Boy's magic to get you and Parpi to fly to New York? You didn't come to my high school graduation."

"Blame it on the big Boy, Mags, Sweetie! He gives Ejay everything he wants."

"But you don't, right Maamie Daley?"

"I cannot tell a lie, Mags, Sweetie," she said blushing. "You are right. I am guilty, too. You call it Ejay's magic. Vee and Sym kept their children too close, and Sadie rebelled. You and Syd started visiting us from America when you were little, and you fit into our mould. I know that not all American children are like you. I ran into Penny Donoghue and her husband Ben just after you and Syd returned to America. They had lived in America for a long time, and their granddaughter went to visit them…"

"Caroline Donoghue?"

"Yes. Do you know her?"

"She was on the same flight to New York with us. She said she hates Montserrat."

"Penny told me she felt like strangling Caroline. She told them she would never come back to Montserrat, and they were happy to hear it. Penny said what hurt her most, was that she had taken care of Caroline since her birth, because she was a nurse who worked the afternoon shift, and she was available. She said she is partly to blame for Caroline's behavior."

"I didn't like Caroline, Maamie Daley, and neither did Syd."

I knew that Auntie Vera was good at decorating, so I invited her to help me with the decoration. She was glad to do so. Mom told me that Vera did not come to New York to work, but Auntie Vera told her she did not mind helping me. We went to the basement where Auntie Vera took over. The result was far better than I could have imagined. Uncle Sym joined with the Daley men. Their private party began with them playing dominoes, drinking beer, and recalling their childhood in Montserrat.

They could not keep Maamie Daley out of the kitchen. Our house was full of Daleys, but they did not act like guests. Like Maamie Daley, everybody pitched in, and helped us to prepare for the party. They helped in the preparation of more food and pastry. Our house smelled like a gourmet restaurant.

Ejay was the guest of honor and the disc jockey. He was the tallest of the Daley men, and he was handsome. Three of his girlfriends showed up at the party. Mom and Dad said nothing to him in words, but their countenances spoke volumes. I thought that the axe would have fallen at any moment. Maybe they kept quiet in deference to Maamie and Parpi Daley. Dad could not really hide his displeasure.

Ejay said, "Don't worry about my girls, Dad. I can handle them."

"Why did you invite three girls, Ejay? Come on!"

"Dad, it's cool," Ejay insisted.

Maamie Daley, who was within earshot of their conversation, laughed and covered her mouth. I supposed that Vincent and James Daley had prepared her for the coming of age of Ejay Daley, Parpi's Little Boy.

"Tunny, Little Boy is a Daley," she said finally. "Let the boy fly his flag."[21] Parpi Daley smiled sheepishly, but said nothing.

Dad stared in disbelief at his mother. He scratched his head. He did not utter a word.

Tanya Rhodes, the most possessive of Ejay's three girlfriends, decided

---

21   Leave the boy alone

to object to the presence of her rivals. She demanded that Ejay get rid of Erica Carmichael and Maya Golden.

"Look Tanya," Ejay said, as I listened carefully. "My grandparents are here. Cool it, or take a hike!"

"Shut up, Ejay. Who do you think you're talking to?"

"Tanya, three of my best friends happen to be girls. Erica, Maya, and you are my friends. I have no favorite."

"But you took me to the prom," she defended.

"So what! I don't recall saying, 'I do?'"

"I do, what?" Tanya asked.

At that moment, Dad approached Ejay, and Tanya backed off. He invited Ejay to accompany him. I saw Tanya jawing with Erica and Maya. I wished I could have eavesdropped on their conversation. I kept an eye on them, hoping to nip any altercation in the bud. However, the three of them picked up plates, filled them with food, sat, and ate. Each took a bottle of beer. After they had drunk them, they left together.

Ejay returned. I asked him about the mess with his girlfriends. He laughed awkwardly.

"Mags," he said, "I'll dump all three of them. Mom said I'm too young to be committed to any special girl. You know what, Mags? Women are getting to be more trouble that I bargained for. They are just not worth it."

"Is that so?" I asked. "Most guys I know start with one woman. Maybe your trouble is greed."

"Mags, I hang with girls. They're more fun than guys, but when they start that possessive mess…"

"Ejay, if I were any of those girls, I wouldn't hang with you."

"That's okay, Maggie," he said. "You'll never understand, being that you're a woman."

The party was in full swing, by then. Hard liquor and beer flowed freely. Some of my good relatives were intoxicated, to put it politely. The basement and the patio were full. People were dancing everywhere. The door was open to let in the night breeze.

Suddenly there was a lull. Uncle Sym and Auntie Vera screamed and ran towards the door. I looked. It was Sadie with a little boy, about two, clinging to her jeans. Someone turned on the lights. Maamie and Parpi Daley ran to greet them. Auntie Vera cried on her daughter's shoulders. Uncle Sym picked up the baby who cried and reached for his mother.

"Jesse, it's your Grandpa," Sadie said. "Don't cry."

Auntie Vera pulled Uncle Sym and the baby into her embrace. They clung to Sadie. The baby stopped crying and began to play with his grandfather's glasses.

Syd and I embraced Sadie for a long time. Keith held on to her, in his turn. Shortly afterwards, a tall, athletic looking young man entered. He had car keys in his hand. He stood at the door and observed the scene. Jesse shouted, "Daddy! Daddy!" I saw Maamie Daley do a double take. I knew immediately that he was not Sadie's first husband.

Sadie said, "Everybody, this is my husband, Roosevelt Washington, of Atlanta, Georgia. Just call him Rozy."

It was as if we had rehearsed. We shouted, "Hello Roosevelt Washington of Atlanta, Georgia! Hello, Rozy!"

He said, "Hello everybody," and waved his hand nervously. We took turns welcoming him onto our crazy family.

Soon Maamie and Parpi Daley had Sadie to themselves. Jesse seemed to have taken to Auntie Vera, much to her delight. Syd and Keith asked Rozy to join them. He adjusted rather quickly, ate of the good food, had a few drinks, and started to dance. I saw when he congratulated Ejay.

When I got a chance to speak to Sadie alone, I sensed how happy she was. She was beaming. She was crazy about Roosevelt Washington. I asked her where she had met him. She was very willing to tell me their story.

"You know that I was in London with my first husband. One afternoon after work, I went to Marks and Spencer to buy a handbag. Rozy was looking at the handbags, also. He laid one aside, and I picked it up. He asked me if I liked it, and I said yes."

"Oh," he said, holding up another handbag, "I was just trying to choose between that one and this one."

"If you want it…"

"No. That's okay. I want to buy my godmother a nice leather pocketbook. She and my godfather helped Dad raise me when my mother passed away. I was only two years old. I'll be returning home tomorrow evening."

"Where is home?"

"Atlanta, Georgia."

"I know from your accent that you're an American."

"And you. You are from the Caribbean."

"Yes, from Montserrat."

"I know Montserrat. I used to go to St. Kitts with my godparents. They are Kittitians. Their former neighbors were Montserratians who had retired in Montserrat, and one summer we spent a week there with them. I'm Roosevelt 'Rozy' Washington," he added extending his hand. "I was named for two presidents. My parents had great expectations for me." He laughed.

"We shook hands. I did not tell him my name. He asked me to help him to pick a pocketbook, and I suggested that he take the one he had in his hand. I didn't buy a bag. He asked me for my address, but I didn't think it was necessary."

"Where is husband number one?"

"Don't ask." She smiled. "When we got to London, he went crazy. He became a classic womanizer. He had just turned forty, and must have had the "forty's jitters." I hardly saw him. He was always away on weekends. One weekend, he was in Rome, the other in Paris. He pushed his luck when he decided to quit his evening nightclub job. He was a bouncer.

"All the men in my family are workers, even Grandpa Duby. People told me he brought his harlots to our flat while I was at work. I just knew I wasn't going to support him. However, I didn't have to give him a penny. His women saw to that. You know Mags, one of them dared to call me. She complained that he had taken on another concubine.

"I guess we islanders are somewhat slow in those matters. However, I offered to kick her arse if she ever telephoned my house again. She never did.

"When things got worse, I gave up the flat, got a room with some friends, and filed for divorce. I had just heard from the lawyer that my divorce was final the afternoon I saw Rozy for the first time. I wasn't ready for a new relationship, and I sure like hell wasn't looking for another husband."

"So…"

"So, Mr. Washington returned to America as he had said, but he was back in London three months later. As destiny would have it, we saw each other again inside Marks and Spencer."

'I can't believe it's you,' he said holding my hand. I promptly released it from his grasp.

"He had startled me. I did not recognize him."

"It's me, Rozy," he said.

"It was a rainy, foggy, and dank afternoon; one of those days for which London is famous. When I first saw him, he wore a goatee, but then, he was clean-shaven. He wouldn't let me go."

"You've got to have dinner with me," he said holding my hand again. "I've been standing here in Marks and Spencer, hoping you would…"

I stared at him. He said "Honest!" He released my hand and crossed his heart. Then, he said that he didn't even know my name. I told it to him. I was hungry, so I accepted his invitation to dinner. He took me to a fine restaurant, and we had a cozy table in the rear. Do you know that fool proposed to me? I told him I would never get married again. He told me to consider my first marriage a 'non-affair.' I had never heard such nonsense in my life.

"It never happened," he said. "I am your soul mate, Sadie. What were the odds that we would meet again? We did. You've got to marry me."

"I don't know you, so the answer is still 'no,'" I said. "Somewhere along the way, I mentioned where I lived. He offered to take me home. I said it was not necessary. When we left the restaurant, I ran into a neighbor of mine, Harmon Wesley.

"Rozy said, 'Harmon?'

"Harmon said, 'Rozy! What in hell are you doing back in London? I tried to reach you in Georgia."

I learned that they had met in a course in Leeds, and that they had become friends.

Harmon told me that he had visited Rozy in Atlanta, that he knew his father, and that he was a fine guy. He told me that he had tried to hook him up with his cousin, but it didn't work out.

"We've stayed in touch by telephone and e-mail for two years," he said.

"Rozy Washington is good at staying in touch. After he had telephoned me many times, I began to call him. If he were not at home, I spoke to his father or to his father's girlfriend, Essie May Devine. His father invited me to Atlanta. We didn't tell Rozy. At the airport, I recognized his Theodore Washington immediately because Rozy looked just like him. It was a chance for me to visit that part of America.

"Rozy came home, carrying a new VCR, so he rang the bell. I opened the door. He almost had a coronary. He handed the VCR to his father, picked me up, spun me around, and planted a kiss squarely on my lips.

"His family treated me so well, that it was as if we had known each other forever. His father and Essie showered me with gifts and told me great things about Rozy. His godmother, Daphne Springer, told me about the Chambers, from St. John's, Montserrat, who were their friends in St. Kitts, but who had retired back home.

"Rozy and I got engaged. I returned to London. Three months later,

Rozy, his father, Essie and Daphne came to London to attend our very private, small wedding. Harmon Wesley was also there.

"Our American guests spent two weeks in London. Rozy and I showed them the city. They spent a few days in Paris, and a weekend in Rome. Rozy had two extra weeks. Before he returned to Georgia, we went to the American Embassy and he applied for my visa. I got it rather quickly. The rest is our story."

"Wonderful," I said. We embraced. "I love your story, Sadie; an international romance, if you ask me. Not bad for a girl from the little Island of Montserrat."

"Not bad," she agreed.

"Did you see Uncle Paul while you were in London?" I asked.

"No. His was one address I never learned. I know Uncle Bern's address in LaSalle, Quebec, Canada, Uncle Tunny's in St. Albans, New York, and Uncle Sol's in South Orange, New Jersey, U.S.A., but I had no clue where to find Uncle Paul. I was living incognito in London, anyway."

"That's right. You had fallen out of grace with the Daley's and Duberry's, you bad girl!"

"They are glad enough to see me, now, Mags. I think Jesse has won them. They like my Rozy, too. Only you asked me for my first husband."

"Rozy is a very likable guy, and little Jesse is adorable. He reminds me of Ejay when he was little."

"Maggie, I was shocked to see Ejay. He is so mature."

"Oh, yes. He had three girls here tonight. We almost had a situation. Imagine, Sadie, Maamie Daley told Dad to leave Ejay alone."

Maamie Daley approached us and hugged Sadie. I heard her whisper, "Sweetie, you look happy. My spirit takes your young man. This is the right one."

"Thanks, Maamie Daley," Sadie said beaming.

"You're welcome Sadie, Sweetie, but how did you know about the party?"

"Uncle Tunny invited me. I knew Uncle Tunny's address and telephone number long before Keith and I came to Maggie's graduation party. Rozy told me it was time for me to get back in touch with my family, not so much for him, but for Jesse. He did not know his mother. I dialed the number and Uncle Tunny answered. He invited me. I told him not to say anything. I didn't tell him about my family. I didn't know you were going to be here.

"You're right, Maamie Daley. I am happy. Rozy is a great guy. Nobody has scolded me about my divorce yet, so I think we can safely come to Montserrat. I'm longing to see Grandpa Duby, too. Rozy wants to return to the island. I've told him so much about you all."

"Return to the Island?" Maamie Daley asked, quizzically.

"Yes, Maamie Daley. He had visited it when he was small with his godparents from St. Kitts."

"That's amazing. Very few Americans know about Montserrat. I'm as happy as a lark, Sadie, Sweetie. Seeing you just makes this party more wonderful. If Vera and Sym scold you, they'll have to deal with your Parpi and me. Isn't that so, Boy?"

"Of course, Shug," Parpi said smiling.

"Now, go and bring our great-grand child and Rozy and present them to us personally, as you ought, Sadie, Sweetie."

"Yes ma'am."

I saw the spark in Maamie and Parpi's eyes as they cuddled little Jesse Washington, while Rozy and Sadie looked on admiringly. Syd and Ejay were snapping photos of everyone. I closed my eyes and visualized Jesse running through the Big House in Montserrat. It made me wish I were a child again. Where have all the years gone?

Ejay, "Little Boy" Daley, accomplished what my Dad, his siblings, and I had not. He spoke one sentence, and my grandparents decided to travel from Montserrat by air, and enjoyed their flight. Because of their decision, the majority of the Daley clan met at our home to reunite with them, and Sadie and her family joined the reunion. Ejay was the last of Maamie and Parpi Daley's grandchildren, and the last to live with them in their flat in the Big House. He had put his grandparents on the move. Ejay had magic.

Chapter XIII

Maamie and Parpi
Daley on the Move

Uncle Sym, Auntie Vera, Maamie and Parpi Daley drove to Georgia with Sadie and her family. Uncle Sol followed two days later for their return to New York. Keith rode with him. They spent nine days in Georgia, and returned to New York. Keith joined Uncle Sol, and took the Montserratian visitors to many places of interest in New York and New Jersey. Auntie Vera raved about the shopping malls in New Jersey and Pennsylvania. I took her to my beautician. She got a stylish haircut. She had her nails done at a popular nail salon. She was ecstatic about her manicure. After six weeks, Auntie Vera, Uncle Sym and Keith returned home. They said they had fun, and vowed they would return some day.

Maamie and Parpi Daley stayed with us until late fall. We took them on the subway to Manhattan to satisfy their curiosity of the New York underground. They liked it, so we took advantage of their fascination with our underground, and stopped driving into the city.

Upon speaking of the subway, Parpi declared, "Shug, now we know how lizards feel. The only difference is they don't pay for their trip underground."

"Boy, only you can compare the subway in this city with lizards' holes in Montserrat." She laughed, and so did we.

Since Uncle Sol and Keith had taken them on many tours of New York and vicinity, we took them to our nation's capital, and to the Great Blacks in Wax Museum in Baltimore, Maryland. They never grew tired. Maamie Daley's gray hair was not a good measure of her stamina.

They asked to return to Harlem. They said they had never seen so many black people in one place. One day, we had just finished having lunch in a small restaurant on 125th Street in Harlem. I went to the counter to pay the bill while the others engaged in their after-lunch chitchat. A lady on line behind me touched me on the shoulder.

"Excuse me, Miss, is that teacher Maggie sitting at your table?"

"Who?" I asked.

"The lady in the green dress," she said.

"Teacher Maggie? No, she is my grandmother. I'm afraid you're mistaken."

"I'm Nancy Farrell from Kinsale Village, Montserrat. I am sure that's teacher Maggie. I cried the day we learned that she would not return to school because she had married Mr. Gabriel Daley and …"

"Yes, she is," I said. "Excuse me, but I didn't know my grandmother was a teacher."

"She was a great teacher. I'll come over and greet her. Please let me surprise her."

As she had promised, Nancy Farrell came to our table after she had paid her bill.

"Good afternoon, Teacher Maggie," she said. "I'm sure you do not remember me…"

Everyone at the table waited to see what would come to light. Maamie and Parpi Daley looked quizzically at the graying woman.

Maamie Daley finally spoke. "You must be Nancy Farrell," she said. "You continue to look just like your grandmother Lucy Farrell. Didn't you promise to kill my Boy because he wouldn't let me return to the classroom?"

Nancy Farrell blushed. Maamie and Parpi laughed. Nancy relaxed.

"I left Montserrat when I was ten, Teacher Maggie, but as you can see, I have never forgotten you. I am a registered nurse, and everyone likes to read my charts. I mention your name when they congratulate me for my beautiful penmanship. Mr. Daley, you do not have to worry any more. I am no longer insane. I am in the business of saving lives."

Maamie stood and embraced Nancy Farrell, and so did Parpi. We exchanged addresses and telephone numbers. The following week, she invited Maamie and Parpi to lunch at the United Nations Delegates' dining hall. We accompanied them.

Nancy invited us to her home in Harlem, a brownstone on "the hill." That was how we referred to anything west of Bradhurst Avenue. We once lived at the bottom of the hill. We met her husband, Douglas Cumberbatch, who was from Barbados. It turned out that he and Uncle Chris Ford were classmates in their youth. What a coincidence!

That evening, at home, we tried to find out why Maamie Daley had concealed her teaching experience at the Kinsale Village School. She explained it quite simply.

"I was very bright," she said. "They chose me to be a pupil teacher, and trained me. I taught Junior A and Junior B for three years, and the first standard, for two years before Boy took me out of the classroom." She shoved him gently. "Don't you remember how I taught penmanship to you, Mags, Sweetie, and Syd, Sadie, Sweetie, and Keith?" she asked.

Syd said, "And the time table, and phonetic spelling, but Mom was alarmed when she saw our 'copy books', one year. We spelt funny. She wrote you, and told you to lay off the spelling. Then she sent you words like 'labor, center, and program, and check'. You are a good teacher, Maamie Daley. Dad said they could not speak the Montserrat lingo in your presence. You made them speak 'the king's English."

"Yes, Maamie Daley," I said. "Syd is right. Mom was so glad to hear that you got us to pick up our 'copybooks' and pencils while we were in Montserrat, supposedly on vacation. We were volunteers on Parpi Daley's farm, because we did not earn a salary. It sure beat watching the tube here in New York. You should have told us that you were a schoolteacher."

"My Shug gave it up to be my private teacher," Parpi Daley said. "My mother was just like Shug. She was also a pupil teacher. Shug continued to polish my English after we got married. She was very strict with Little Boy, too. He learned his timetable fast. He was not a happy boy, especially when the other children were outside playing. I think that was why he learned it so quickly. She worked harder with him on his handwriting."

"Maamie taught all of us," Dad said, and he left and returned with his first copybook.

Maamie Daley took it, and went through it page by page. She looked at all the notations she had made for her baby boy, Tunny Daley. All of us examined it, in our turn. Dad's notebook was neat, but the letters were as large as the full moon. We stood and applauded Maamie Daley. She blushed and beckoned us to sit down.

"Thank you, family," she said. "However, I must tell you that all mothers are teachers. We are the first teachers of our children."

"Let's hear it for our mothers," Ejay said. He stood and applauded. We joined in his applause.

"Fathers are teachers, too," Maamie Daley said. "My Boy taught his boys carpentry, farming, and many of his tricks, but he taught them well."

Parpi Daley blushed.

Mom shouted, "Put your hands together and let us applaud our fathers." Everybody applauded. Maamie hugged her Boy, and kissed him on his baldhead.

Ejay declared, "I am a proud father. Thank you, guys."

Dad said, "Say what, Ejay?"

Everybody waited anxiously to hear the youngest grandson's explanation.

I said, "Ejay, you said you are a proud father."

"Just testing you, guys," he said.

There were loud "Oh's" and laughter led by Little Boy Daley.

Since their meeting in Harlem, Nancy Farrell Cumberbatch kept in touch with Maamie and Parpi Daley, and with my family.

I noticed that Maamie grew sad around mealtime. She was uneasy, and kept looking towards the kitchen. I said, "Mom, please let Maamie Daley cook now and then. I think she misses being in the kitchen."

"But she is here on vacation, Maggie."

"Let her cook! Please!"

Mom acquiesced, and Maamie was in Paradise in our kitchen in St. Albans. Soon, Mom became a helper in her own kitchen and liked her new role. She learned a lot from Maamie Daley, and the rest of us relished the delicious meals. Thank God. One of Dad and Uncle Sol's hobbies was deep-sea fishing. We often had fresh fish. We froze the excess fish, and Maamie Daley lectured us on eating twice-dead fish.

I said, "But Maamie, how could we eat live fish? We're not seals."

"You know what I mean," she said. "Fish should go from the sea to the stove and then to the table. That's fresh fish. Must you put fish and meat in the freezer, Lisa?"

"Yes, Maamie Daley; to preserve them," Mom said.

"To kill them again," she said. "Sym clubs fish with mallets and you use a freezer."

Parpi Daley began to get a potbelly, and Maamie Daley became alarmed. "Oh no," she told him. "Not you, Boy! I don't want a big belly man."

"But Shug…"

"Don't you 'but Shug' me", she said. "You're eating too much. You are not at the farm where you can work it off, Boy."

To diffuse that situation, Dad introduced them to his exercise room in the basement. Parpi Daley worked to exhaustion, and so did Maamie. They took early morning walks in Roy Wilkins's Park, but refused to go to the swimming pool. They doubted that swimming pools were sanitary. The exercises did the trick. Soon, Parpi's potbelly disappeared. Maamie Daley monitored his consumption of Virginia ham. Parpi Daley often devoured large thick slices at one sitting.

I always suspected that Ejay had inherited Maamie Daley's entrepreneur spirit. He learned how to "turn his hand." He had gotten some trinkets, and secured a spot in a local flea market, where he "turned his hand" on weekends. One Saturday, Maamie and Parpi Daley accompanied him. They helped him, and he felt confident enough to leave them in charge when he returned home for more supply. It was a pleasure to listen to Maamie Daley when she spoke of her experience in the flea market.

"I turned my hand in America, buddy," she said, beaming. "Boy shook his head when I pocketed the money. I wished I had my pinafore."

"Maamie Daley," I said, "once a *crabbit* woman, always a *crabbit* woman. Did you marry any items?"

She laughed. "That wouldn't work here, Mags, Sweetie. I noticed that other vendors had the same items that Little Boy had, but Ejay is a charmer. The girls came, they stared at him, he winked, worked his magic, and they bought his goods."

Maamie and Parpi Daley did not want to take any money from Ejay for their days at the flee market, but he gave them one hundred dollars, each.

"You can't say you never worked in America, Maamie and Parpi Daley," he said. "Welcome to the American dream. Don't mention it however. You'll have to pay tax."

He hugged Maamie Daley and rubbed Parpi Daley's bald crown.

Parpi Daley beamed, and said, "Little Boy, I am proud of you."

Of course, they vowed never to break their one hundred dollar bills.

Syd brought Tabitha to New York to meet Maamie and Parpi Daley. Syd loved her, but he must have given her an ultimatum. Days later, they flew to San Francisco, took a cruise to Alaska, and married on board. Tabitha said she did not want a big wedding. When they returned from their honeymoon, they moved to Roswell, Georgia, and stayed in touch with Sadie and Rozy who had bought a home in Lithonia. Maamie and Parpi Daley were pleased. Maamie Daley said she hoped that one day, we, in America, would all live in walking distance from one another. Then, she reconsidered and said that she knew that might be impossible in these big countries.

Dad said, "Maamie, we live better apart. Everybody here likes his or her own space. We get together on festive occasions. The telephone makes it easy to communicate."

"Tunny, is that what they call being Americanized?"

Dad laughed and said, "Maybe, Maamie."

Parpi and Maamie Daley had planned to be away from home for one year. They spent a month with Uncle Sol and his girlfriend in New Jersey and then left for Montreal. They would spend a month there with Uncle Bern and his family. After that, they would go to Barbados to be with Auntie Ellie and her family.

While they were in Montreal, we spoke to them every night. Then Maamie Daley started a correspondence with me. I responded by telephone.

"My dearest namesake, Sweetie: Here we are in Montreal, my Boy and I. Imagine we thought we would never leave the Emerald Isle of Montserrat! Sometimes, I have to pinch myself, and ask, "Is this really you, Magdalene Elizabeth Corbett Daley?" The pinches hurt. I wince and I know it is I.

"Bern and James drove us to Niagara Falls, and we spent two days in Toronto. When I saw the great volume of water, and heard its roaring force, I remembered our little Great Alps Water Fall in Montserrat, and I chuckled. Boy said there was nothing wrong with Montserrat's waterfall. He reminded me that Montserrat is a small island.

"Boy has taken up with Vincent Daley who drives an inter-city bus part-time between Montreal and Quebec City on weekends. Boy is getting to know the Province of Quebec very well. You should hear him 'parlay fransay'. Last week-end, Vincent was free, and he took us to Quebec City. While we were there, we took a boat ride on the St. Lawrence River as far as the Montmorency Falls. We stayed at a small hotel on Rue St. Jean. We will send you photos of us there.

"Later that evening, Boy and I were dressed to kill. Becky and Bern had bought us new outfits. Boy looked handsome in his dark brown suit and light yellow shirt. Of course, we needed Eskimo clothes. It was cold, and we wore overcoats. We had dinner at the Chateau Frontenac. Can you imagine that they had frogs' legs on the menu at an extremely high price? Why would we let Vincent spend so much money for frogs' legs that are so abundant at our farm in Montserrat? To tell you the truth, I didn't eat them back home, and I certainly did not eat them at the Chateau, either. We returned to Montreal the following morning. Boy is feeling very comfortable in North America. I believe he can settle here. However, I still yearn for my little Montserrat.

"Oh Mags, Sweetie, on Saturday morning it snowed. Everyone was surprised. They claimed it was an early snow. My body shivered with excitement. Montreal resembled a bride waiting for her groom. Then, I looked out of the backdoor and saw icicles hanging from the roofs and glistening in the morning light. I breathed deeply. Boy and I were delighted.

"Boy begged to go out and join the children playing in the little park across the street. Bern, Becky and James were home. They gave us warm clothing. They held our hands, told us to plant our feet firmly and walk. We had no boots, but Becky lent me a pair of hers, and Vincent's boots were perfect for Boy. When we entered the park, an adolescent hit Boy with a snowball. He saw the youngster who had thrown it. Boy stooped, gathered up two handfuls of snow, formed his ball, aimed and brought the boy down. Everybody applauded him. He was the hero of the moment. You should have seen him. I closed my eyes and remembered him, at thirteen, when he first returned home from St. Kitts with Mother Daley. I believe it was what you call 'love at first sight.' Of course, I dared not tell my parents I was in love, but later, I got my Boy.

"In two weeks, we will leave for Barbados. Bern and Becky feel that we will not appreciate spending a full winter in Montreal. Furthermore, they have to work, and we will be alone in the house during the day. They say we are outdoors people. Anyhow, our time with them will soon end.

"Mags, Sweetie, hurry and get married! Find yourself a good man and settle down. When you get older, your children will honor you. I pray that you'll get a man like my Boy Daley."

At that point, I recognized Parpi's handwriting. "Mags, I felt like a little boy again, when I threw snowballs in the park. New York and Montreal are wonderful. I think I can stay through the winter, but Bern and Becky know this place, and I bow to them. We are tropical people, after all. Say hello to everybody. Your Parpi Daley."

"Love you Maggie, Sweetie, namesake. Give our regards to everybody. Love, Maamie Daley."

I never answered Maamie's letters. The next letter came from Barbados. I continued to talk to her on the telephone.

"Sweetie namesake, Barbados has changed, but we suspected it, because Montserrat is changing, too. Ellie has a beautiful home here in St. Philips, and we are outdoors again. We will stay here for two months. Boy said we should drop in on Montserrat before we leave for England. If we don't get there, Paul will be peeved. It was so good to see him at your place in New York. Yolanda and Christa Ford will be getting married next June. Since they were born together, it is good that they will marry together. Their young men are cousins. They are all fine young people. We will return to Barbados for the wedding.

"Boy and the Ford household send their best wishes to you. Marc Ford resembles the Fords and the Daleys. We heard from Sadie last week. I guess you know that she has a little girl named Vera Rose Simone Washington. She named her for her husband and her parents. I know you prefer to speak to me, but write me sometimes, please. Love. Your Maamie Daley.

"P.S. Maggie, Sweetie, I feel so blessed. A little woman, who turned her hand in the little Island of Montserrat, now has offspring in Barbados, Canada, London, Georgia, New York, and God knows where else. Just pray for Boy and me. I love all of you." Maamie Daley.

"Dearest Maamie Daley: As you know, I have received your letters and I am delighted with all the good news you send me. Ejay says that he will visit you in Barbados before you leave. I did not know that Sadie was pregnant, but we'll definitely congratulate her and Rozy.

"Good news! Uncle Sol has introduced me to a handsome young man. He claims that he is madly in love with me, but I will not rush into anything. His name is Duke Randall. His mother is Bermudian, and his father is a New Yorker. I don't know what will become of it, but I will not make a commitment as yet, although he is pushing me to do so.

"I'll let you know when I make my decision. Dad likes Duke. I think he figures it's time for me to get married, and he would welcome anyone I bring home, especially since Uncle Sol is a friend of Duke's parents. Mom is not overly enthusiastic. However, that's life. Imagine, Maamie Daley, I'll be the first in the family to marry into royalty. He's Duke and I'll be Duchess Maggie. Laugh!

"I like Duke. I've met his family and they like me. He takes me to exciting places. He teaches foreign languages, and I get to practice French with him. He also helps in his father's dry cleaning business on weekends. Please tell Parpi about my good news. When they meet, he can "parlez a little français" with him, too.

"Maamie Daley, if I accept Duke's constant proposal, I will not get married next year. Let Yolanda and Christa Ford enjoy the limelight. I may attend their marriage in Barbados in June. I have often thought of all of our relatives in Canada, England, and in different States in this country. You have a right to be proud. I am so happy that you have overcome your fear of flying. The world is at your fingertips, now, Maamie.

"Take care and God bless you and Parpi Daley. Love, your Mags, Sweetie."

Maamie Daley could not wait to answer my letter. She telephoned me. She told me that my good news was exactly what she and Boy were praying for. She said she would write to Solomon and thank him, personally. I told her that she should not be partial to me. She said I was her namesake, and those who did not like it could "lump" it.

"Don't forget, Mags, Sweetie, your grandmother prays for all of you, daily. Please pray, too. Prayers work."

Maamie and Parpi Daley spent Christmas with Auntie Ellie, Uncle Chris and their family in Barbados. She and her Boy had a great time. They returned to Montserrat, briefly. It was wonderful that Ejay had started all their travels with his insistence that they attend his party. He did not go to Barbados, as he had planned. He was too busy, "turning his hand", and the Christmas season was very profitable in that business.

Uncle Paul went to Montserrat and took his parents to London. Maamie Daley told me that they had a very good time, because they were with Paul and his family. They liked London. She complained that the churches were practically empty on Sundays. She could not believe that those empty pews were in churches in the great England that had sent so many missionaries to all parts of the world.

Uncle Paul and his family took them to Birmingham, Manchester, Preston and Leeds, where many Montserratians, including some distant relatives lived. They spent a week in Paris with Verona Daley, and one weekend in Rome. They returned to Montserrat, satisfied, because according to Maamie Daley, she knew where their children and their families "called home." She said that Verona Daley lived and worked for a British firm in Paris. She returned to England with them, but could only spend three days there.

"Mags, Sweetie, Verona, my British Sweetie resembles me. My Boy is the one whom most of you resemble, but Verona does look like me. She has my 'body language,' too, as she puts it. Verona has a little girl called Paula. She told me she wanted a child but did not want the commitment of marriage. She said something about her biological clock ticking out. I did not quite understand what she meant. That's not my style, but I will not judge her. Paula is an adorable and loving child. When Verona told me what her salary was, I was amazed. No wonder you modern women are so independent. You, Mags, Sweetie, know that I handle the purse in the Big House. My Boy did not challenge my independence.

"Darius Daley is a sweetheart, a fine young man who is still at home with his parents. I have invited them to Montserrat. I have no favorites among my daughters-in-law, but Alexandra Bridgewater Daley, is a charmer. Your mother, Lisa, and Bern's wife, Rebecca, are all good, loving women. Thank God, five of my children have chosen well, and I hope that you, my grandchildren, will have lasting relationships, too. I pray for Sol whenever I think of him. He is not comfortable speaking about his family. May the Lord reunite him with his children one of these good days! God has helped Sadie. She is happy with Rozy Washington. Sym Duberry is like a son to me, and Chris Ford is an angel. Boy and I are truly blessed. Your Ejay is fascinated with women. I hope he'll find just one. I pray for that, too. " To imitate folks I've met along the way, 'Luv ya!' Maamie.

I always shared my correspondence with Maamie Daley, with my parents. Duke knew the names of all my relatives wherever they were in the world.

Chapter XIV

Another Generation of Daleys on the Move

Tunny, my Dad, was Auntie Vera's confidant. He was her source of consolation when things went wrong. I imagine it was because they were the two youngest children. It seemed that Keith had taken up with Dionne Marie Wilkins, the daughter of *high mucky mucks*, Anderson and Chloe Wilkins. They were not happy with Dionne Marie's lifestyle, but it seemed that they were even more unhappy with her choice of boyfriends.

The high mucky mucks were the people of West Indians' upper class. They lived in mansions, called estates, and they were surrounded by maids, man servants, chauffeurs, and field hands. They owned vast acres of land and commercial establishments. Ultimately, many of them became hoteliers, as islands' tourism increased. Members of the middle and lower classes, whose children socialized with high mucky mucks, considered themselves lucky. However, the Duberrys did not.

Auntie Vera told Dad that young people would do better if they stayed in their own milieu. It made for a much happier existence. She said young women like Dionne Marie Wilkins did not make good wives, because they could not do the ordinary household chores. She added, "Such unions just don't last, Tunny. She wouldn't be able to fry an egg for my son."

She added that the Wilkins flattered Keith, because Dionne Marie decided that she wanted him.

"They always give Dionne whatever she wants. Keith is a poor boy from a working family. His father is a mere fisherman, and his grandparents are farmers. It does not matter that I have earned my university degree in

111

accounting. In Montserrat, old money has more value than the new. My Keith is more than a carpenter. He is an all around builder with knowledge of blueprint. He has earned certificates in plumbing, and electricity, and has amassed a rather large savings account. He drives a jeep. He is destined to inherit Duberry and Daley land."

Auntie Vera went on to say that Dionne Marie was a dunce in secondary school, who showed little interest in the academics, so she was among the students at the bottom of her class. She liked to go island hopping on a whim, leaving Montserrat to shop in St. Martin, Puerto Rico, and Miami, returning home with her luggage full of the latest styles. She had an eccentric side, too. She dressed according to her moods, sometimes overdressing, other times not. People say she was "spoiled rotten." Chloe Wilkins was not pleased with her daughter's behavior. Her sons were model mucky mucks, who were very good examples of what the offspring of high mucky mucks should be. They were educated abroad, and returned home to be with their father in the family's business.

Dionne Marie was absent from the island for two years, after she received her certificates from the Grammar School. She took up with Keith upon her return. They had met at school, although she was popular island wide. She would appear at his worksite at the end of his workday, and they rode off in his jeep.

Auntie Vera was livid. She told Dad that when Dionne Marie came to the Big House, she absented herself. Uncle Sym tended not to interfere in his children's affairs of the heart. Sadie and Keith often confided in him. He spoke to them and left them to their will. They claimed that Auntie Vera was too emotional and extremely "meddlesome."

Auntie Vera realized that her long conversations with Dad were costing her a fortune, so she decided to write to him. He read her letters aloud to Mom, Ejay and me.

"Tunny, I am miffed that my boy, Keith, would take up with a trollop like Dionne Marie. She had her eyes on him since grammar school, went away, and returned to seduce him. I heard that Chloe would be glad to get her off her hands.

"Imagine, they came here late one night looking for her. They woke up our household. Do they think Maamie and Parpi Daley are running a cathouse? I was sure Keith and Dionne Marie were at Parpi's cabin, but I said nothing. I am sorry I made curtains for the windows there. Trust me Tunny! Keith will be sorry, when she 'dumps him,' as you say in America."

Ejay interrupted. "Dad, Keith told me he is having the time of his life. He said he's going to ride this romance out, and when it ends, it ends. He said that Dionne Marie is hot, and that he is basking in her heat with umbrellas for his shade."

Alarmed, Mom exclaimed, "Emanuel Jay Daley!"

"Mom, I swear that's what Keith said," Ejay said laughing.

I said, "Dad, I remember the Wilkins' Estate. They did not count the Daleys among their friends. Auntie Vera ought to respect Keith's privacy, however. He is grown."

"I'll let Vera know how you feel, Mags," Dad said. "Thanks for your comments."

"No, Tunny," Mom said. "Do not let Vee know that you have violated her confidence. Humor her."

"Okay, Lisa. Vera goes on to say, 'They'd better elope. I will not attend the wedding.' I know Vera. She means every word."

"Dad, you know what Keith means by umbrellas, right?'

"No, Ejay. What? Educate me, Son."

"He uses the best condoms on the market. That Duberry boy is no fool."

Ejay looked at our parents and me, burst out laughing, and left the room. No one uttered a word.

In another letter, some three months later, Auntie Vera wrote, "Tunny, eloping is out of the question. The Wilkins called us to plan the fiasco. I told Mr. Keith that I would not attend the wedding whether it is big or small. Vera Duberry will not be the laughingstock of this island. He and his blushing lady ran off to St. Kitts where they were married. After three weeks, the groom returned home, alone. It must have been prearranged, because he went straight to his in-laws' estate. He said that Dionne Marie had gone off to St. Martin with her cousins to shop for their new condominium, a wedding gift from her parents. Does that sound like proper behavior of a newly wed woman, to you, Tunny? Why was Keith so obstinate?"

"Maybe it's because he is a man, Dad, and Auntie Vera still thinks he is a little pickny," Ejay said.

The letters arrived often, and when she was most annoyed with Keith's stupidity, she would still telephone Dad. He humored her by calling sometimes, but he, too, wrote to her often.

"Oh Tunny, Keith and his blushing bride will never live happily in their condo," she wrote. "It seemed that what Dionne Marie really wanted was a means out of her parents' jurisdiction. She spends more time off island than at the condominium. Mr. Keith took us there when Duby blessed it. It is elaborate. Dionne Marie had a lot to say about how happy they are there. However, Keith is not happy. He is jittery and disgusted. We hear all kinds of rumors, but he does not tell us anything. Keith was such a levelheaded young man. I hope he doesn't find solace in alcohol like his grandfather, Duby."

She signed off "with best regards to your household."

Not long after, Auntie Vera wrote to tell Dad that Keith's brief marriage to Dionne Marie ended in an annulment. She married one of her father's associates, a much older man. They had a big wedding in Tortola. She said she heard that Anderson and Chloe paid off Keith, but he never discussed the Wilkins or Dionne Marie with his family.

She declared, "My son was a 'bought man,' Tunny. Where did I go wrong? I always told my children that their father and I would pay for their university education, and I kept my promise. Master Keith got his education in piecemeal. A certificate here; a certificate there! Maamie says I'm too damn intrusive..."

That letter ended with tear drops.

Since Syd got married, Mom and Dad were anxiously awaiting their grandchildren, in spite of what he had told Mom. I had a man in my life who had charmed my parents. Dad liked Duke from the start, but Mom grew to like him. Some day, Ejay would get serious and find the right girl. Our Ford cousins, Yolanda and Christa would be married soon. I thought how fortunate Maamie and Parpi Daley were to be alive to see their grandchildren fully grown. Then I realized that of all the grandchildren, Auntie Vera's Sadie and Keith, the Montserratians, were the closest to them, and then Ejay, Syd, and I, the New Yorkers. Sadie had given them their first great-grandchildren.

Early in June, just before I left for Barbados, Duke proposed to me, and I accepted his proposal. He gave me a beautiful pear-shaped diamond ring. We had a family gathering. My best friend, Melissa Fields, was there. She had decided to travel to Barbados with me. Duke's parents and his sister, Cassandra, were also present. Duke's father, Sinclair Randall, was much older than his mother, Marianne. Syd and Tabitha returned to New York for the affair. Of course, Uncle Sol and his girlfriend were also present.

Ejay provided the music. Cassandra could not keep her eyes off him. Ejay was still a playboy, and Mom was unhappy with his exploits. We had a noisy buffet in our dining and living rooms. We danced to ballroom music, and then Syd, Tabitha, Duke and I went to a club for the evening. We did not know what had happened during our absence. We left Cassandra and Ejay with the older adults. However, the following day, I overheard part of a conversation between my parents, when I passed by their room.

Dad said, "Lisa, leave Ejay alone. He's a young Daley, for God's sake."

"He's totally irresponsible, and now he's hitting on Cassandra Randall. What effect will it have on Maggie's relationship with Duke, when he dumps Cassandra?"

"Who says he will dump Cassandra? Has he told you he likes her?"

"Did you see how he was coming on to her?"

"Did you see how she was all over him?"

"Oh you men!" Mom complained.

I hated to eavesdrop, but I had to listen to the whole conversation.

"Maggie is old enough to know what she wants, and so is Duke. If I must tell you, Cassandra is just like Ejay. Sinclair told me she has been giving him hell since she started high school," Dad said.

"He admitted that he spoiled her rotten, and that Marianne is not happy about it. When she talks about it, he tells her she is his only daughter. Cassie gets everything she wants from him."

"Ejay is every inch a Daley. You should know it, dear. We're hot stuff."

"Be serious, Tunny. And stop the Daley myth."

"I'm dead serious," he said in a cocky tone, and added, "Myth? My dear, is your memory defective?"

I knocked and waited.

"Who is it?" Dad asked.

Mom opened the door. "Oh Maggie, you're home." Mom rushed to say. "Come in."

I entered and hugged Mom and Dad. Their little spat had ended.

One afternoon, Ejay told me, "Maggie, I'm into panties and it's great."

I said, "Oh my God, you're A.C., D.C.!"

He laughed. "No way! Hell no! Not this boy! I am a Daley. Why do you think Parpi Daley calls Maamie, 'Shug'? We Daley men stir the sugar in women. Dad's no slouch either. Just ask Mom."

"Ask me what?" Mom asked entering the room.

"Ma, tell Maggie..."

I shouted, "Ejay, stop it! You're crazy."

"Sex is a natural act," he said. "In Montserrat, even the lizards do it."

Mom shook her head. "What kind of conversation are you two..."

"Ma, tell Maggie that Dad's hot stuff. He's a Daley."

"I'll do no such thing. Have some respect, Emanuel Jay," she said." She was smiling broadly when she left the room.

Ejay laughed until tears filled his eyes. "Now, as I was saying, I'm into panties." He looked at me quizzically. "You're a seven," he said shaking his head.

"You sell panties, Ejay?"

"Bingo! The father of this guy I met in my small business class manufactures female underwear. One day we were chatting. When I told him I sold stuff in the flea market, he told me that his father is looking for buyers for his surplus goods. I got a real good deal from him."

"You're just like Maamie Daley, Ejay?"

"Yep! Come visit me in the flea market sometimes. Don't go away." He said. "I'll be right back."

He went into his room and brought back some thongs and bikini panties."

"Get out of town," I said. "I won't wear anything like those."

"Get with it, Maggie" he said. "Come on! Ring Duke's chime! Cassie likes them, and boy, is she ringing mine."

"Duke doesn't need it," I said laughing. "Now, about this Cassie affair; Mom is concerned."

"I don't know why. The Randalls love me. They're not concerned. Father Randall asked me to take care of Cassie for him. They love you, too, Mags. They can't wait for your wedding."

"Really?" I asked curiously. "By the way, Ejay, how much did you make last week-end?"

"Close to $1,500.00."

"Clear profit?"

"Yep! I told you I got a great deal."

"Congratulations Ejay," I said hugging him. "You really know how to 'turn your hands.'"

"Maggie, the girls keep bothering me. I'm so damn handsome, I'm worried." He laughed. "Imagine this chick came to buy some thongs. She was with her man. Later, she returned with him, bought thirty dollars more, and slipped me a note. 'I love your body. You've got it on, you great big Teddy Bear. You are so fine! Here's my number. Call me. Candy.'

"What did you do?"

"I'm a big guy, but her dude is huge and ugly. I don't play those games. I choose my sweeties."

I remembered Maamie Daley, but I also thought that they call candies sweeties in Montserrat, and I laughed. "Good, but be careful out there, Ejay!" I said.

"In the first place, I don't want any ugly woman making a move on me. Besides, she has a flat, broad butt. I wondered how she was going to wear those thongs she bought. Forget about her. In the second place, Cassie is very jealous, Mags. I tolerate her jealousy because I like her, and because Father Randall trusts me." He winked at me. "She is a rebel, you know. She is the only girl in my life right now. You know that symbolic wad and load that Maamie Daley described to you? Well, I'm finding out that one woman is the wad; two or more, the load."

"Hurrah for you, little brother. That's a new twist," I said.

"I first found out about that other wad at my graduation, and not long after, at a dance when two of my girls fought. When the bouncer separated the girls, this gay DJ, I know, asked them what the hell they were fighting about. 'Ladies,' he said. 'I don't know why you're fighting. Ejay is all mine.' The girls stopped their mess, and ran like hell out of the joint. I thanked him for saving my arse, and told him never say that again, even in jest."

'I'm cool, Ejay,' he said. 'Everybody knows you are all man.'

"I said, 'Don't you ever forget it, Al!'"

"Let's get back to business, Mags. I need your opinion. Do you think Mom can use a dozen thongs for her birthday?"

"Ejay, you're a troublemaker," I said brushing him off, though Mom was slim and curvaceous.

We laughed and slapped high fives.

The wedding in Barbados was wonderful. I did not know that Yolanda and Christa were so identical. They were tall young ladies, just like Maamie Daley and Auntie Ellie. Yolanda wore Maamie Daley's wedding gown, and Christa wore her Grandmother Ford's gown. They were elegant, in a sophisticated manner. I thought it was wonderful that Auntie Ellie and Uncle Chris had asked Uncle Bern to walk Christa down the aisle, since he had no daughters. The brides beamed, and their grooms smiled broadly, as they waited for them at the altar. They had a grand service at their church, where the choirs and solos were superb.

Marc Ford was somewhat shy, but he overcame his bashfulness to celebrate his sisters, who adored him. The other ushers and bridesmaids looked as if they had stepped off the pages of a bridal magazine.

They invited all the family members present to accompany them to the photo shoots. Maamie Daley got her wish that God would smile on the day. Blue skies covered the island, and flowers were in bloom everywhere. The brides and grooms posed for photos on the seashore, in valleys, and in parks. The Daley and Ford clans seemed innumerable. The photographers and videographers had their hands full that sunny afternoon.

Auntie Ellie and the Best women had decorated the reception hall with the input of the brides. Everyone marveled at their expertise. They had chosen red and white for their decorations, and the roses and all variety of tropical flowers gave the hall a Caribbean touch that was quite refreshing.

The food was delicious, and abundant. They had ordered the champagne from the Island of Martinique, and it was excellent. The Best Caterers went overboard to celebrate their daughters. Melissa told me that it was the best wedding she had ever attended.

The music was hot, and we were in a dancing mood. They played rock' Hip Hop, Calypso, and more Calypso, Latin, Waltz and Quadrille for the elderly folks. Maamie and Parpi Daley were by far the best dancers of the Quadrille.

I met many of my cousins for the first time. Uncle Paul, Auntie Alexandra, and their children, Darius and Verona, and Verona's little charmer, Paula Alexandra Daley Lambert, had flown in from London. Paula hugged me tightly.

I told her, "You are a beautiful little girl, Paula. You will be a queen, some day."

No," she said, "Maggie, I will be a princess. That is what Mémé said."

"Who is Mémé?"

"My grandmother; my Daddy's Mom..."

"Thank God," I thought. "Paula knows her Daddy's family."

Then she said, "I love Maamie and Parpi Daley very much, you know. Maamie Daley told me that I am their first great-granddaughter. Parpi spoke French with me. He is funny." She laughed.

I told her, "My fiancé speaks French, and I speak a little French, too."

"When you come to Paris, I will introduce you to my friends, Maggie.

I like you. You know that Maamie Daley calls me 'Paula, Sweetie'. Then she whispered in my ear, "Mommy says, 'Paula, you are my only treasure,' but I need a little brother, Maggie. She loves you. She told me so. Maybe you can ask her for me."

"I'll try, Paula," I said.

She thanked me, kissed me, and ran to Auntie Alexandra. When I told Verona what Paula had said, she told me, "Maggie, it's a wonder she did not beg you to ask me to marry her father. Monsieur Yves Lambert adores her, and she loves him. Did she tell you that she has a little sister?"

"No."

"Yes, Yves got married after I told him, in no uncertain terms, that I would not marry him. Paula is very jealous of Yvette."

Our conversation switched to our Canadian cousins. The presence of their parents did not deter Vincent and James Daley. I had a special spot in my heart for them. They were there "raising hell," as they would put it.

Verona said, "Maggie, James and Vincent are very charming. I wish Ejay had stayed a little longer. Our uncles are fine, but the second generation of Daley men is gorgeous."

"Our generation of Daley women is not shabby, either. I have Maamie Daley's name but you have her stature and beauty, Verona." She blushed.

Keith could not make it. He said he would spend a week in Barbados with the Bests when they return from their honeymoon. Uncle Sol, my parents and Ejay attended the ceremonies, but flew back home together the following afternoon. Sadie, Rozy, and their little ones popped in for the wedding, stayed two days, and returned to Georgia. Syd and Tabitha did not make it. Auntie Vera and Uncle Sym were in the mix. They beamed with pride when Sadie and her family arrived. They introduced them to all the Daleys, present.

"I am the youngest, Maggie," Auntie Vera told me. "I became a grandparent before Bern, Ellie, and Tunny. Sol never speaks of his children. I call them the missing link in the Daley's chain. Maamie and Parpi lament that they are not in touch with us. Only Paul and I are grandparents. I am one proud grandmother," she concluded.

"You have a right to be proud, Auntie Vera," I said. "Jesse and Vera Rose are wonderful. Paula Daley is also a little jewel."

"Have you called her, 'Paula Daley?'" Auntie Vera asked me.

"No."

"Then, please don't. She will correct you, 'Paula Daley Lambert.'

Maamie is right. Alexandra is a charming woman. Have you noticed how much Verona looks like Maamie? I close my eyes, and I see my mother in her youth. It's remarkable. I told her and her brother that they must come to Montserrat. They promised me that they would be there soon."

"Oh yes, I know. Maamie Daley had already told me about little Paula's insistence on her full name, Auntie Vera."

Yolanda and Christa Ford Best, were secondary schoolteachers, and planned to settle in Barbados. Their husbands, Jonathan and Roland Best, who were first cousins, ran a sizable boarding house, and a small restaurant. They also catered weddings and other festivities. The two elder Mrs. Best and Roland's grandmother were licensed chefs. Roland's sister, Angela Best Clarke, was the manager, and Jonathan's brother, Glenn, their international consultant. He lived in Miami, Florida. They served home-cooked meals, and sold "take-out meals."

Melissa and I had a late breakfast at the **Best in Town** one morning. It was delicious. We especially liked their flying fish. I took home pounds of frozen flying fish to share with Duke and his family. Dad and Mom had also taken some home.

When I saw the ripe mangoes on the trees on Uncle Chris' property, Maamie Daley asked me to make them a mango pie. I chose some firm, but ripe mangoes and made two pies. They enjoyed them. We shared the recipe with them. They taught me how to make a flaky crust. The pie was an immediate hit in the *Best 'N Town*. The Bests could not wait for the newlyweds to return home to taste my pies.

I enjoyed Barbados, especially because I was with my cousins who spoke with many accents. I wished it were possible to see them more often. I was elated to see how happy Maamie and Parpi Daley were with the gathering of their children, grandchildren, great-grandchildren and other relatives. Melissa and I spent ten days in Barbados after the festivities. I spoke to Duke often, giving him a blow-by-blow account of the celebrations in Barbados.

I returned home to the exciting news that Ejay and Cassandra had eloped. Mom was still skeptical about their relationship. Ejay was not rude to Mom, but he ignored all her advice. That made her angry. Ejay called their tiffs "friendly misunderstandings".

"Mom, let Dad explain things to you. He knows about male hormones.

Most women don't understand. I told you we're rebels. Don't worry, however, Mom. I hear rebels make sober parents."

Mom said, "Can you imagine this young whippersnapper, telling me, his gray-haired mother, that I do not understand male hormones. Emanuel Jay Daley, you have lost your mind. You are young and full of yourself, but since you and Mags have decided to join us and the Randalls in a 'royal bond,' I hope you know what you are doing."

Ejay always turned on his charm, when dealing with Mom. He hugged her and kissed the top of her head. She pretended she did not care, but she adored her "baby boy."

The Randalls promptly prepared a blessing of their marriage at their church. Cassandra wore her mother's wedding gown, and Ejay a rented tuxedo for the wedding album. They had a large family reception for Ejay and Cassie. Syd, Rozy, Sadie, Jesse and Vera Rose were there. Vincent, James, Uncle Bern and Auntie Becky drove down from Canada and went straight to Uncle Sol in New Jersey. They arrived together in Uncle Sol's new Town Car.

Mom had told them that we would handle the cooking, and handle it, she did. Mom was good at doling out assignments. It turned out to be an "everybody brings a dish" affair, and it was well organized. Every item on Mom's list was checked off and returned to her. She had the hot food tables set apart from the cold salads. Auntie Becky, Mom, Sadie, Melissa and I were the servers. The Randall family was small, but they showed up bearing gifts of food and wares.

Mom Randall told Mom, "Lisa, I am glad you handled it. I could never have accomplished what you did."

"Thank you, Marianne. Congratulations to you, too! You worked your butt off."

We danced well into the night, and collapsed the following day.

Sinclair and Marianne Randall moved downstairs in their two-family home in Queens Village, remodeled their upstairs apartment and gave it to "the kids". Ejay liked his new living arrangement. It was almost the same deal that Maamie and Parpi Daley had given Auntie Vera and her family at the Big House in Montserrat. They paid no rent.

Duke told me, "Father admires his Emanuel. He never calls him 'Ejay.' He likes his entrepreneur spirit. He says he'll give him and Cass the other two family homes he owns in Queens Village, when his tenants move.

Mother surprises me. She agrees, because she thinks Ejay is a wonderful young man, too. She calls him 'Son.' Maggie, guess what? Cassie is pregnant. My parents are ecstatic."

"Cassie is pregnant? My God, they didn't waste any time."

"Why do you think they eloped? Cassie was a little on the wild side. I am glad Ejay has married her. She used to give Father 'horrors'. Mom and Dad spoiled her. You know she got a degree in teaching, and then decided she didn't want to teach. She's supposedly studying business. She works with Father in his dry cleaning business when she feels like it.

"Father spoiled us, because he was married for years to his first wife who did not conceive. However, I never took advantage of his generosity. He had met and married Mother two years after he lost his wife. The Randalls were not pleased and neither was her family. My grandparents were still alive at the time. They said Mother would take Father for a ride, because that's what young women do to older men who didn't act their age. People thought Mother was his daughter, and we were his grandchildren. Cassie defended him when she was little. She was always sassy. She let an elderly woman have it one day when she came to pick up her garment.

"'Good afternoon, Mr. Randall,' she said. 'How is your little granddaughter?'"

"She popped up like toast from behind the counter, and asked the woman, 'Are you speaking about me? My name is Cassandra Denise Randall. Mr. Sinclair Randall is my father. When you ask him for me, ask for his daughter.'

"The lady paused, looked at her, quickly paid for her dry cleaning, and left.

"Cassie sucked her teeth and said, 'These people make me sick, Father. The next time, I'll really let her have it.' She'll be a good mother. She has had a lot of practice with her doll collection."

"Old Syd and Tabitha better get going. Ejay is going to give my parents their first grandchild," I said.

"And mine too. So Mags, why not let's set the date?"

"Okay Duke. We'll get married early next year."

He held me tight and kissed me. "I love you, my duchess," he said.

"And I love you, my Duke."

Mom relaxed when she heard of Cass' pregnancy. She and her Tunny were elated. She told me she was happy that the Randalls had accepted Ejay and me. "They are a fine family."

Because of Duke's pleasant demeanor, Mom had long decided that he was worthy of me and cooked his favorite dishes when he visited us. Mother and Father Randall did the same thing for me at their house.

Duke began to drop by occasionally, but when we said goodbye one evening he told me he would come by on Sunday. He had been pushing me to set the date for the celebration of our marriage, and I was ready to do so. When I told Mom, she told me to invite his parents. Duke agreed. I prepared dinner that day. They arrived with a basket of fruits, and red roses for Mom and for me.

The six of us ate, chatted, and laughed together for a while. Duke stood, cleared his, held my left hand, and placed a diamond bracelet on it. We kissed while our parents applauded. After we had received our congratulatory embrace from them, we shared a glass of fine champagne, and set our wedding date for the second Saturday in the month of September.

Duke had told me that his father had an awesome voice. Sinclair Randall stood, and told us that he considered Sol to be the blood brother he had never had.

He said that his children were lucky to get into the Daley family.

Dad interrupted him and said that it was we who were lucky to join with the Randalls.

Father Randall added, "I consider myself a lucky man. My Duke has a sober head, but my little girl has certainly been tamed by your Emanuel. I am so happy that I am here to celebrate this moment with you. I shall now sing "Blessed Be the Tie That Binds".

He sang a cappella, but no instrument was needed. Father Randall's voice filled our home. Mom embraced Mom Randall. Dad wiped his tears, but I did not wipe mine. I had heard that hymn many times, but Father Randall's version of it hit home. I felt Duke's arm tighten around me. Dad embraced Mom and Mom Randall, and Father Randall joined in our embrace at the end of his song.

We shouted, "Bravo! Bravo!"

I felt that we Daleys were bonded with the Randalls forever. Later, the memory of that song deepened for all of us who were privileged to hear it that Sunday afternoon.

When Duke learned that I had prepared the dinner, he held his stomach, faced the full-length mirror on the wall, and smiled.

"Honey," he pleaded, "please don't cook like this every day; promise?"

"No," I said. "Maamie Daley would be horrified."

"We won't have that," he said, hugging me and laughing hysterically.

I silently thanked God that Uncle Sol had met Sinclair Randall when the firm for which he used to work sent him to Sinclair's dry cleaning store to fix some machinery. Later, he met Sinclair and his children one Mothers' Day at his church in New Jersey, which was also Sinclair's mother's church. They became good friends.

Uncle Sol spoke of Mrs. Randall's son's solo that had brought everyone to their feet on that day, but his rendition was one of the best I'd ever heard.

Early in 1989, Mom and Dad were horrified when I told them that Duke and I would visit Maamie and Parpi Daley for Easter.

"What?" I asked.

"Family morals, Maggie," Dad said. "Maamie would never hold her head high in Montserrat again if you enter into her house with a man. Do you remember Vee's remarks about the cathouse?"

"We're engaged, Dad. I believe Maamie is more modern than you are. She did not judge Verona."

"You are not married," Mom said. "Tell you what, speak to Duke, go to City Hall, get your marriage license, and have the celebration at the church as you planned. My generation began to bend the morality rules, but your generation has turned morality upside down, and trampled on it, Mags. I guess I'll keep my old values."

"Good idea, Lisa," Dad said.

"Good idea that I've kept my values or good idea that the kids should go to City Hall and get their license before going to Montserrat?"

"Good ideas all around," Dad said, 'But Lisa, I'd bet that somewhere you either have Caribbean blood in your veins, or you got it by osmosis. Where is the American daring spirit?"

"I do not want my daughter to be the one who shocks Maamie Daley," she said. "She shares a great bond with Maggie because of her name."

"Paul's daughter had a baby out of wedlock," Dad said. "He is very proud of his granddaughter, and Maamie and Parpi love little Paula."

"That may be true, but I'd rather that Maggie not shock them."

My parents and I spoke to Duke, and he agreed. We got our blood test, and filed our application. Duke's parents and mine accompanied us to City Hall, and witnessed our getting our marriage license. Dad telephoned

Maamie and Parpi Daley and explained that we rushed the legal part of our marriage, because we wanted to spend Easter with them.

"Maamie, you will be present when Rev. Spooner blesses their union in September."

"Of course, Tunny," Maamie told him. "Boy and I will be there in the flesh or in the Spirit."

Mom, Dad, Father and Mom Randall, Ejay, Cassie and Uncle Sol celebrated Duke and me in our basement. Cassie and Mom Randall truly went overboard to entertain us. Uncle Sol brought the champagne. He and his girlfriend had a misunderstanding, so she did not come with him.

Ejay said, "Maggie and Duke, you are not teenagers. Cassie and I are in it for the long run. You are older than we are, so just hang in there. It'll not be easy. All the best!"

Duke stood and hugged him. Ejay picked me up, and kissed my forehead.

Cassie said, "Duke, thank you for putting up with me in my 'terror' years. If I were the older one, I would never have tolerated that kind of nonsense. I love you very much. Maggie, I love you twice as much as before, Sister and Sister-law." She hugged and kissed Duke and me.

Sinclair Randall said, "Duke, the survival of the Randall's name lies squarely on your shoulders. I love you, Maggie, our new daughter. Please be happy and make our son happy."

He hugged us.

Tunny, my Dad, said, "Maggie, I'll save my speech for the church ceremonies. In the meantime, may you and Duke find lasting happiness in each other's care" Dad embraced us.

Mom stood, but she broke into tears, and just hugged and held on to Duke and me. After regaining her composure, she said, "Maggie, I am so happy to be here to see you in the arms of a loving husband. I have prayed for this moment all my life. Duke, please take care of my daughter."

"I guarantee you that he will, Lisa," Mom Randall said, "because if he doesn't, Sinclair and I will go upside his head."

I asked Father Randall to sing "Blessed Be the Tie That Binds". He did, and we applauded him and hugged him.

We waltzed with each other and then with our parents. The prelude to our marriage ceremony was a memorable affair. Two days later, we left for Montserrat.

Chapter XV

Maamie and Parpi Daley, Always in Our Thoughts

Duke and I knew we had planned wisely when we landed in the island. We found out that Maamie and Parpi Daley were lonely. There were no children's voices in the Big House. Ejay had not kept his promise. He did not move to Montserrat. Keith had modernized Grandpa Duby's house and moved in with him. Auntie Vera and Uncle Sym had become couch potatoes. The island had plunged headlong into the twentieth century mode, and like many families, they had cable TV. They were history and nature fanatics. They looked at educational programs; thank God. The occupants of the Big House did not have after dinner conversations any more. Maamie and Parpi Daley preferred to read and discuss their Bible after dinner. Auntie Vera and Uncle Sym watched TV in their own quarters. The Big House had lost its bonding powers. I wondered where our Daley jumbies were.

Maamie Daley must have written to Sadie and Rozy and told them that Duke and I would be in Montserrat. To our surprise, they joined us there. Jesse and his little sister, Vera Rose, were no little angels, but Uncle Sym and Auntie Vera loved all their antics. Keith brought Grandpa Duby to the Big House to meet his great-grandchildren.

Sadie told Vera Rose, "This is your Grandpa Duby."

"Duby," she said. "That sounds funny." Sadie laughed, and Vera Rose laughed, too. Grandpa Duby kissed her. She stared at him, and laughed again.

Grandpa Duby got on the floor with them, and Jesse got on his back. Jesse said, "Look Mommy, Grandpa Duby is my horsy."

Maamie and Parpi Daley adored their great-grandchildren as much as they loved their grandchildren. I thought it was wonderful to watch the generations multiply in our family. I knew that my grandparents felt very special.

I had told Duke so much about the Big House, that he was quite familiar with it when we arrived there. He liked the layout of the Big House, and the cistern system. Parpi Daley explained its construction to him. They enjoyed many long conversations. Duke admired him and Maamie Daley, because he did not know any of his grandparents.

One evening, Duke, Rozy, Sadie and I were alone with Maamie and Parpi Daley. Suddenly, Rozy stared at Parpi Daley and asked, "Is your nickname Desperate, Parpi Daley."

Parpi Daley straightened up in his seat, and stared at him.

"Who told you, Son, Shug? Nobody has called me that for years."

"No, sir," Rozy said. "My godmother's friend, Mr. Chambers, introduced me to you in Town when I was little. You were standing at the Clock Stand. Mr. Chambers was the chief of police in St. Kitts for years. My godmother knew him there when she was a girl."

"You mean Farthing? Norman Chambers?"

"Yes, sir! When he died, my godmother returned to Montserrat for his funeral," Rozy said.

"It's a small world, Rozy," Sadie said. "I know you said you were in Montserrat, but I didn't know that you knew my grandfather." She wrapped her arms around Rozy, and asked, "Parpi Daley, why did they call you Desperate?"

Maamie Daley responded. "Sadie, Sweetie, Boy was a nervous type when he first moved back to Montserrat with his Kittitian[22] mother. She had left his father and returned to her native land, St. Kitts. Boy wanted to go back to his grandparents, because he didn't like Montserrat. Besides, his father used to strap him. One day, when he tried to escape to St. Kitts on a sloop, they stopped him on the pier. His father was not far behind. He had his razor strap wrapped around his hand, ready to teach 'that little scamp a lesson.'

"Natty Daley shouted, 'Hold that boy! Hold that scamp!' A man grabbed Boy, and he yelled, 'Mister, let me go! Can't you see I'm desperate?'

---

22   A native of the Leeward Island of St. Kitts

The man did not release him. Boy kicked him on the shin, released his hand, and leaped into the sea. His father jumped in behind him, dragged him to the pier, and started to beat him. His mother appeared out of nowhere.

'Natty Daley, if you hit Gabriel again, I'll take my son, and return to St. Kitts for good! For good!" she screamed. Do you hear me?'

"He released Boy, and he ran to his mother. She called her husband a brute, and left in a huff. My mother was on the pier that day. She told me about it when she got home. We heard the end of the quarrel that afternoon. When Natty Daley realized we were listening to their confusion, he locked his door.

"Boy, didn't you tell me you loved your father."

"Yes, I grew to love him, especially since he never hit me again. That's why I left the scolding of our children to you for the most part, Shug," he said jostling her lovingly. "Montserratians are fond of giving people nicknames. From that moment on, they called Boy 'Desperate,'" Maamie concluded.

"Parpi, what's a farthing?" I asked.

"When we used pound, shilling, and pence, we also had a ha'penny, a penny and a farthing. A farthing was one quarter of a penny. Norman Chambers went around collecting farthings. He used to buy them from us. I wonder what became of his collection. His father was a boatswain, and they moved to St. Kitts when we were young men. Wait! I still have a few farthings in a bottle, somewhere."

Parpi Daley left and returned with ten farthings. We examined them, and returned them to him. They were made of copper and resembled the American penny. One was dated 1919, eight from the 1920's through the 40's. The date on the tenth one was not legible. Maamie Daley told us when they were children one farthing bought two or three jawbreakers, or one sugar cake or coconut candy, depending on the vendors.

Later, Parpi Daley gave me one farthing and also sent one to Syd.

Then Rozy said, "Maamie Daley, have you ever been to a jumbie dance?"

Maamie stared at him. "Are you really an American, Rozy Washington? Where did you hear about the jumbie dance?"

"The year I came here with my godmother, they had a jumbie dance at Mr. Chambers' house. They believed that some envious person had bewitched their home, and they wanted to consult their jumbies. I got real scared that night when my godmother told me what it was all about.

I remember that the music was hot, and they did and said crazy things. They hurled glasses of rum outside at a coconut palm, and they hit it, and fell to the ground, without spilling a drop. The man, who *turned*, (assumed the spirit of the ancestor, who wanted to be heard,) had a weird look on his face. When he reached for me, I split. Later, my godmother came out and got me. She kept me at her side, but I sensed that she was scared too."

"Maamie Daley," I said. "Rozy is not from Montserrat, but he has been to a jumbie dance. Can't we have one, please?"

"My mother put an end to jumbie dances in our house. There's no curse on this Big House. She said I was getting too deeply involved in them. The music is tantalizing. Boy and I don't bother with them, either. Anyhow, Olivia Barzey's granddaughter, Charlene, is visiting from England. She is giving a jumbie dance for her, to settle a family matter. You remember Olivia, my good friend in Gingoes. They invited Boy and me to their home for one on Friday night. I was wondering whether we should go, but since you're curious, you, Duke, Rozy and Sadie can come with us."

When Auntie Vera came home, I told her that we would be going to a jumbie dance in Gingoes. She said that they should ban jumbies and jumbie names, and jumbie dances, because the dances could get quite sinister. She was happy that they were not popular any more.

"What's a jumbie name?" I asked.

"I was named for Maamie's grandmother, Vera Corbett. Tunny was named for our great-grandfather, Nathaniel Daley's father. According to the culture, children who are born in the year an elder dies, or soon thereafter, must carry his or her name."

"I'm glad I have Maamie Daley's name."

"You and I are named for my great aunt, Mags. They called her Madge in the family," Maamie said.

"Wow, I have a jumbie name," I said. "I didn't know that. I am an American with my jumbie name, Duke."

"I think that's a great custom," Duke said.

Auntie Vera told Duke and me she had defied the jumbie-name myth when she named her children "Sadie and Keith". However, she learned later that Sadie was the modern name for Sarah, and a cousin by the name of Sarah Molyneux had died the year that Sadie was born.

That Friday night, we arrived at the Barzeys around 9:40 p.m. We used flashlights (searchlights in Montserrat) to brighten our way. We used a narrow pathway from our home to the Barzeys. It was pitch black.

The place was abuzz with music and revelers. They served plenty of food, desserts, and drinks. Rum was plentiful, and the bartender was generous. The band, comprised of a fiddler, two goatskin drummers and a concertina player, was playing a hot piece. The music grew intense. Maamie asked her friends to serve us goat water. It was excellent. Duke and Rozy asked for more, and got it. I asked for a second serving of coconut tart.

They dimmed the lights off around 11:00 o'clock. By then, some folks were dancing themselves into a frenzy, while others were clapping and tapping their feet rhythmically. Parpi Daley tapped his feet wildly, too. As my pupils adjusted to the darkness, I saw the faces of those around me. Some seemed to be in a trance, while others sipped alcohol nonchalantly.

Suddenly, someone said, "Nellie Brown is here." Maamie Daley's eyes beamed. The music lulled, the musicians wiped their foreheads, drank more rum, and asked for goat water. They paused, ate the goat water, drank more rum, and began to play again.

Rozy huddled us together, and whispered, "Nellie Brown was the youngest dancer at the Chambers the night I witnessed my first jumbie dance. She *turned* into a relative who had died in her adolescence, and who had a message for the family. I was too scared to find out what the message was, so I ran like hell to my room."

Nellie was dressed in a white flare skirt and a printed, frilly blouse. She had wrapped her head in Montserrat's traditional bandana, the kind that some vendors wore in the market. The audience had formed a circle. They took their places as if they were led by invisible guides. Nellie started slowly, stomping on her right foot, dipping and swirling as she moved around the ring. She increased her stomping to the tempo of the music. They passed her a drink of white rum, and then another. She leaned back and threw each drink in the back of her throat. She then began to twirl, dip and stomp first to the right and then to the left. Each stomp of her right foot landed with a thud on the hardwood floor. Her bandanna fell off, and her long hair swirled around her head with each movement. She stopped abruptly.

"Charlene O'Garro, come out! Where is Charlene?" she asked.

A slim, young woman stepped out of a room and stood in front of Nellie. Nellie began her rhythmic dance again, moving slowly around Charlene with her hands clasped behind her back. The drummers beat their instruments with the heels of their hands, and twirled their fingers around them. They made the sound of "Woo! Woo!" That is the reason a jumbie dance is also called a "woo woo" dance. The scene was eerie. The music penetrated the semi-dark house.

Nellie continued to dance around Charlene, with her hands still clasped behind her back. Her movements were dazzling. She jerked her head menacingly. Suddenly, Charlene's slim body began to twitch rhythmically. I heard a British accent say something I could not understand. It seemed that Charlene was speaking, but I did not see her lips move. "My Lord, she's a ventriloquist," I thought.

The entire dialogue was in the Montserratian lingo. ("Charlene, you coom. So you lef Inglunt aftoo twenty-five years. A wha mek you cheeange you niam? Cityra Amina. De inishuls aar de siam. Charlene Ann. The inishals no enuff. Me want me niam.").

"Charlene, you came. You finally left England after twenty-five years. Why did you change your name? I want my name. I want my name. Cityrah Amina. Charlene Ann! The initials are not enough. Charlene. I want my name!"

Nellie danced around Charlene again. She stood like a statue in the circle. Nellie continued to dance around her, and with each twirl, she shouted that she wanted her name. My heart thumped in rhythm with the drums. Perspiration drenched my face. I was too petrified to wipe it. Nellie opened her arms widely, and indicated she was going to exit the circle. She went to the liquor table, poured a generous drink of rum and drank it. Her countenance was spooky. I closed my eyes to keep from becoming dizzy, but the music reverberated in my brains.

I heard a familiar voice say, "Your grandmother wants her name. Give Cityrah to her. She is here now, and is waiting for your answer!"

Suddenly, there were three dancers in the ring. The third one was Maamie Daley. The musicians increased the tempo of the music.

Nellie's face was rigid, showing the intensity with which she *turned*. "Give Cityrah her name, Charlene!" She said, as she twirled. Parpi Daley stood. He stomped in place, and clapped rhythmically. His head jerked sadistically. He stared at Maamie Daley as the beat increased. She stomped and twirled. She did not speak the Montserrat patois.

Maamie Daley and Nellie Brown seemed to have rehearsed each move together. They twirled and dipped in unison. Her friend, Mrs. Barzey, shouted, "Give Mummah her name, Charlene. Change your health! Give Mummah her name!"

Charlene began to *turn* slowly, then she, too, began to dip, swirl, and stomp at the speed of giddiness. "Yes!' she said. "Yes! Yes!"

"What is your name, little girl?" Maamie Daley asked in a British accent.

I dammed the thought of the evil medium that was operating through my grandmother. Maamie does not speak like that! She poured herself a glass of rum and drank it. I was alarmed.

I heard Sadie whisper, "Maamie does not drink."

"Cityrah Amina O'Garro," Charlene responded in a child's voice, as her body swirled rhythmically although the musicians had lessened the tempo. Beads of sweat covered her brow. The two women retreated, moving backwards out of the ring. Charlene danced herself into frenzy. The large beads on her forehead ran freely on her face. She held her skirt, waltzed around the ring, and collapsed on the floor. She stayed in that position for a while, then she knelt with her toes curled under her. She leaned forward, and lowered her head. Her long, black hair covered her face. Other players entered the ring. They threw bottles of rum around the ring. I watched as the new arrival caught each one, drank of it, and passed it around the ring. They did not spill a drop. A rhythmic chant ensued. The fiddler and the drummers joined in a chant. The spectators applauded, and I, too, joined nervously in their applause.

A middle age couple picked up Charlene, and escorted her out of the room. I wondered if she would abide by the decision she had made to return to her jumbie name. I thought that Cityrah Amina O'Garro was a heavy load for a beautiful modern young woman to carry. She would definitely need a good wad, maybe the nickname, **Ceetie**.

I felt Duke's arm tighten around me. Rozy and Sadie were already clinging closely to each other. I did not understand what I had seen. I had no idea when we left the Big House that Maamie Daley would be one of the players in the jumbie dance theatrics. I saw clearly why my great-grandmother had forbidden the dance in her house.

At daybreak, we walked home silently. The cool morning breeze did not erase the woo woo sound from my brain. Parpi and Maamie Daley walked arm in arm ahead of us. I held tightly to Duke's hand, but Sadie and Rozy walked briskly side by side. We arrived at the Big House rather quickly. I wished I could have spoken to Auntie Vera while my head was still buzzing with the rhythm of the goatskin drums.

Before we went to bed that morning, Rozy told us, "Now I remember why the Chamber's jumbie dance scared the hell out of me, when I was little. I recall grabbing my godmother's arm before I split."

"Weird," I said. "That was so weird! Did you guys see Maamie Daley?"

"How could we have missed her? Rozy asked. "Walking home, she acted as if nothing had happened."

"Cityrah Amina O'Garro! They can call her Ceetee, for short." I mused. Then I asked Sadie the question that troubled me most. "Do you think Charlene is going to change her name?"

"If she believed what happened in that house last night, yes, she would. Do you believe in it, Mags?" Sadie asked.

"If my jumbie name is part of a ritual, I guess so."

"Well, there you go, Duke," Sadie said. "Mama did not give Keith or me jumbie names, and we are still here," she said laughing.

"What do you mean, Sadie?" he asked. "Do people really believe that the kid will die if they don't…"

"Yep," Sadie said. "My parents, especially Vera Daley Duberry, did not believe in that stuff. From what I gathered she named Keith from some guy she had met in college."

Duke and I slept soundly until noon. Auntie Vera knocked to say she just wanted to see if everything was okay with us. She said that Sadie and Rozy were already up. After Duke and I ate breakfast, I had a private chat with Auntie Vera. I told her what we had witnessed.

"Our grandmother Daley wanted no part of it in what is now the Big House, because one dancer had turned and conjured up an evil ancestor. He frightened the hell out of us, children, swinging his cutlass around the room as he *turned*. When he pulled a short rope with a noose from his satchel, we children ran out of the house, screaming. We were not the only ones who ran for our lives.

Someone outside said, "Why the hell would *Crazy Bucky,* the cutlass man, come back? Oh, Gad! I forgot his mother was a Daley. He came back to settle the score."

"They caught your father in Trials. He ran the fastest to get away from our house. I won't tell you what else took place that night, and neither will Tunny. None of us ever spoke of it again."

"How come Parpi Daley let his mother rule in his house."

"While she was alive, she was the absolute lady of the house. Remember, we lived in her house. I was the smallest, but I remember that she did not like Maamie. She thought Parpi was a 'prince'. Actually, that was her nickname for him, 'Prince Daley.' She paused. Then she added, "Maggie, if you ask Maamie about the role she played last night, she will not remember what happened, not if it was a true jumbie dance. Believe or don't believe what you saw, but do not ask her anything. All I can tell you is that Cityrah

Amina O'Garro, the elder, had rivaled her for Parpi's love when they were young. It's a wonder she should use Maamie as a medium to get to her granddaughter. I think Grandma Daley preferred her for Parpi, but old Boy loved his Shug from the start. According to Maamie, he threatened to move in with the Corbetts. That would have been the ultimate insult. She either loved or tolerated Maamie for the rest of her life. My Sym loves me. Your Duke loves you, too, Maggie. I know when a man loves a woman."

I told Duke what Auntie Vera had said, but we never discussed it further. Sadie told me that she had never gone to a jumbie dance before, but they used to discuss them when "children were seen and not heard". She said that when she heard that Rozy had met Parpi Daley when he was little, it confirmed that she had the right man.

"Mags, it's so great to be back here with you in the Big House. Can you believe that I have two little ones tagging behind me? My little Vera Rose is giving Jesse a fit. Sometimes, I have to get real stern with her, and threaten her father. Rozy spoils her. Hurry and get pregnant Maggie. I want our children to romp together here in the Big House. I'll get in touch with Ejay when his baby comes along."

Easter Sunday was special. Sadie, Rozy, Jesse and Vera Rose did not travel with us to church, but they joined us when we entered. Keith and Grandpa Duby were not there. The church was full. Maamie and Parpi Daley were as proud as peacocks.

Duke could not understand where all the people had come from. He was amazed to see that St. Anthony's Anglican Church was full to its capacity. He enjoyed the singing of the old hymns, and paid close attention to the parson's sermon. It was not I, but Maamie Daley, who introduced Duke to everyone after the service. Sadie also introduced her family to the folks.

We saw the Barzeys at church. We could not have missed Cityrah. She had smiled and greeted everyone to whom her grandmother introduced to her, as Cityrah Amina O'Garro. She wore a light green silk dress, white shoes and bag, and pearl necklace and earrings. She greeted us, as if we were old friends. I wished I had the time to know her better. Her grandmother had asked the parson to pray for her safe journey back to London. She would leave on Easter Monday. He prayed long and loud.

I was sure that he had heard of the jumbie dance. At one point, he closed the Bible, held it above his head, and shouted, "All the answers are found in God's Word, my friends." He scrutinized the congregation with his large protruding eyes.

When we said good-bye to Cityrah, Duke said, "Duchess, that's a gorgeous woman. I don't think she will honor that 'jumbie dance stuff.'"

"According to what Auntie Vera told me, the penalty for non-compliance, is death of the newborn child, and Sadie confirmed it."

He stared at me, and said, "Are you kidding? I didn't know it could get that serious." Then, he pondered for a while, and added, "But Charlene is a fully grown woman. She seems mentally sound to me."

"Duke," I said "sometimes what we believe can kill us. I wonder who Bucky Daley was."

Auntie Vera had attended the sunrise service, and she had brunch ready when we got home. Maamie Daley said we should have invited Keith and Grandpa Duby to church and then to the Big House. Keith was not a church going man, and I was sure that Grandpa Duby was out somewhere preaching his roadside sermons for those who did not attend any church.

Auntie Vera showed off her expertise in the kitchen. She made Johnnycakes. They were delicious, light, fluffy, and crispy. Jesse and Vera Rose ate like adults.

Sadie said, "Jesse, when we go home to Georgia, I'm going to put you on a diet. Mama, look what you have done. Jesse has a potbelly, and Vera Rose's face is as large as the full moon."

Vera Rose started to cry and ran to her father. Rozy picked her up.

"I don't like you, Mommy," she declared. "You are mean." She hugged her father tightly around his neck, and pouted.

"I am sorry, Vera Rose, but it is true," Sadie said.

Rozy asked her to apologize to her mother and she did.

We spent Easter Monday at a picnic on the beach. Easter was a two-day celebration in Montserrat. Jesse and Vera Rose had a ball. Keith had dropped Grandpa Duby off at the Big House. He spoke to Uncle Sym and Auntie Vera, and they answered him.

Jesse said, "Uncle Keith," ran to him, got his hug, and then ran to Grandpa Duby who scooped him up, and clung to him. The iceberg that was the relationship between Grandpa Duby and Uncle Sym was melting, thanks to Sadie, Rozy and their children.

We had taken boxes of franks and hamburgers with us, and saved them for that day on the beach. The men set up the portable grill. Auntie Vera made breadfruit salad, which was far tastier than potato salad. Like my mango pies, that was a new treat in the island. They said that it was introduced by a certain Mrs. Ellie Wade who was a Montserratian hotelier.

I ran into Mrs. Wade one afternoon in Town, introduced myself, and asked her about the breadfruit salad. She told me the secret was to choose a very ripe breadfruit. I realized then that Auntie Vera had already known that.

Sadie told me that Auntie Vera had looked at Grandpa Duby, shrugged her shoulders, and whispered, "What the heck!" then hugged him and kissed him. He was one happy camper.

Later Sadie announced, "I'll return often because of my grandparents, Grandpa Duby, and Maamie and Parpi Daley. My parents can come to see us. They are still young. Grandpa Duby is a sweetheart. Rozy adores him."

Sadie, Rozy and their children spent three days with Grandpa Duby and Keith. Maamie and Parpi Daley, and Auntie Vera and Uncle Sym accompanied them to the airport.

Duke had rented a car. We said good-bye to Sadie and her family at the Big House, and set out for our trip to the villages in the north. When we got to St. Peters, Duke parked the car, and we hiked up to Zion, shouting the hymn loudly and clearly. We thought we heard our voices echoing in the Jacky Ghaut below, but it was residents and day workers who had joined in our chorus.

We drove carefully down Fogarty Hill. I breathed a sigh of relief when we got to Soldier Ghaut. Soon, we were driving into Cudjoehead. Duke and I learned the history of that roadside village. It was named for Cudjoe, a slave who had defied his master, and who was beheaded to teach the others the consequences of disobedience.

We drank coconut water in Davy Hill, and bought fruits from roadside vendors in St. John's. We saw the island of Redonda basking in the daylight. I wanted to visit that rock island. Duke laughed when we got to Dick Hill. I asked him why he was laughing. He did not reply. I told him that only an American would have such thoughts. He laughed even louder. We paused to pick mangoes and ate them. We viewed the sea and the villages all around when we got to Geralds. The mountains were beguilingly green.

I thought, "Oh beautiful Emerald Isle of Montserrat, please bloom verdant forever!"

We were happy that Duke had videoed all those scenes. Just a few months later, Hurricane Hugo swept the island, clean. We thought of the coconut palms, the tamarind, mango, soursop and sugar apple and all the other fruit and non-fruit trees that made the island glow verdantly.

I was amazed at the beauty of the rolling hills in the north. I had recently learned that the word "Montserrat" means serrated mountains. I associated the word "serrated" with sierra. Awesome! On our way back, Duke drove over Fogarty Hill as if it were just a simple road. I wondered why it was such a frightening place for me, when I was little. We drank lots of water at Runaway Ghaut. We knew we would return to Montserrat, because according to the legend, if one drinks of that never-ending stream, one must return.

We swam on most of the beaches in the island that week, something that I had not done before. We spent a night in Parpi's **hide away villa**, where The Mighty Watchman was our spy and protector. Duke was fascinated, because he had visited the volcano in Hawaii, but he got much closer to the Soufriere Hills volcano, Parpi Daley's "Mighty Watchman". We picked sulfur off the rocks, dangled our toes in the streams that flowed freely near the volcano, and leaped barefooted from rock to rock.

I showed Duke the old jackass's grave. We saw the old latrine where I had encountered the snake. It was sealed and shuttered. We managed to pry the door open, using a cutlass, and Duke took photos of me standing at the door. We resealed the door of the latrine, forever. Keith and his friends had added a private room and a flush toilet to Parpi's little villa. I understood why Keith and Dionne Marie had their romantic escapades there.

I was not as brave as Duke. I did not accept Uncle Sym's invitation to join him on a one-day outing on his fishing boat. I spent the time with Maamie and Parpi Daley, but it was not the same. I missed Sadie, Keith and Syd. I begged Duke to take close-up photos of Redonda. I thought that Montserrat should arrange weekly and maybe even daily excursions to Redonda. That rock island is definitely in its territorial waters.

I joined my grandparents for a light chat while Duke was away.

"Maamie, what do you think of Duke?" I asked, sitting at her feet with my head on her lap.

"He's a fine young man, Mags, Sweetie. I must thank Solomon Daley again," she said, smoothing my hair.

"And you Parpi?"

"I predict that you will always be happy, Maggie. Shug is right. I only wish you had met him before, and that you were bringing your babies home to meet us, like Sadie and Rozy. When Shug told Sadie you were coming, she decided to come. I wish they could have spent more time with us. Did you see my Vee, Mags? Now you know how Shug and I feel about you, our grandchildren. You are the greatest treasures in the world. We will dance at your wedding ceremony. That will be our greatest pleasure."

I hugged him and kissed his shiny forehead. I kissed Maamie Daley and sat between the two of them on the sofa. When I was with Maamie and Parpi Daley, I felt complete.

Duke returned from his fishing trip with his personal fish tales. How quickly he had acquired the ways of the Caribbean fishermen!

"Duchess, Uncle Sym was surprised at my fishing expertise. I used to go fishing with my father when I was little."

One evening, we sat together on the back verandah. We sipped on fresh coconut water. It was mellow and refreshing. Uncle Sym used it to chase his rum. Auntie Vera kept her eyes on him. At one point, she cleared her throat, and he covered the bottle. It would have been his third drink.

Maamie Daley, Parpi Daley, Auntie Vera and Uncle Sym were in a counseling mood. They spoke to Duke and me of the attributes that make a marriage work.

"Settle your disagreements immediately," Maamie Daley said. "Remember, teeth will bite tongue, but they have to exist together."

Auntie Vera and Uncle Sym smiled. That was the same advice they had received years ago when they got married.

"We can see that you're in love," Auntie Vera said, "but be sure to like each other. When love fades, you will stay together because you like one another. Be each other's best friend. We live here with Maamie and Parpi, but they never interfere in our affairs. I do not suggest that you live with your parents after your marriage celebration. America is different. I don't believe that it would work there. I wish you the same measure of happiness that Sym and I have enjoyed these many years."

Uncle Sym said, "I will drink to that." He stared at Auntie Vera, and filled his glass with coconut water.

Parpi Daley said, "Likewise," and Uncle Sym filled Parpi's glass with coconut water.

Duke and I thanked them. Duke said, "I am glad Mags and I had a chance to come here. I have learned much about your family. Mr. Daley, now Uncle Sol, and my Father have been friends since I was little. I am so happy that I am now a part of the Daley family. I love you, Maamie and Parpi Daley, Uncle Sym and Auntie Vera. Thank you for welcoming me into your family. I adore my in-laws, Tunny and Lisa Daley, and my parents love Mags. We have turned it into a royal family. Your Little Boy, Ejay, and my sister Cassandra are now husband and wife. They are expecting their first little one. The rest is up to my duchess and me, and we love one another."

They pulled out a bottle of fine wine and toasted us. The following day was Saturday. We had planned to spend the evening with Keith. He still checked on Maamie and Parpi Daley on Saturdays in the market. However, Parpi Daley had trained Percy to take over the farm, and Percy's brother joined him. They handled most of the work, but Maamie Daley still helped with the cooking at the farm, and the vending in the market.

Keith came to the Big House to pick us up. Grandpa Duby was with him. He dropped him off at the Clock Stand in Plymouth, where he would preach sermons of gloom and doom. Keith reminded him that Maamie Daley had invited them to Sunday dinner. Keith took us to a friend's surprise birthday party in Hope, Salem. It was a blast. Maamie and Parpi Daley were still up when we got home. When I told her where Keith had dropped off Grandpa Duby, she was happy.

"Duberry has returned to his childhood love of God," she said. "When we had island-wide Sunday school Bible contests, Duberry often won.

"I wish Duberry had never taken to the bottle. I know his wife's long illness had contributed to it. His daughter, Lydia, told me that he expected her to do the dutiful thing and stay with him when her mother passed away, but she could not. She said when her mother was ill, she had to clean up his drunken vomit, and she was repulsed by it.

"I begged Sym to be lenient with Duberry, but he was not. It surprised me that Vee was cruel to Duby, too. I guess she was sticking to her man. Sebastian felt abandoned, so he made rum his steadfast companion.

"Now, you know Mags, Sweetie, why I am so proud that Duberry has retuned to the God of his childhood."

Chapter XVI

Sebastian Duberry Faces Himself

Grandpa Duby had found religion, indeed. However, he lost his good drinking buddies. They said he was a fake, but Keith said he hadn't backslid. He told us that a number of nurses at the clinic had admonished Grandpa Duby and given him the ultimatum, "Give up liquor, or die!"

One doctor told him, "Duberry, you're drinking your way into hell. Get ready to meet the devil."

Evidently, he hated the devil. He stared at the doctor and staggered out of his office. His mother had always sermonized about hell, its damnation and its fire. Keith said he sat and stared at the bottle of rum while banging his glass on the table. He cried profusely, but did not pour a drink. Keith said it seemed that he didn't enjoy alcohol any more. Keith was right.

Grandpa Duby told Duke and me, "I was lost in the spirit of the bottle, but I have been reunited with the Holy Spirit. Hallelujah!"

Grandpa Duby never mentioned the doctors' warnings.

"When my boy, Keith, became of age," Grandpa Duby continued," he modernized my house and moved in with me. He told me he would have none of my drinking and vomiting. I eat regularly now. Sym knew that I started hurting when I lost his mother and his sister moved out of my house and lived in a flat in Town. She brought shame on my house. Young unmarried women just didn't leave their parents' home. Sym shunned me because I drank heavily. Your Auntie Vera took his side. Then Lydia left the island without saying good-bye to me. That hit me like a stab to my heart. I heard she had met a rich man in Trinidad when she went there on holiday. He came right here to Montserrat to get her. She introduced him to everybody but to me. I heard they got married and have a family.

She never respected me, as a daughter should. I lost the two women in my life.

"If I had any sense, I would have quit drinking liquor years ago. My grandchildren, Keith and Sadie, respect me. They used to hide to visit me, especially on Saturdays. I love them very much. I am bigger than liquor now. I cleaned up every day: bathed, shaved, and wore clean clothes. I didn't want them to see me in my drunken state.

"I cursed Sym and Vera. Yes I did. Rum possessed me, then. Rum is a cussed companion. I did not respect myself. If I was still drinking, Maggie and Gabe would never have invited me to dinner."

Uncle Sym and Auntie Vera had entered the room and listened silently as Grandpa Duby presented his case.

"You may ask what changed me. Well, here it is. I owe my change to Jesus. It had to be my Savior who guided me to reread the book of Job. I lost a wife and a daughter, and I crumbled like the unbeliever I had become. Job had lost everything, but he never lost his faith in God." He shook his head and started to cry.

"Yes, I try to share what I have learned about the Lord with my fellow Montserratians, but they laugh at me. That's okay. I know we are in for a rude awakening in this little island. I have visions of gloom. I am no Jeremiah or Ezekiel, but I have God on my side.

"I had a powerful vision. Yes, I did. An elderly man with a walking stick led me to a strange house. Before entering, he plucked a handful of grass. He brewed it, gave it to me, and told me to drink it. After I did, I fell into a dead sleep. When I woke up, he poured a glass of rum and a cup of the brew, and placed them on the table. I reached for the cup, and drank all the liquid, though it was bitter like gall. To this day, I do not recall seeing the man's face. He shook his head, smashed the bottle and the glass of rum on the floor and left through the back door. I ran behind him, but he vanished before my eyes.

"I jumped up. I was so drunk I had wet myself. I ran to the back of my house, collected a handful of the bush that grew there, and brewed it. I poured a cupful and drank it. I vomited so much I thought I would die. However, I felt great, minutes later. I drank more of it. Following that experience, every time I reached for a drink, I saw a vision of the elderly man. I dreamed of him again after I stopped drinking the brew. He raised the cane to strike me. I kept on drinking the brew. I never vomited again, and I lost the taste for liquor.

"One day, some old drinking buddies dropped by to ask why I had stopped coming to the saloon. I told them I didn't drink any more, because I had religion. Instead of rolling out glasses, I pulled out my Bible.

"'Duby,' one said, "You are a damn liar. Look, you have your glass and all your bottles lined up on the table.'

"I began to break every bottle of liquor I owned in their presence. When I reached for the last bottle of rum, one of them knocked me down, grabbed it and ran. I fell and struck my head. I bled. I grabbed a towel, wrapped my head and ran to my cousin's house. Flossie Duberry was a nurse. I was sure she would help me.

"She said, 'Sebastian Duberry, go away, you old cuss! Don't come here to blight my house. I warned you years ago to stay away from rum. Grand-Mummah would kill you if she was still alive, and Grand-Puppa would skin you like they skinned the old wife fish.'

"She thought I was still a drunken cuss. I left, feeling like a wounded dog. A neighbor took care of me. She was elderly, but strong. She treated my wound, prayed with me, and I fell asleep in her house.

"Years later when Flossy took sick, someone came to my house to get me. I went to her bedside and prayed with her. She held my hand and cried."

"The man who cured you was our great-grandfather, Isaiah Duberry" she said. "He was not pleased that I had turned you away."

"What are you saying, Flossy?" I asked her.

"He spoke to me in a dream, Sebastian. Please forgive me. Please pray for me again." "I prayed with my cousin, and visited her every day. I was there the day she took a turn for the worse, and breathed her last. I forgave her and prayed that God would have mercy on her. 'God bless you, Sebastian,' she whispered. 'You are a good man.'"

He showed us the scar on his forehead, and added, "This is my reminder of the day I gave up rum."

At that point, he read us a poem he had written called "I Owe My Recovery to Jesus."

> "I am out of the gutter; I now feel clean,
> I was a tramp, and I was quite mean,
> I was full of anger, trials. and fuss.
> I owe my recovery to my Jesus.
>
> My Lord rescued me and held me tight,
> He was so strong I could not fight.

I struggled but He wouldn't let me go,
I know it was because He loved me so.

Now I'm no longer a slave, to rum bound,
He lifted me up and turned me around.
Rum no longer has any power over me,
My Lord has touched and set me free.

Please do not tempt me with your rum,
For my triumph over liquor is won.
I'm done with cussing; no fear; no ruckus.
I do owe my recovery to my Lord Jesus.

We applauded Duby. Uncle Sym blushed. Auntie Vera stood, and hugged and kissed Sebastian Duberry. I heard her whisper "I'm sorry, Duby. Please forgive me."

He nodded, and they sobbed in their long embrace. I brushed involuntary tears as I joined in their embrace. Uncle Sym and Duke also joined us. There was therapy in that hug.

I wished Sadie were there to witness the scene. However, she telephoned Grandpa Duby from Atlanta once a week since her visit. She had invited him to visit them, but he told her he had a mission to deliver God's message to every corner of Montserrat. He preached in the market place, on the beaches, and whenever he had an audience. People remembered him as the old drunk, Duby Duberry. He did not seem to mind.

Later when we were alone, Duke told me to add Grandpa Duby to our guest list.

"Of course," I told him. "Keith will arrange everything."

"Do you think he'll come, Duchess?"

"Yes. Keith has a great rapport with him. He'll be there, I'm confident."

Chapter XVII

The Daleys and the Randalls

I could not wait to get back to New York to ask Dad about his experience with jumbie dances. He stared at Duke and me, while Mom waited to hear about a secret that Tunny had never shared with her. At least, she knew that a jumbie was the Montserrat's corruption of the word zombie.

"Sadie, Rozy, Duke and I went to a jumbie dance with Maamie and Parpi Daley, and Maamie Daley got down, Dad."

"No, she didn't 'get down.' Montserratians say she 'turned.'"

"You're right, Dad. That's what they said. How come you never told us about the time they called you inside the ring, and you ran clear past Trials Village?"

"Maggie, every time they had a jumbie dance anywhere in the Daley family, they looked for us Daley boys to beat us. The spirits were supposed to be saying how bad we were. Bern, Sol, and Paul always got enough food, and liquor and ran somewhere to eat and drink. When I was big enough, I followed them.

"There was a man called Uriel Browne who had it in for us, Daley boys. He was the son of Parpi's godmother. He said we were a bunch of scamps, and he was right. Whenever he turned, he pulled his belt off and lashed us. One night, it was not his turning and the jumbies that flattened him and made him writhe on the floor. Bern had given him one cuff and knocked him out.

"The next day, Parpi gave Bern a five pound note; and told him to take us to Town and treat us. He said, 'Bernard Daley, I was waiting for you to stand up like a man and defend yourself. You say you want to go to Canada, I say yes, Son. You are ready.'"

"The night I ran like hell to escape Uriel's lashes, my brothers had already migrated. I am sure it was Vee who told you about it. She called me a coward and said I should have given Uriel Browne more of what Bern had given to him. No jumbie dancer ever hit my sisters.

"Vee was not easy, you know. She had a violent temper when we were small. She got her share of lashes from Maamie Daley. She used to cuss people out and take her lumps. Ellie was always more ladylike."

"Parpi Daley said that, Dad."

"Yes, my father is a great guy. Maamie belted our butts at the slightest provocation, but Parpi took care of us when we committed serious acts."

"Maamie Daley is sweet to us, Dad."

"She is your grandmother, dear. That's how grandparents are, so hurry up and bring on my grandchildren."

"Is that how you're going to be with your grandchildren, Dad? Sweet?"

"Absolutely! I'm going to be their lollypop," he said beaming. "Speaking about grandchildren, Christa and Yolanda are due any day now."

"Really, Dad?" I asked.

"Yes," he said. "They seem to do everything together. They are in their ninth month."

"That's wonderful. Maamie Daley didn't say anything to me."

"They will surprise them when the babies are born. Ellie just slipped and told me, so mum is the word."

'Thanks for letting me know, Dad."

Mom asked him, "Lollipop, eh, Tunny?"

Dad smiled broadly.

"I can't wait to congratulate Ellie and Chris. We'll all be grandparents soon. Maggie, did you really witness the jumbie dance?" Mom asked.

"Yes, Mom! Guess who asked Maamie Daley about it?"

"Who? You?"

"No. It was Rozy Washington."

"Sadie's husband?" she asked amazed.

"Yes Mom. He went to Montserrat when he was ten years old with his godmother who is from St. Kitts. He said the jumbie dance he saw then had scared the hell out of him. And guess what, Dad? Did you know that Parpi Daley's nickname was 'Desperate,' when he was little?"

"I heard some of his old cronies call him that, but I never thought much of it."

"Well Rozy knew that, too. He remembered seeing him in Town. Mr. Chambers, their host in Montserrat, called Parpi Daley, 'Desperate'."...

"Farthing? I knew Farthing. He was the one who always called Parpi, Desperate."

"We wanted to know what a farthing was, and Parpi Daley showed one to us."

"What is a farthing?" Mom asked.

"It's one quarter of a penny, Honey. We used that currency in Montserrat, when we were little. Our currency was the British 'pound, shilling, and pence.'"

"Dad, Parpi gave me one that year when I left Montserrat," I said.

"I ran for mine, and showed it to Mom. She stared at it, squinting to read all the inscriptions.

"You've got to tell me about that some day, Tunny. Promise?" Mom asked.

"I promise, Sweetheart," Dad said.

One month before the celebration of our marriage, Sinclair Randall died suddenly. Duke was distraught. His father had been the inspiration of his life. Cassandra was depressed, Mom Randall, confused. Mom and Dad became a good support for them. I asked Duke to postpone our celebration, but he said, "No!" It was the first time that I had experienced the death of someone so close to me. I liked old Sinclair. I didn't know his age until he died. He was eighty-five, chronologically, but about sixty plus in physique and in spirit.

At the funeral service, Duke honored his father. "Father, when I was six, you took me to school, and when I had trouble adjusting, you took me home and continued to teach me there with the permission of the Superintendant of Schools. You were my father and my teacher. My friends said you were old enough to be my grandfather. They were right. How lucky I was to have a father and grandfather in one package! I drew strength from you, because you were strong, physically and spiritually. You taught me patience, because you were patient. When I was afraid, you placed your arm around me and reassured me. I am thirty-five now, and I have had you for these many years. Thank you Father.

"You once told me, 'Son, by all odds, I shouldn't have celebrated your birth. I was fifty years old when you were born. God did not bless my first marriage with any offspring. You came along in the first year of my new union. You are my little champion. Next to God and the Holy Family, I love you most.'

"Father, you have prepared me well for life, and I love you. Father, you met my soul mate, and you loved her. My only regret is that you will never hold my son in your arms, but you will see him from Heaven."

He walked over to the casket, kissed his father's forehead, and sat. Cassandra stood. She wore a black veil that covered her face. Ejay and Dad supported her.

She said, "Daddy I love you. If my baby is a boy, I will name him Sinclair Randall Daley. She paused. "I know that I was the rebel who often tested your patience, but I have your counseling locked deep in my heart. Yes, Daddy, I, this 'little brat,' remember every advice you ever gave me. I am sorry for all the times that I caused you pain. I love you, and I will remember you as long as I live. I did not have the chance to ask you to forgive me, but I've asked God, and I'm sure He has. When I said that I would name my child for you, he leaped in my womb. You will live on in my son, Daddy."

She placed her right palm on his forehead. She stared at him. Ejay and Dad embraced her and returned her to her seat.

Uncle Sol spoke glowingly of his friend, and said he was happy to have "Randall's children in his family." He spoke of how much he had learned from Randall on their fishing trips, and in ordinary life's situations.

"Marianne," he said, "you had a classy husband. Duke and Cassie, your father cherished you. Please, come to me for help, if you need it. I'll be there for you."

Uncle Sol shook hands with everyone in the mourners' pews, and embraced Mom Randall, Duke, Cassie, Ejay and me.

The following day on their way back from the cemetery, Cassie went into labor. Five hours later, she gave birth to Sinclair Randall Daley, to the delight of two doting grandmothers and one energetic grandfather. Of course, this adoring aunt was elated, too. We visited them in the hospital.

Ejay, Duke and Mom Randall went to the hospital to get Cassie and her baby. Mom Randall spoke of how precious he was, but begged Cassie and Ejay not to spoil him. They nicknamed him Randy.

Maamie and Parpi Daley had invited Mom Randall to spend two weeks in Montserrat after the funeral. My parents gave her the roundtrip ticket, so she went, though it was hard for her to leave little Randy. She called from Montserrat every evening to check on Randy's progress. Mom Randall returned to New York with Maamie Daley's wedding gown. The dress was a celebrity. It first appeared in Montserrat eons ago, in Barbados, not so long ago, and then New York. It was ageless. The fabric glistened in white elegance. Mom said we would never find lace and sateen like that again in this "phony world." I knew I would be overjoyed to wear it.

"Mom Randall, what did you think of Montserrat?" I asked.

"It's beautiful. I loved the beaches. Maamie Daley is a fantastic cook. I had to beg her not to serve me. You know how I feel about my weight. I went swimming with Maamie and Parpi Daley every morning, at sunrise. I broke down when I thought how much Sinclair would have appreciated those beaches and the good morning swim. Maamie Daley and Vee consoled me. Of course, I thought of Randy all the time. Keith gave me a tour of the Emerald Isle, and Vera had a family dinner for me. I admire Grandpa Duby. He had dinner with us twice."

"I am glad you had fun. I love Grandpa Duby, and you know how I feel about Montserrat."

"I knew many Montserratians in Bermuda when I was little. One of my best friends in school was a Katy Skerritt. Her parents moved the family to Birmingham, England. I never heard from Katy again, but I can now say I've been to Montserrat. I should have enquired about her when I was there."

"It's a small world," I said. "You may just run into her again some day, Mom Randall, now that you have an interest in the Emerald Isle of the Caribbean."

"It would be nice to see her again," Mom Randall said.

While Mom Randall was there, Yolanda and Christa Ford Best, Auntie Ellie, and Uncle Chris arrived in Montserrat. They surprised Maamie and Parpi Daley with their sons, Jonathan and Roland Best, Jr. She said they were ecstatic. She brought us photos of the babies who resembled their moms, and could easily be mistaken for twins. Jonathan Jr. was one week older than his cousin. Mom Randall said that she wanted to steal the babies. She told us that we would be seeing them at the wedding.

Of course Maamie Daley called to brag about her new great-grandsons. She said that Parpi was elated because she herself always thought that Ellie was his favorite child although he denied it. Maamie Daley never admitted that Tunny Daley was her favorite child, either.

The Daleys descended upon us a few days before Duke and I took our vows, but we had ample room for them. Yolanda and Christa Ford Best, their husbands and Verona Daley had secretly arranged for a Daley-family dinner at Uncle Sol's home on Friday evening. Maamie Daley and

Auntie Vera had a hand in it, too, although Maamie had to divide her time entertaining her baby great-grandsons. Jonathan and Roland Best and Randy Randall almost stole our show, but Duke and I did not mind.

They had a combination of Barbadian and Montserratian food. Mom Randall made her delicious potato salad. Naturally, the Bests asked for the recipe. They made breadfruit salad that was ultra tasty. They set up a special table for Duke and me, and served us. I reminded them that I had to fit in a wedding gown, but I ate everything on my plate, especially Barbadian style flying fish. I felt ashamed to ask for more.

They followed with moments of counseling, and Duke and I listened intently. Parpi Daley said, "Maggie, you have Shug's name, and in many ways you are like her. I predict that your union will last as long as ours." He shook Duke's hand, and embraced him. He hugged me and kissed me.

My parents' tenant had finally vacated their apartment, and our basement was huge. Dad pitched a tent, and spruced up our patio. They asked Duke and me to stay away, and we did. When we returned late on the eve of our exchange of vows, we entered an elegantly decorated reception hall. Yolanda and Christa Best, Auntie Vera, Mom Randal, Auntie Ellie, and indeed all the women with decorating skills, had created a masterpiece. Duke and I cried.

Auntie Vera scolded us. She said to Duke, "Now sir, tears do not become a duke. Cut it out! None of those tears, tomorrow. I did not know your father, but from what I've learned of him, I know he will want you to be brave, and enjoy one of the best moments of your life." She picked up a napkin and dried his tears. I held tightly to his hand.

Mom Randall's brother, Carleton Sanders, had flown in from Bermuda. At the final rehearsal, Duke broke down when his uncle escorted Mom Randall down the aisle. Thank God, Duke's good friend and best man, Joseph White, was there! He counseled Duke. Parpi Daley and my uncles had a long talk with him after the rehearsal. Auntie Vera did not scold him again, but hugged him. However, I, too, felt the absence of Sinclair Randall.

Nature, our uninvited guest, provided the "something blue", on our wedding day. The skies were cloudless and blue, and a wonderful breeze filled the air. The borrowed wedding gown got its share of applause, too. My new four-inch heels helped me to do justice to the gown. No one applauded me more than its original model, Maamie Daley.

The Daleys and the Randalls, my maid of honor, Melissa Fields, Duke's best man, Joseph White, and all our invited guests made our celebration a remarkable affair. We had put our recent loss aside and had a wonderful time at our reception. Duke toasted me.

"Duchess," he said, "This will be my 'daily' prayer, to love you more and more." He kissed me.

The entire Daley clan stood and applauded him. Whether Duke intended a pun, or not, it was spark that ignited our celebration.

I answered Duke in kind, "Look at me!" I said. "I learned from my grandmother, my adoring Maamie Daley, that my great-grandmother Daley had nicknamed my grandfather, my beloved Parpi Daley, 'Prince.' However, I have married into royalty. You are my soul mate, my husband, and my duke. I am the Daley of your daily prayer, so we will always pray together."

Duke hugged and kissed me, and the wedding guests tapped on their glasses for more kisses. We acquiesced.

Ejay stood, and asked Mom, Dad, Cassandra, Mom Randall, Duke and me to stand. He reached for Randy, and held him facing our guests. Randy smiled broadly. The guests applauded. Ejay simply said, "Speaking of royalty...!"

Duke threw his head back, and laughed loudly.

"We are the Randalls-Daleys, and the Daleys-Randalls," Ejay continued. "Friends, welcome to our kingdom, in the County of Queens!

The guests stood and applauded, as Duke and I embraced Ejay. Mom, Dad, Mom Randall and my uncles toasted us. I thought, "I am so happy we are having this celebration, for Duke' sake"

We ate, and danced, exchanging partners along the way. We went through all the rituals: the throwing of the bridal bouquet, and the removal of the garter. Maamie and Parpi showed their alarm when they covered their mouths. Melissa caught the bridal bouquet, and a friend of the Bests caught the garter. Duke and I hugged and kissed my grandparents, and our parents, and joined our guests in a hot reggae. Minutes after 2:00 a.m., my man and I slipped away to our reserved room at our favorite hideaway.

Mom and Dad told us days later that the celebration ended at 4:00 a.m. Mom Randall told us afterwards, that having her brother present, and the joy of the Daley clan really gave her a lift.

She voiced the rhetorical question, "Why am I sad, when Sinclair is dancing in Heaven? My husband loved to dance."

Duke and I postponed our long honeymoon for a while. He was still helping his mother and Cassandra with his father's affairs. Though we had tried hard to put forth a good front, we still felt the loss of Sinclair. Uncle Sol told us that time would be the greatest comforter.

Cassandra remained somewhat depressed. I told her, "Cassie, mourn for Father Randall. However, you are still lucky. You have a brand new Sinclair, and everybody agrees that he looks like your Dad. Do you remember how the baby leaped in your womb when you pledged to name him Sinclair Randal? That was a good omen."

"It's the strangest thing, Maggie," she said. "I couldn't believe it at first, but Randy does resemble my father. I hope your Dad is not jealous."

"Jealous? Dad? No way! He brags about his grandson so much, you'll think he's the only grandfather on earth."

The Montserratians were the last to return home. Keith knew New York well enough to show Grandpa Duby the city, while Auntie Vera shopped fanatically. I only went with her on one of her shopping sprees. Maamie, Parpi Daley and Grandpa Duby spent time with Uncle Sol in New Jersey. Vincent Daley drove to New York, and took them to Montreal for one week. Auntie Vera, Uncle Sym, Keith, Maamie, and Parpi Daley went to Georgia to spend five days with Sadie, Rozy and the kids, and visited Syd and Tabitha. Maamie declared that she loved Georgia, even more than New York and Montreal. It reminded her of Montserrat.

Maamie and Parpie decided that they should spend some time with the Fords and Bests in Barbados, so they would plan their visit when they returned home. She asked us not to say anything to Ellie and the children. She chuckled mischievously when she added that she too could plan a surprise.

When our guests had finally returned home, Duke said, "Duchess, we didn't have a honeymoon right away, but I would make it up to you. I truly feel married now." He held his ring finger up, and stared at his ring. "We'll fly to Montserrat and go to the hide-away under the Mighty Watchman on Parpi Daley's farm. Keith told me I would be amazed at what he has done there."

We asked Mom and Dad for the apartment, and they said yes. It was a three-bedroom apartment, with a bay window overlooking a small playground. Mom took pride in her lawn and rosebushes. She had won many "Best Lawn in the Village" prizes. Dad planted vegetables every year, and his garden was quite productive. Maamie and Parpi Daley had marveled that Tunny's "little garden" had produced so much vegetables. They praised Dad for his ingenuity.

I told them, "Dad does not have the variety you have, but at least for three months a year, we have fresh corn, beans, okras, squash, thyme, rosemary and basil. Dad plants sweet potatoes and they are good, but not as sweet and dry as yours are. We don't have a Mighty Watchman looking over our little vegetable garden, just some evil looking scarecrows that Dad made. You trained him well, Parpi Daley." Parpi chuckled and kissed Maamie on her cheek.

Duke loved the apartment. Uncle Bern had converted our attic into a peaceful hideaway. I loved the spiral stairway that led to it. Mom and Dad spent many a cozy hour there, away from Ejay and his antics. Syd and I were far quieter than my little brother was. I told Mom that she could still use it. She reminded me that she had the basement with its large bathroom and that she had just added her Jacuzzi.

Duke promptly set up his office in the attic. Ejay still stored some of his merchandise in one of the walk-in closets. Duke said it was time for him to take them out. Ejay apologized and moved them. He had his own attic with ample space. Ejay liked the spiral stair case and said it "added a touch of elegance to the space." He had one built.

That summer, Duke and I went to Montserrat. We spent our first week at the Parpi Daley's "love nest under the volcano", as Duke had dubbed it. Keith and his friends had truly transformed the hideaway into a little villa fit for a duke and his duchess. Maamie Daley and Auntie Vera had made new curtains and new straw mats for our honeymoon.

At daybreak, we bathed naked as birds in a brook under the rising sun, and then foraged for food. Duke and I liked soursop, and we feasted on it and other fruits every morning. The dates and plums were scrumptious. We traveled by day, ate dinner at the Big House and returned to our lovers' roost at night.

We returned to New York after three weeks. I was sure that I was pregnant.

"Oops! False alarm!"

In the month of September 1989, hurricane Hugo devastated more than ninety percent of Montserrat. The Big House stood firmly, having experienced little damage. Uncle Sym got hurt when he ventured outside in the eye of the storm. He lived for a short while afterwards and died of his head injury. Duke could not accompany me because of his job, but he flew in for his funeral, and burial Sadie and her children were especially saddened. Rozy Washington was a great comforter, and she leaned on him a lot.

Many of us went home for his funeral. None of us was prepared for what we saw in Montserrat. I could not believe that it was the same island Duke and I had visited only a short while earlier. Hurricane Hugo had brought the island to its knees. Its scars were deep.

I believe that Uncle Sym's death was harder on the family because of the circumstances under which he died. Maamie and Parpi Daley were stalwart in their understanding of death, but they, too, were truly sad.

Grandpa Duby was dutifully sad. However, they claimed that he accepted the death of his only son better than he had accepted his wife's passing. He said it was God's will.

"The Lord giveth and the Lord hath taken away. Blessed be the name of the Lord," he said, and then added, "What pains me most is that my Lydia does not know that her brother has passed away."

Many folks came to seek a decent hot meal, and we were happy to feed them. Food was scarce, but he went home prepared for the emergency. Normally, at wakes, alcohol flowed, and so it did at Uncle Sym's wake. Grandpa Duby never tasted a drop of it. His former drinking buddies were there. They cried for Uncle Sym and drowned their sorrows in rum that they chased with gin and Scotch.

Maamie Daley said, "God has certainly redeemed Duberry. He has the Spirit of the Living God now. He has no need for rum."

Parpi Daley said, "Duby is a better man than me. May the Lord grant that I never have to bury any of my boys! I cherished Simeon. He lived under my roof longer than any of my sons. Who would have thought that Duby would face Sym's death with such strength?"

Maamie Daley said, "Boy, Duby is a true believer. His strength comes from the Lord."

Auntie Vera bore her loss well. It was Mom Randall's turn to console her, and she did. Maamie Daley cried long for Uncle Sym, but she was also concerned about her daughter. She said that Uncle Sym had spoiled Auntie Vera by catering to her every whim, and she was afraid that no other man would coddle her. Sadie and her family spent one month with her mother. It was after they left that Auntie Vera broke down. Sadie had invited her to go to Georgia at least for a few weeks, but she declined.

"Keith and I had a long talk. He said when his mother was acting so bravely, she was pretending, but she cried for his father in private. He said that Parpi Daley comforted him, and that Maamie Daley hugged him as if he were still a child. She spoke no words, but he knew exactly what she was thinking.

"Keith added that he wished his mother had accepted Sadie and Rozy's second invitation to go to Georgia. He thought that the change would be good for her. He said that Hugo had destroyed Dub Me On, but his father had good insurance. 'Dada was a good father, Duke. He let Mama have her way up to a point, but when he got stern, she backed off. I loved my father. Grandpa Duby is a strong man, and we respect one another. He loved Dada, and Dada loved him. Their long dispute was over of his drinking. I doubted his new-found faith, but who am I to judge him? He has me reading my Bible now.'"

Duke said he told him, "Keith, you know I share your pain. Father adored me. My sister puzzled him, but when she married Ejay, she stopped her wild ways, and they got along better. I love your family, Keith, including Grandpa Duby. You love one another. Maamie and Parpi Daley got over their fear of flying, and visited their children from North America to Europe, and Barbados. They are great, Keith."

"Thank you, Duke," he said. "Welcome on board."

Grandpa Duby's house was practically destroyed, and he and Keith moved back to the Big House, temporarily. Keith worked frantically to repair Duby's house. Everyone had vowed to rebuild. The insurance companies, most of them located in London, processed their claims quickly, and paid them for heir losses. Keith was busy. Duke said he was drowning his sorrows in his work.

Keith liked Duke. Keith was a man of few words, but he was most talkative when my husband was around. Auntie Vera and Mom Randall became fast friends. They promised to communicate by telephone and by mail.

I cried when I saw that the calabash trees were no longer there. However, Parpi Daley assured me that in years to come, more calabash trees would grow again in the big yard.

"The hurricane of 1928," he explained, "had mashed up the big yard, too. You would never know it. But, this is the Emerald Isle. It will be green again."

Parpi, I said, "I am so happy I got my calabashes years ago." He hugged me.

I went into the old kitchen, converted into a living quarter by Uncle Sym, and saw his empty hammock there. I cried. Why did it survive Hugo? Death had silenced a great storyteller. I thought I heard his voice and saw his hammock moving. I ran out of the old kitchen, found Duke, and hugged him tightly.

Duke and I returned to Montserrat in the summer of 1990 with more food stuff for the family and for some poor folks of the villages. We were surprised to see how quickly the plants had begun to grow again. Parpi Daley was right. He gladly showed me all the baby calabash trees.

Dad had sent Parpi Daley all kinds of plant seeds earlier in the year, and so did Auntie Ellie from Barbados. Parpi's farm produced vegetables as in the years before Hugo. Percy and his brother did most of the work. Duke and I went to the market with them one Saturday. Maamie's marriage of the vegetables delighted him. Parpi was her spy. As far as Duke was concerned, Parpi Daley was more like a detective. Duke observed everything. Later, he told me that Maamie Daley was a shrewd entrepreneur. I wished she had asked Duke and me to help her. While we were mingling with the other shoppers, we heard a familiar voice rising above the hubbub.

"I know that voice," Duke said.

I listened again, and said, "Of course. It's Grandpa Duby."

We stood on the steps of the market and listened to him. "Oh Montserrat, your day of weeping is coming. God does not like what he sees, and he cares less for what He hears. Some low-life idiots are hoping for another Hugo, because the insurance companies paid off, big. If I was still the old cuss I used to be, I would have challenged them. I lost my son, Sym to Hugo's wrath," he said, reaching for his handkerchief and drying his tears. "What if we were all dead? Put your greed aside.

He raised the Bible. This great book says, 'Turn back to God before it's too late.' He sent Hugo, a rampaging messenger, and we still do not heed His message. Each lesson will be more striking until we fall on our knees and give God the glory."

Someone yelled, "Who is making that racket?"

"It's Sebastian Duberry. You know the old drunk. He found religion."

Laughter filled the marketplace.

An elderly woman said, "He's lambasting Montserrat. However, we know, he is right. We Montserratians are too damn gluttonous. We haven't learned much from Hugo."

Grandpa Duby continued, "Go to your Bible, Montserrat. Hugo was only the wad."

"There's that wad again," I told Duke.

"What's a wad?" Duke asked.

I explained it to Duke, as Maamie Daley had told it to me. I told him that Grandpa Duby spoke of the wad in a figurative sense, as when Maamie Daley had spoken of the burden Sadie must bear for being the first divorcee among the Daley and Duberry women.

"Montserrat, you have turned a deaf ear on God," Grandpa Duby continued. "From Genesis to Ephesians, we learn of mighty winds. We have had our Hugo. I give you Isaiah 29:6. 'You will be punished by the Lord of Hosts with thunder, earthquake and great noise, with storm and tempest, and the flame of devouring fire.' He laid his Bible aside, cupped his mouth, and shouted, "Hello out there, Montserrat! Are you listening? We have had the thunder, the winds and the earthquakes. Watch out for the devouring flames!"

"Where will the fire come from Duby?" a young man asked mockingly. "From the rum in your belly?"

"You may mock me today, but look to the mountains. For centuries, those volcanoes have been belching at us, a little smoke here, a little sulfur there. Where will the fire come from? Just look to the mountains! Montserratians, pick up your Bibles, read the Word, and obey the Lord. Hugo visited us, and we have survived. I lost my son, but God has given me the courage to carry on. Go to Isaiah again and read for yourselves, about "the flame of devouring fire." May God never visit us with the flame that I dream of at night! May God have mercy on Montserrat!"

The chorus of a hymn that Maamie Daley always sang rose above the hullabaloo. It was "Yield Not to Temptation." When he got to the chorus, his voice rose high above the hubbub. Duke and I joined him and sang along. Some folks in the marketplace joined in the chorus.

In the summer of 1991, when Duke and I returned to Montserrat, we were surprised at the restoration. Maamie and Parpi Daley had aged more rapidly in that short span than they had in all the years we had known them. Yet, their sons had bought them a car, and Maamie and Parpi Daley traveled all over the Island much to the dismay of some of the younger drivers. The young drivers were not kind to the elderly ones. Parpi Daley told us about an incident he had faced one day when he was going to the Bay to get some fish.

A young driver tailgated him and shouted, "Get off the road old man. A car is not a jackass!"

Parpi Daley said to the arrogant young man, "No. You are the jackass.

If you touch my car, I'll take my '*cutlass*' (machete) to you, and bring my jackass to kick you." Parpi Daley said he turned the ignition off, jumped out of his car, opened the trunk, and pulled out his cutlass. The young driver sped away.

Maamie Daley was not pleased, and she told him so. He insisted that the young man was a damn idiot. Maamie Daley told him, "You are a damn fool, Boy. There is no fool like an old fool. You should know better."

Parpi Daley said he told her that she was right, and their little dispute ended immediately.

Parpi Daley had not given up his old donkey, though he finally leased the farm to their helper Percy Matthews and his brothers, Ned and Charlie. The young men bought a second truck and a tractor, and the donkey was no longer useful for them. The Matthews and their helpers handled all the production and sales of their produce. Ned drove from village to village selling fresh vegetables from the back of one of their trucks.

Maamie Daley would no longer marry vegetables in the market. It was the end of a personal era for me. Parpi Daley did not intrude on the Matthews. He rode his donkey to the base of the Mighty Watchman to get spring water for their use at the Big House, admired the greening of his land, and then returned home. Of course, his home garden produced more than they could use, so he continued to donate some to the elderly of the village. His present Friend and Foe were mere puppies, and he was in the process of training them. He cared for his donkey, bathed him weekly, and cooked the food for his hogs. His goats and sheep were also getting special care. Maamie Daley said she never knew a donkey was a pet.

"A jackass, she maintained, "is still a jackass for all that." She warned Boy not to take him into her house.

When Sadie visited with Jesse and Vera Rose, Parpi Daley taught Jesse how to ride his donkey. He was fascinated with the animal, and wanted to live with Parpi Daley. Unlike Mom and Dad, Sadie did not leave Jesse in Montserrat with her mother and her grandparents.

She said that she told her husband, "Rozy, we'll take Jesse to a petting zoo when we get home."

A clever little rascal with an Associate Degree had become the Maamie Daley of our generation. Ejay worked hard at everything. His selling of merchandise in flea markets paid off richly. He didn't know why Mom was fussing that he had no BA or BS degree. He showed her his earnings for one week. She was surprised, but not impressed. Mom still insisted that, "the bachelor of arts or of science, was the way to go."

"I studied my butt off at The Borough of Manhattan Community College," he said. "Mom knows I'm not one for the books. Cassie and I had a good start. Father Randall gave us a house. I praise the no-nonsense teaching I had in Montserrat, Mags. Every afternoon Maamie Daley took me to task. She told me 'It seems that you will be the last of your generation of Daleys. My great-grandchildren will look up to you. Some will call you, 'Uncle Ejay, others 'Cousin Ejay.' Let them speak well of you.' She sure knew how to build my ego. I remember things I learned there. I crammed here just to get the grade. However, my greatest course was the psychology of sizing up people, and my greatest professors were the streets."

He paused for a moment, and shouted. "Baa! Bull shit!" Then he laughed until his eyes watered. It was only a little later that I realized he was poking fun at the B.A. and B.S. degrees. I could not join him in that view.

"Ejay," I said, "no matter how Mom fusses, you'll do it your way. All, I say is, 'Do it your way, little brother.'"

Ejay hugged me, and thanked me for my support.

I knew that Ejay had entertained the selling spirit, since he met Maamie Daley in Montserrat. Earning a BA or BS did not guarantee financial success. Before Randy was born, he worked full time and "turned his hand" part time. After the baby arrived, Ejay worked part time and spent quality time with his son. He was an excellent father. He took him to school, and picked him up. Randy was curious, and smart, and Ejay taught him many things.

"I keep my job in order to secure my health plan coverage. Cassie and I plan to have another baby soon. Mom Randall will retire and take care of Randy's sister or brother."

"That's wonderful, Ejay," I said, "especially in these days of child abuse. I guess when I have mine she'll do the same for Duke and me. I'm so glad you've nicknamed him, Randy."

"Yes," Ejay said. "He should like that. Sinclair was kind of heavy for a cute little baldhead guy."

"Are you saying he needed a wad when he was born?" I asked.

Ejay laughed. "Maggie, your nephew had no hair, then. My boy will carry no load, because I'll always be there for him. However, look at his curly hair now. He gets his haircuts regularly. I don't want anybody thinking he is a girl. ."

"Daddy Ejay, you go, boy! However, remember the bit about 'There's not a child so small and weak, but has his little cross to take'! I paused and hummed the hymn, 'We Are but Little Children Weak'. By the way Ejay, I'm sure Maamie Daley told you that someone in our generation would have twins."

"Cassie and I will handle them, Maggie," Ejay said confidently. "My Cassie is a good mother."

"Exceptional!" I said. "To tell you the truth, Ejay, I am surprised that she breastfed Randy. She handles him like a pro."

"Father Randall's death really shocked her. He had spoiled her by giving her everything she wanted. She knows that Mom Randall will not coddle her. Why should she? Cassie is a mother and a full-grown woman. You talk of my head for business, but Cassie is brilliant. She helps her mother with her father's affairs. I'm encouraging her to go to Law School."

"You, Ejay?" I asked him?"

"Trust me Maggie, it's Cassie's idea. I'm just supporting her. Maggie, Duke was pushing Mom Randall to sell the dry cleaning business. He said it was too burdensome for his mother. He made a deal with two brothers. Cassie jumped in and said, 'No way! My father invested too much in this business.' She told the buyers straight, 'You will not rob us. It won't happen on my watch.'

"Duke was shocked. Mom Randall said nothing. They had a family conference, and Cassie won. Two months later, they were offered $50,000 more. What do you think of my Cassie?"

"Duke told me about it. I think Cassie is brilliant."

"Now, Mom Randall will be free to travel. She and Auntie Vera will be taking a cruise early next year. They'll meet in Miami," Ejay said approvingly.

"So I heard," I said. "Good for them!"

I listened to Ejay, and I admired him. He was a tall, imposing man, who was quite mature for his age. He had left his womanizing behind, and Cassie gave up her wildness. Sometimes, I laughed when I telephoned them late on Saturday evenings, and they were at home with their son.

Ejay did so well financially, that he and Cassie had invested in a three-family building. She used the money from her inheritance from her father, and Ejay added his savings from the selling of merchandise. However, Mom still wanted him to go back to college and complete his BA. He turned a deaf ear to her every time.

"Mom and I will never see eye to eye, Maggie. The next time she tells me about getting my degree, I'll tell her to get her doctorate."

Duke and I were having trouble conceiving. We had two false alarms. We were getting anxious. My biological clock was ticking. My nephew was getting bigger. Almost five years had passed since hurricane Hugo roared like a raging lion and tore up the Emerald Isle. I started eating raw peanuts, making fresh eggnog, and doing some of the crazy things I had heard of in Montserrat.

Finally it happened, thank God. On the day I returned from my obstetrician with my good news, I called Duke at school during his free period. I could still hear his scream. Ejay's son was going on five.

When we hung up, I got a call from Keith. He had taken up with an older woman, Winifred Martin. She was ten years his senior. Auntie Vera did not accept her. It was the most extensive conversation I ever had with Keith. He had a friend at the Cable and Wireless, and he paid minimally for the call.

"Maggie, can you imagine my mother? She is the first to say that Maamie and Parpi Daley never meddled in her and Dada's business, and now she is ready to dip into mine again. I had finished the repairs of Grandpa Duby's house, but he did not return home until recently. He visits Maamie and Parpi Daley frequently, and occasionally they drop in to see us. Grandpa Duby cooks a mean fish stew, and he prepares it for Maamie and Parpi Daley when they come. They're getting along just fine.

"I had met Winnie while I was repairing some minor damages to her house. She has a Big House with a rental flat. Your Auntie Vee says that she will be visiting Sadie and her family often. I hope she'll stay there for a long time. Maggie, Winnie is pregnant." He paused.

"Congratulations Keith! I just learned this morning that I am pregnant, too, and you are the second to know. Don't say anything to Maamie and Parpi Daley. I'll telephone them."

"Congratulations, too, Maggie. Can you imagine? I can't wait to hold my first child in my arms. Mama must be crazy. Maamie and Parpi Daley can't live forever. Mothers are closer to their daughters, and Sadie keeps inviting Mama to live in America. I plan to stay right here in Montserrat. If I don't, when they are all gone, who will maintain the Big House? I will not permit Mama to ruin my life. Like you, Americans say, 'No way! Hell no!' She had enough to say about Dionne Marie. She said I had made a mistake. Yes, but it was my mistake."

"Good for you, Keith. I'm with you one hundred percent."

"Thanks, Maggie, and congratulations again to you and Duke! I'm happy to have you on my side, along with Grandpa Duby, and Maamie and Parpi Daley. Now, do you understand why Sadie did not confide in Mama? Lucky for her, she is married to an American."

When Duke got home bearing two dozen red roses, he picked me up and almost smothered me with kisses. Mom and Dad came upstairs to congratulate him. They had already congratulated me. We heard the key in the door. It was Ejay, Cassie, and Randy smiling all over himself. I kissed him. They told us how happy they were that we would soon be delighting in the joys of parenting. They did not stay for a long time. They were about to leave us to revel in our good news, when Randy told me that his nursery teacher's name was Mrs. Pinter, and that she was strict.

"She likes me, Auntie Maggie, because I'm obedient."

"That's nice, Randy," I said. "Learn all you can so you can teach your baby cousin."

"Where is he?" he asked.

"In my stomach," I said beaming.

"When is he coming out, Auntie?"

"Soon," I said. "Your Uncle Duke and I can't wait to welcome him."

"Please let me know when he comes," Randy said.

"Oh yes. You'll be double first cousins. Your daddy is my brother and your mommy is your uncle Duke's sister.

"Really?" he asked, quite puzzled.

"Come Son, let's leave now," Ejay said. "I'll explain it to you."

"Okay, Daddy," he said.

He ran to me, kissed me, kissed Duke, and waved goodbye.

Soon after they left, I discussed Keith's plight with Duke. He told me that Auntie Vera was a hypocrite. He remembered her counseling in Montserrat.

Later, Duke telephoned Keith to congratulate him and to tell him to hold fast to his decision.

"Don't let your mother, or any one, tell you what to do, Keith. Be a man! We will always be there for you. I heard that your mother and mine would be traveling together sometime next year. Mother is so not into interfering in grown-ups lives, that I'm sure some of her ways will rub off on Auntie Vera."

Keith thanked Duke profusely.

Not long thereafter, I learned that I was carrying twins. The pregnancy was a good one according to all the experts in my family. Duke was happy. He told me that they would be two boys.

Chapter XVIII

The Mighty Watchman as a Thief

In 1995, at the beginning of June, Mom, Dad, Mom Randall, Ejay, Cassandra and Randy went to Montserrat for three weeks. Randy liked the Big House and all the animals on Parpi Daley's farm. He adored the donkey. Ejay relived part of his childhood with his wife and son. Mom liked to be there, too, especially with her Tunny and Randy. She liked the beaches.

While Parpi Daley had leased the farm to the Matthews brothers, the cabin was not a part of the deal. He told them that they could use it, but when his children and grandchildren came home "from America," they might want to stay there. He was right. Mom and Dad spent one night there. She spoke of her early morning "dip" in one of the pools of warm water. Dad described it as a second honeymoon. Ejay, Cassie, and Randy also had their night at the villa. However, Ejay said that Montserrat was intensely hot.

"Maggie, even the breezes from the sea are hot," he told me on the telephone. He added that they spent hours at the beach, and Randy loves the sea. He swims like a *crapaud* (frog). I wish you were here to see him. He runs from Auntie Vera's apartment to Maamie and Parpi Daley's apartment in record time. He likes to fling stones. He doesn't take too easily to other children. Randy preferred to be alone."

Ejay said that Maamie and Parpi Daley stared at him with Randy, and hugged them frequently. They remarked how big he had grown. Randy surprised him by clinging to his great-grandparents. He did not like strangers. When he told them how surprised he and Cassie were, Maamie

Daley told them, "Randy smells the blood. Children sense to whom they belong."

They had not long returned to New York when the Mighty Watchman, the Soufriere Hills volcano, began to erupt. On July 18, 1995, it spewed ashes on the eastern part of the Island. The wind blew them to the west, south, and parts of the north. We, abroad, were more perturbed than the folks were in Montserrat. Maamie and Parpi Daley remained optimistic. Duke demanded that we get them out of the island immediately.

"Montserrat is a tiny Island," he maintained. "An erupting volcano is not a hurricane."

Dad said, "They say they're fine. Let's wait and see."

Uncle Bern and Auntie Becky had built their retirement home in her native St. Croix in the American Virgin Islands. They were just about to relocate, leaving their children in charge of their property in Montreal. They visited New York. We had an important family meeting at our home. Uncle Sol also joined us.

"Sol and Tunny, your parents are the most bull headed people I know. We'll have enough space for them in St. Croix. Have you spoken to them?" Auntie Becky asked.

"Maamie asked me what I was getting upset about," Dad said.

"Parpi said whatever Maamie decides is fine by him," Uncle Sol said.

"I tell you, they are stubborn and selfish," Auntie Becky said.

Uncle Bern made one final effort. Two months after he arrived in St. Croix, he visited Montserrat armed with masks, canned food and dry goods. Auntie Ellie and Uncle Chris joined him there. They did not like what they saw. Maamie and Parpi Daley stood firmly on their decision to remain in Montserrat. Auntie Vera said she would not leave her job and sacrifice her pension. She said she had been with her parents since her birth, and would continue to take care of them.

Uncle Bern said that Auntie Ellie cried as she told them, "Maamie and Parpi, come to Barbados stay with us for a month, then go and spend a month in St. Croix with Bern and Becky. That will give you a chance to think..."

Uncle Bern said he was surprised when Parpi Daley interrupted Ellie.

"Ellie and Becky, I know that you are concerned about Shug and me. Shug and I are living on borrowed time. Remember, wherever I am, Shug is happy, and wherever she is, I am happy. We are happy together here in Montserrat. The Mighty Watchman will not rob us of our happiness."

Uncle Bern told my Dad that they saw the futility of their visit, when Maamie hugged and kissed Parpi Daley, and they stayed embraced for a long time. He said that their farewell was long, and teary.

We pleaded with them by telephone, but neither Maamie nor Parpi Daley relented. Meanwhile, the Mighty Watchman refused to be silent. It had been dormant for four centuries and wanted to be seen and heard. I told Maamie Daley of the report that we had seen on CNN. She said they were lying.

"Mags, Sweetie, we have it on good authority that they're trying to drive us out, so they can seize our land. Boy and I were born here, and only God can separate us from what is ours. We Daleys and Corbetts joined our properties together, and Boy and I will be here as long as God gives us breath. We got over our fear of flying and flew to North America, Barbados, and Europe. We're not afraid any more. Hugo did not uproot us; and neither will the Mighty Watchman at Chances."

"Chances?" I asked.

"Mags, Sweetie, don't you remember Chances Peak, Boy's Mighty Watchman, the highest peak in Montserrat? That's where most of the volcanic activity is. Chances Peak will spit on us, but it will not uproot us."

"Of course, I remember. Maamie Daley, you know those emissions of sulfuric gases that you told us were good for our health?"

Yes. They…"

"They were not," I interrupted. "They're killer gases."

"Your Uncle Bern and Auntie Ellie got to you, too, eh? To hear them tell it, Boy and I will be dead before long. Why Mags, Bern left enough masks here to supply the entire island. Tell you what, except for the heat, the ashes remind me of your snow. If Boy dares to leave his motorcar outside, he has to clean it every morning. I told him we were too old to be bothering with a motor car, but he will not get rid of it. He's just as married to his motor car as he is to his jackass."

"Maamie, you and Parpi Daley can leave Montserrat for a little while. You can go to St. Croix, Barbados, Atlanta, London…"

"And New York! Ellie Ford wants us in Barbados. Bern wants us in St. Croix. Tunny, and you want us in New York. Solomon wants us in New Jersey. Paul wants us in London. Boy and I are the most wanted people in Montserrat. However, the answer to all of you is still 'No!'"

"Maamie Daley, you make yourselves sound like criminals, 'most wanted,'" I said. "That's funny." I laughed and she chuckled.

"Anyhow, Sweetie, we won't be leaving, just yet. Boy says when The Mighty Watchman stops vomiting, everything will go back to normal, and we'll still take our chances here at the Big House." She laughed again. I could imagine how her laughter lit up her face.

"An erupting volcano is not a joke, Maamie Daley," I said, but it is funny. "So you and your Boy will take your chances." She laughed again.

Things did not return to normal. The volcano went berserk not long thereafter, blew its top, and thousands of Montserratians fled from the island. They had established a safety zone in the north, and housed many evacuees there. During that period, tons of ashes and magma buried Parpi Daley's farm, the old house, and their village. They escaped with the bare minimum, their evacuation suitcases that they were told to prepare when the eruptions intensified. Keith had taken Parpi's car to the North, packed with linen, dishes, clothing, and other small items, so they, too, were spared. Keith had arranged for them to stay with his girlfriend in Olveston.

When Auntie Vera called with the bad news, Dad was horrified. She asked that I listen in on the call.

Dad said, "Vee, tell Maamie and Parpi that I want all of you to get out! Please! We will send you to Bern and Becky in St. Croix or to Ellie in Barbados."

"The ashes have invaded Antigua and St. Croix too, Tunny," Auntie Vera told him. "Bern and Becky may consider returning to Montreal."

"Really?" Dad asked. "Bern didn't say anything to me."

"He is still very upset that Maamie and Parpi didn't pack up and go to St. Croix with him. He calls often enough, and his message is the same. 'Vee, get out!' I reminded him that St. Croix is getting ashes too. He said that might be so, but they didn't have the fire and the destruction."

"What about Keith?" Dad asked her.

"He is there," she said without enthusiasm. "Parpi is depressed. He had to leave his jackass behind. Every morning, he looks towards the east and south, and shudders. He doesn't say much, but he stays close to his Shug."

"What about Friend and Foe?"

"I wish you didn't ask. They broke their chains and fled. We haven't seen them since. Tunny, the roar from the Mighty Watchman, sounded like a boom out of hell. That was the rude awakening."

Soon after Auntie Vera called, more villages fell. They began to get ashes in the safety zone in the north. Later, they had the vomiting of pebbles, and pyroclastic flow. Uncle Sol, Dad, Uncle Bern and Uncle Paul met in Antigua and made a desperate trip to Montserrat to speak to Maamie and Parpi Daley again. They joined their parents and Keith at Winifred's place. The men had taken sleeping bags with them, on Uncle Bern's suggestion. Grandpa Duby was also there. Auntie Vera stayed with a friend in St. Johns. For the first time, she did not live under the same roof as her parents.

Keith telephoned me. "Maggie," he said, "Hello. The uncles are here on a hopeless mission. If they had called me, I would have told them so. Winnie is fine. I love her. The uncles have taken my side in the feud with Mama. They like Winnie. They are trying to reason with Maamie Daley. Your Auntie Vee is exactly like her bullheaded husband, Sym Duberry, and her parents. However, I'm just as bull headed as all of them. I am a Daley and a Duberry. Maamie Daley is stubborn, too. I guess the Corbetts were just as stubborn as the Daleys were. Winnie is carrying my baby, and when he is born, I'm going to give her an ultimatum. She didn't want to marry me because of Mama. She's ten years older than I am; so what? I know what I want and whom I want, and Vera Duberry is not going to rule me. She is my mother; not my judge. I will not disrespect her, but I'll maintain my stance.

"Grandpa Duby knows he cannot return to Cork Hill. He is now at the Home for the Aged, but he comes home for his meals. He feels he can preach to the elderly more effectively than he did to the young. Half of them are hard of hearing, anyhow. However, they shout 'Hallelujah' when he shouts it, and they applaud him. They sing the hymns loud and clear, but off-key most of the time. He sees to their welfare, and works to keep the place clean. He is happy. Maamie and Parpi are too concerned about the Big House to worry about anyone else."

"Keith, are you wearing your masks?"

"Absolutely! Especially me. I have to be outdoors a lot, and I want to see my son."

"Of course, Keith! You can't be too bullheaded. Is the Big House totally buried?"

"Completely! Grandpa Duby's house is only partially buried for now, but it won't be long."

"Did you lose a lot, too?"

"Maggie, I'm young. Hope is on my side. Of course, I could go before

Maamie and Parpi Daley, but the odds are in my favor. I can feel their pain, Maggie. They are hurting."

"Keith, for the first time in my life, I have no desire to visit Montserrat. Last night I concluded that I am simply afraid. Now I know how Maamie and Parpi Daley felt about flying."

"Uncle Bern and the others added another bathroom to Winnie's house. They also helped me with the room I was adding to it. Maamie and Parpi Daley say they are comfortable, but let's face it, Maggie; it is not 'the Big House'. However, they are very grateful. Winnie and I have moved into the new room. I've got to go. So long, Mags!"

"Bye, Keith."

Dad was depressed when he returned home,. He did not understand why his parents and even his sister, Vera, could not see the danger of the situation. Mom cheered him up. He spoke of Winnie and the health of her unborn child. He said he and his brothers wore their masks although they were uncomfortable, so they "could get the message." Then he broke down and cried. Mom and I hugged him.

"Lisa, I don't think I am a coward, but I was happy to leave my homeland. Montserrat is too small for one tiny part to remain safe. Please, family, let us keep on praying for everyone who is still in the island."

A month later, Keith called to say that Winnie had given birth to their son, and that they named him Simeon Keith Duberry. He said he was the prettiest baby he had ever seen, and that everyone agreed with him. We congratulated him, and prepared to send him gifts. Auntie Ellie had already sent gifts for the baby before he was born. He said that Winnie and the baby were just fine, and he was the happiest man on earth.

"I am a father, Maggie," he said. "If the Mighty Watchman still existed, I would shout it from its summit!"

Duke congratulated Keith, as he waited anxiously for the birth of our babies. Everyone was happy for them, but Maamie and Parpi Daley were ecstatic.

About a week after I had spoken to Keith, a worker from UPS, the delivery service, rang our bell. It was a package from Syd addressed to me. I was quite surprised, because I had never received anything from Syd. The insulated package measured fifteen by nineteen. Bubble wraps protected the content. My heart pounded when I opened it. It reminded me of how anxious I was when I saw the contents of my Christmas and birthday boxes when I was little.

There were two paintings. I looked at the first one, and my heart beat with joy. It was the Big House in its splendor. The original kitchen, the cistern under the calabash tree, and the old jackass that Parpi Daley had kissed good-bye before we buried him, were all there. Tears filled my eyes. I hurried to uncover the second painting. It was Maamie Daley at the market place, standing tall and firm as she eyed her clients. She wore her pinafore with its long pockets and her bandana. Parpi Daley was not far away talking to his friends, and Sadie, Keith, the artist himself, and I were scattered about, no doubt, spying for Maamie Daley. It was signed with Syd's fancy writing style, Syd Murray Daley. It was the first time, as far back as I could remember that he had used his middle name.

I closed my eyes. I could visualize Parpi calling us for our visit to the candy shop. It was then that my tears really flowed.

I yelled, "Dad, Mom, come quickly!"

I held the painting of the Big House up as they entered the dining room where I had unpacked the paintings. Dad's mouth fell open. Mom took the painting from me and examined it. I saw Dad looking at the painting of the marketplace with his mother, his Maamie and my Maamie Daley. It was the second time that I had seen him cry, so I hugged and kissed him.

"Who sent you this?" Mom asked.

"Look at the signature in the lower right-hand corner, Mom," I said.

"Syd!" she screamed. "I knew my son was talented, but…" she paused. "Maybe I should never have suggested that he consider majoring in art. These are magnificent. Remember, Maggie, children never listen to their parents."

"Don't I listen to you, Mom?" I asked hugging and kissing her.

"Sometimes," she said, kissing my cheek. "However, I am glad you married Duke."

Dad wiped the tears. He stooped and picked up an envelope that must have fallen from the package.

"It's for you, Maggie," he said.

It was a note from Syd. "Hello Sis, I was examining my photos one day, and when I saw those represented here, I cried. I bought everything that I needed, canvas, paint, brushes, oils, and started to paint. Mom often told me that I should be an artist. I locked myself in my basement, and here are the results of my endeavor. Of course, yours are copies. The originals will go to Maamie and Parpi Daley. I made two copies, one for you and the other for me. Tabitha could not believe her eyes. She did not know I have 'this hidden talent.' Now, she wants me to paint her portrait. Women! I am not a portrait painter. However, doesn't the scene at the market look real? Notice, I added myself to it. Please comment. Your brother, Syd."

After my parents had read the note, Dad said, "My son, Syd, has done a wonderful thing. I am so proud of him. While the rest of us are trying to get Maamie and Parpi to leave the island, Syd will give them gifts that will bond them to it forever." He broke down, and Mom hugged him and cried with him.

I telephoned Syd, but he was not at home. I left a voice mail. Tabitha returned my call that evening.

"Mags, Syd is in Montserrat. When he said he was going to mail the paintings to Maamie and Parpi Daley, I suggested that he take them. He asked me if I didn't know that the volcano is erupting there. I told him he would be fine. Therefore, he went. He called to say that next to marrying me, it was the best decision he had ever made. He said he videoed Maamie and Parpi Daley from the moment he entered their home. He said they were overjoyed to see him, but when they saw those paintings, they cried, as did everyone in the house. He said, 'Tabby, do you know that there are truly tears of joy? It was a happy moment.'"

"Tabitha, thanks so much for sharing that with me. I'll tell Mom and Dad. I'll speak to Syd."

Syd called me on the eve of his return to Georgia. I told him that everyone here cried, too, when we saw what he had recreated. I told him that he is a magnificent artist, and that he must continue to paint.

I said, "Syd, I will let the world know about our Maamie and Parpi Daley. You must prepare the cover for my book. I know the title already. It will be simply, *Maamie and Parpi Daley of Montserrat*, written by Magdalene Elizabeth Daley, II, and illustrated by Syd Murray Daley. Duke will have to forgive me. I will not use my marriage name."

I spoke to everyone briefly, congratulating Maamie and Parpi Daley for the birth of their new great-grandson.

Maamie Daley said, "Mags, Sweetie, Syd and Simmy have arrived. Syd brought us the original paintings of all the things that are so dear to us, the Big House, Friend and Foe, the stone oven, the big yard, the market! Did you see me in my pinafore, Mags, Sweetie?

"Baby Simmy brought us a breath of fresh air, and new hope. Where there is life, there is hope, after all else is lost.

"Syd said he sent you copies of his paintings. We are in our joy, first to see Syd, and then to see his artwork. The old house lives again! The market is still alive. I can't stop looking at them. Everybody here thinks Syd is the greatest artist on earth. He said he started painting the farm, and he would post it to us. Boy can't wait. I laughed so much when I saw Friend and Foe sitting in command of the farm. Our home and property are living history now, Mags, Sweetie. Syd has seen to that. Good-bye. I love you."

"I love you, too, Maamie Daley," I whispered softly.

She did not tell me that Friend and Foe had run away.

Chapter XIX

Mom's Premonition, Syd's Revelation

Syd's trip had brought great joy to Maamie and Parpi Daley, Auntie Vera, and all who knew and cherished the scenes that Syd's talent had recreated.

That morning, before he left Montserrat, he telephoned Mom to say that he had changed his mind and would stop over briefly in New York to see us. He reminded her that he hated to change planes in Puerto Rico, because he remembered how the strict custom's officers there had harassed us when we were children.

We waited for Syd, so we would have dinner together, in family. Ejay, Cassandra, and Randy joined us. Mom prepared a feast for her older son, the artist. All of us enjoyed it: braised pork chops smothered in onions and green pepper, broccoli, and baked white potatoes. I made a mango pie, because Syd was there when I made the first one in Montserrat, and he liked it. We always had ginger beer and sorrel in our refrigerator, or in our earthen jars.

We had a noisy dinner. After dinner, Syd shared a cocktail with Mom, Ejay, Cassandra, and Duke. Dad and I drank more ginger beer.

Syd said calmly, "Mom, the strangest thing happened on the flight from Puerto Rico."

"What, Syd?" she asked.

"I met a man who knew you when you were a little girl."

"Me? What? Who?" Mom asked, baffled.

While the rest of us listened carefully, awed by what Syd had said, Mom listened intently. She and Dad sat together on the couch while Syd spoke. She held Dad's hand. Syd said that the man seated next to him had introduced himself to him soon after the flight started, but that they paused to listen to and watch the in-flight safety demonstration.

"Yes, you, Mom. Your name was not Lisa Evelyn Murray. It was Dorotea Ana Pardo Moore."

"Dorotea Ana Pardo Moore? That's a Spanish name. Who was the man, Syd?" Mom leaped to her feet as if she were propelled by a magical force, while listening anxiously to every word that Syd uttered. Dad stood at her side.

"Your brother, Guillermo Antonio Pardo Moore, of the Dominican Republic."

"Syd, I don't have a brother. I told you about my sister, Theresa. She was at Mommy Babs with me in the South Bronx. Then she disappeared."

"Yes, you do, Mom. When you see him, you'll recognize him. He looks just like you. I resemble him, too."

"What about my father, Syd Murray?"

"That was one of his aliases. You should have seen your brother's face when I told him that my name was Syd Murray and explained that you had named me for your father. He cried."

"He did?" Mom asked.

"Yes, Mom," Syd said. .

"Why did you tell him your full name? You don't use your middle name."

"Mom, he said, 'Glad to meet you, Sidney.' So I said, Not Sidney; just Syd. Syd Murray. I thought he was going to burst out of his seat belt."

"'Syd Murray?'" he screamed. Everyone turned to look at us.

I whispered, "Yes, Syd Murray Daley!"

"Syd," he said, choking back a sob, "I am sure that I knew your grandfather, Syd Murray."

"You knew my grandfather?" I asked. "He abandoned Mom when she was little. We turned to face each other. I thought, 'Oh my God! He looks like my mother and me, and he has our large brown eyes!'"

"'Yes,'" he said. "'Syd Murray was one of my father's aliases. Your mother, Dorotea, …'

"Mom's name is Lisa …"

"'Lisa Evelyn Murray,' he interrupted. 'Syd, my father was a con artist. He used to disappear with his friends and return home unannounced. Mama is bilingual. Her parents were Jamaicans and spoke English at home. She worked as an interpreter for English-speaking tourists.

'My mother's cousin, Syd Murray, was the first to migrate to America. He was very generous to all the folks back home. He sent them money and packages. Two years after he got married, he brought his wife, Mercedes,

173

and his little daughter, Lisa Evelyn, home to meet his family. Unfortunately, they died in a horrific car accident in San Pedro de Macoris, where we had relatives. The family was devastated.

'The baby was eighteen months old, and your mother was eleven months old. That was where the drama began. My father seized the opportunity and stole Syd Murray's documents: his naturalization papers, his wife's passport, and his little girl's birth certificate. He wrote to his friends in Yonkers, New York, and told them what had happened. They dealt in identity thefts, alteration of documents, and all of that stuff. One of them was getting married. Papa asked him to send a letter of invitation and a wedding invitation for Mama and me. He did. We got through. We never returned to Santo Domingo. Three months later, Papa and your mother arrived. He told Mama the whole story. Mama was scared, because he told her that she had to keep a low profile, because Immigration could pick her up at any time. He must have sold Mercedes Murray's identity to one of his many girlfriends.

'They registered me in a Catholic school because I was of school age. One afternoon when I got home from school Mama had everything packed. Papa had told Mama that they were looking for us, and we had to get out. We got in one car with our suitcases, and he and Dorotea got into another. They took us to his friends place in Brooklyn. We never saw Papa and your mother again. Mama told me that he adored Dorotea. That's why he named her for his mother, Dorothy Allen.'"

Mom interrupted Syd. "So, I have the identity of the dead child?"

"Yes, Mom. Do you remember being on a plane when you were little?"

"No. I don't," she said, drying her tears.

"Do you know you were born in the Dominican Republic?"

"No. When I first remembered myself, I lived in the South Bronx. Mommy Nixon never told me that I was born in the Dominican Republic. As far as I knew, I was born here in New York. I have my birth certificate."

"Mom, the real Lisa Evelyn Murray, was born in New York. Syd Murray's real name was Jose Antonio Pardo Allen. His father was Dominican."

Syd continued to recount what Guillermo had told him.

"Your mother had many disputes with your father's friends in Brooklyn. They told her she was lazy, and they were tired of her just sitting around, watching novelas. They said they were going to put her and her kid out, because Syd had not sent them any money to take care of them. She was cautious and scared because of her illegal status. Your brother said that his father's friends were not satisfied that your mother was the slave who cleaned, cooked, washed and ironed for their big family. He said they had a little room without windows in the basement.

"One day, she took a chance and went to an employment agency near their supermarket. She got a job working as a babysitter for a rich family in Valley Stream, Long Island. She worked all week, and went home on weekends. They charged her for room and board, and things got a little better for them.

"Your brother said that one weekend when your mother got home, your father's friends told her that Syd had called them to say he would be there next week to get him. It seemed he had hooked up with another woman. Your mother packed their clothes and documents quickly, grabbed him, got a taxi to Penn Station, took the Long Island Railroad and went back to her employers in Valley Stream. She explained her situation to them. They told her they could stay in the servants' quarters. They loved her because their children adored her, and she was teaching them Spanish.

"Your mother's employers, the Fitzgeralds, who were realtors, sponsored her and your brother. After they received the permanent visas, they went looking for you on weekends. They showed your baby photo around. An elderly man recognized you and told them that he had seen you with Syd Murray in the South Bronx. He took them to the address on Fulton Street, without charge. Your South Bronx neighbors told them that as far as they knew, Syd Murray was a nice guy, who worked out of State, and visited his two little girls frequently. They mentioned your sister, Teresa Maria, and Barbara and Franklyn Nixon, your Mommy Babs and Daddy Frankie. Your sister did not disappear, as you thought. Your father had taken her away."

"Why didn't he take me?"

"You were in the hospital with a high fever. The Nixons told him you were in the Bronx Lebanon Hospital. You were actually in St. Barnabas Hospital. Evidently, when he didn't find you in Bronx Lebanon, he left. One of the receptionists there, who knew Frankie and Barbara Nixon, told them that their son-in-law was at the hospital. She had seen him from the inner office.

"Son-in-law?" Mom asked.

"Yes, the Nixons had told their neighbors that Syd Murray was their son-in-law. According to your brother, things were getting too hot for him in the Bronx. He had swindled some old con artist friends from back home in Santo Domingo, and they were looking for him. He was also afraid of the law, fearing they would discover his true identity and deport him.

Mom had a strange look on her face. Then, she said suddenly, "Syd, are you talking about Will?"

Syd's large eyes brown widened. He gulped, and jumped to his feet. "Mom," he said, hugging her, as I have never seen him hug her before, "how did you know your brother's name is Will? He is my uncle. Oh my God! I forgot to mention that he told me he preferred to be called Will; Will Moore. He said his father had named him *Guillermo*, William in English. His mother hated the name, so she called him, Will. He only uses Guillermo Pardo in official situations."

Mom dried her tears. "I don't know why I said Will," she said with quivering lips.

"You had a recall, Mom," Ejay said. "Mom, I think Syd is right. Will Moore is your brother."

Syd spoke more animatedly. He said that Will Moore told him that they did not give up their search for you. They searched for Barbara and Franklin Nixon. After a long while, they found an elderly woman who claimed to be Barbara Nixon's friend.

Syd paused to drink some water, and continued. "She told them that your grandparents, Barbara and Franklin Nixon, sent you to their relatives in East Orange, New Jersey, after they discharged you from St. Barnabas. She said that Barbara had told her that you were their daughter, Regina's child, but that her poor daughter had run away from Syd Murray, because he was abusive. They changed your name to Lisa Nixon, but their daughter did not let them adopt you, legally. The woman was surprised when your biological mother spoke Spanish. She told her all she knew about you. She said she had lost touch with Babs and Frankie Nixon when she went home to Puerto Rico to take care of her ailing father."

Mom spoke softly, wringing her hands. "Mommy and Daddy Nixon were older people, but they loved me, and I adored them. They trained me well. We moved from the South Bronx to Harlem, and then to Brooklyn, where I attended Brooklyn College when I grew up. Yes, I knew that they called me 'Lisa Nixon,' but I also knew my real name. They registered me in school in my correct name, Lisa Evelyn Murray. They never had any biological children. Regina was the tallest doll in Mom Nixon's doll collection. She was my favorite doll." Mom managed to force a smile.

Mom continued. "We lived in Crown Heights, on Lefferts Avenue corner of Nostrand. Daddy Nixon worked as a janitor there, and Mommy Nixon helped him to maintain the building. However, they liked the culture of the city, and took me to all the places of interest. We had a bull dog named Hannibal Nixon, and Daddy Frankie registered the telephone in his name. Now, I understand why. He was afraid that Syd Murray was still looking for me. Maybe that meant that Syd really loved me. Our telephone in the Bronx was in Mommy Babs' name.

"I had a good childhood. Daddy Nixon had an old jalopy, and on weekends, 'We rolled!' She smiled. "His favorite phrase was, 'Wife and Bubbles, let's roll!' That was his nickname for me; 'Bubbles'. He liked to drive to Long Island. We went to Jones Beach, and shopped in flea markets, all over the island. They spoiled me. I was the best dressed girl on our block."

The words were flowing from Mom's lips, but she seemed to be in a trance. Suddenly, Mom stopped speaking.

She took a deep breath and asked, "What about my mother, Syd? Did Will say where my mother is?"

"Yes. He said he could not wait to get home to tell his Mamá that he had met me."

"Will I get to meet them?"

"Yes, Mom, you will meet them. Will and I exchanged telephone numbers, and I gave him this address. I was so excited, I didn't get his."

Mom grew sadder. For some unknown reason, I could not comfort her. I left that to her Tunny. I was trying to recall all that Syd had said.

Maamie Daley often repeated the saying, "God moves in a mysterious way His wonders to perform". She was right.

Around 9:00 p.m., we were lazing around, chatting. Mom played with Randy Daley, and laughed at his frolics. Someone rang the bell. Syd announced that he would get it.

He took a while to return. A tall, fair skin middle-age man with salt and pepper curly hair, and large brown eyes entered holding the hand of a slim, elderly woman. All of us stood in deference of her. She was nimble, and reminded me of Maamie Daley. The elderly woman opened her arms widely. She and Mom walked towards each other, as if they were drawn by a mysterious magnetic force. They ended in each other's arms.

"Dorotea," the lady whispered. "My little Dorotea!" She continued to whisper into Mom's ear, as their tears blended.

Syd said, "Family, meet Uncle Will!"

177

We greeted Will. I stood, introduced myself and gave him a hug. Cassandra followed me, and one by one, we met our new uncle. Randy shook his hand. He stooped to embrace Randy.

My uncle introduced himself as Will Moore. The moment he spoke, I knew he was family. I thought, "Oh my God! He does look like Mom and Syd and, besides, he has Syd's voice tone."

"Syd," he began, "Your name first caught my attention. Mamá and I needed to have a closure in our search for Dorotea. I always felt that we would reunite some day, and this is the day. Syd, you look like my mother, your mother and me, and you have my voice." He walked over to Syd, embraced him, and started to sob. Ejay stood at Will's side.

Mom and my grandmother finally separated. Neither spoke for a while. We waited eagerly, wondering who would utter the first word. Even Randy looked inquisitive. He, too, was probably trying to figure out what was happening. Mom embraced and kissed her brother, Will Moore. They sat with their mother, who removed two photos from her pocket. Mom stared at them, and passed them to Dad. Then I looked at them. One showed a little girl standing alone, marked Dorotea, *dos años,* (age two) The second was a larger photo marked, Guillermo, Mamá y Dorotea. Mom could not stop staring at the photos.

A deafening silence reigned for a while. I passed them to the others. Silence ruled until Ejay spoke.

He said, "Mom, you were a beautiful little girl. If I had seen you first, your Tunny would have had a fight on his hands." He winked at Dad.

Mom laughed. Her mother hugged her and kissed her tear-stained face. We did not exclude Randy. He, too, looked long at the photos. Mom had dried her tears by then.

"Grandma, don't cry any more," he said. "You have a mommy, too."

"You are right, Randy," she said, hugging him.

I thought, "So, that little son-of-a gun understood everything."

Mom said, "Family, this is my mother. Besides the photos that speak for themselves, there are only three persons in this room who knows of the birthmark on my buttock, Tunny, my husband, Will, my brother, and my mother, Carlota Moore. Syd, you have it, too. Ejay, Syd, and Maggie, this is your grandmother."

While we hugged our newfound grandmother, Mom embraced Uncle Will again. At the touch of my grandmother's lips on my forehead, the babies moved within me.

Our grandmother spoke English with a slight Jamaican/Spanish accent. She had learned English from her parents in Santo Domingo, earned a certificate as an interpreter, and interpreted for English-speaking tourists there, and for some private folks.

As we stood close to her, our grandmother spoke. "I am your abuelita Carlota, Carlota Moore Pardo. I have looked for you for a long time." She raised her eyes to Heaven, made the sign of the Cross, and said, "Dear Lord, I thank you. My search is over."

Ejay, proud of the Spanish he had learned in school and from his Hispanic friends, said, *"Abuelita, tú eres muy guapa. Yo soy tu nieto, Ejay."* (Grandma, you are very beautiful. I am your grandson, Ejay."

Syd said nothing in Spanish. Bad boy! He had barely learned enough Spanish to pass the Regents examination. He simply embraced Abuelita Carlota and kissed her forehead. I said, *"Abuelita, tú te pareces mucho a mi mamá. Es un placer conocerte.* (Grandma, you look a lot like my mother. It's a pleasure to meet you.")

Mom took Dad by his hand, and presented him to her mother. Then, Ejay led Randy to Abuelita Carlota. She covered him with kisses while he stared at her. He did not object. He must have "smelled the blood."

Dad said, "Mamá Carlota, thank you for your beautiful daughter. She has highlighted my life. If I wear a glow, it's because of Lisa." Then, he paused. "Dear, will you change your name?"

"Tunny, please give me a chance to digest all of what has happened here tonight. I…"

She broke into sobs again. Abuelita Carlota consoled her daughter, kissing her and playing with her fingers, as one would a tiny baby.

"Mamá, I am sixty-two years old, soon to be sixty-three. But, wait a minute! Lisa Evelyn is sixty-two. How old is Dorotea?"

I thought, 'Did I hear Mom say, 'Mama'?'

"She was one year older than you, dear," Abuelita said. "You were born on October 10, and she, on October 5, the previous year."

"I thought I had no family; that is, until now. I'll keep everything about Lisa Evelyn. It will be easier that way. The Nixons treated me well, because they always wanted a little girl. My children did not know them. Tunny and I were courting when they got sick. They passed away within months of each other. He helped me with all the funeral arrangements.

"Old Babs and Frankie adored each other, and they loved me. Mommy Babs told me to marry Tunny Daley, because he would take care of me. However, now, you are here. You are my biological mother. I share your pain of separation, and I hope that we can build on our mother-daughter relationship. I adore my mother-in-law who accepts me as a daughter. Now, I have two mothers. Will, somewhere in my subconscious, I remembered your name, and I do resemble you and my mother. You tell me that Syd has some of my father's characteristics, but I know he also resembles us. Only God knows why my father lived as he did, but I do not hate him. I do feel sorry for him. I know that he is the loser, for not knowing my family. Please give me time as I figure out what to call you. My children call me Mom."

Mom did not realize that she had already uttered the word "Mama."

Abuelita Carlota grew sad. I stared at her and my uncle. I went to her and hugged her, and Ejay and Syd joined me in one embrace. We sat around and spoke for a long while. Laughter broke the sadness of the encounter. Randy squeezed in beside her, and placed his head on her lap. She stroked his head gently.

"Wow!" I thought. "The Montserratians are right. 'What has not happened in a million years can happen in a day.'

Randy hugged Abuelita Carlota, kissed her, left, and went to play. I was so happy that my mother had found her mother. Thank God, it was Friday. Our meeting lasted well into the wee hours of the new day.

After Abuelita Carlota and Uncle Will left, Mom sat quietly, as if she were in a trance. She knew that she belonged to Carlota and Will Moore. She was the female version of Will.

I said, "Mom, do you want to talk?

She said, "No, thanks. Not now."

Dad looked at the clock, yawned, announced it was 1:05, and stood. He helped Mom up, and held her hand. They said goodnight.

I did not fall asleep right away. I tossed and turned, thinking of how prophetic it was that Mom had named my brother "Syd Murray", hoping that someone would recognize his name, and tell him the whereabouts of his grandfather. I knew if I had seen Uncle Will on the street, I might have made a double take without questioning why he resembled my mother. I fell asleep. I woke up at 9:00. Duke was still asleep. Normally, we were up by 7:00 a.m. on Saturday mornings. The reality of Abuelita Carlota and Uncle Will's visit had anesthetized us.

After taking care of my toiletries, I went downstairs to Mom's apartment. She appeared, yawning, still dressed in her robe. "Maggie, I'll get the breakfast started," she said. "Syd likes pancakes. Do you have any ripe bananas?"

"Yes, Mom, I said. "You go and get dressed. I'll make the pancakes. I'll do breakfast."

I opened the freezer, got two packages of sausages, and a package of bacon. I peeled six apples, and sliced them, went upstairs, asked Duke to join me, and got five ripe bananas. I returned to my task in Mom's kitchen. I blended the apples and bananas with eggs, added my unbleached flower, baking powder, honey, cinnamon, nutmeg, and water. I added cottonseed oil, blended it to a smooth batter, let it rest a while, added vanilla, blended it again, and made a batch of man- sized pancakes. I brewed a pot of coffee and a pot of rich coco tea from Maamie Daley's home-grown coffee and coco beans. The thievery of the Mighty Watchman was also a topic for discussion in our kitchen. There would be no more chocolate or coffee brewed from Maamie's beans.

Syd had also brought mango juice, sliced papaya, manicport, and mango wedges. I placed the pitcher of juice, the bowl of fruits, a teapot of cocoa and a pot of coffee and hot milk on the table. I rolled the cart with the platters of pancakes, bacon, and sausages into the dining room.

"Mom, I'm ready. Get the boys!"

Duke, Ejay, Syd and Dad entered the kitchen laughing hysterically. Ejay declared, "That was a good one, Dad." I knew how proud Dad was to relate to his sons, man-to-man. I was happy that Syd and Ejay were getting along much better. Cassandra and Randy arrived, late as usual.

Ejay recited Uncle Sol's favorite grace. "Thank God. Let's eat."

Mom said, "Ejay, you ought to stop it."

Ejay asked, "Mom, what can this Little Boy Daley possibly tell God that He does not know already?"

Randy surprised everybody. "Daddy," he said, "I am the little boy Daley, not you."

Cassie said, "Tell him, Randy."

Still surprised, we smiled, and we started to eat.

While filling his plate, Syd said, "Mom, this is the first time you will taste honey that comes from a hive I know. I went with Keith to Zion to get it. Maamie Daley sent you a bottle, too. I'm taking mine home."

The clamor of forks tapping the service platters filled the room. It was a pleasure to watch Randy Daley eat like a little man, and drink his cup of coco tea that his mother had cooled for him. She spread honey and homemade butter generously on his pancakes, and he ate and ate.

Everyone praised my pancakes, but Dad did not let it rest. "Lisa, Honey," he declared", yours are good, but Maggie's are better."

"I concede, Tunny," she said. "I imagine Maamie Daley has a lot to do with Maggie's expertise."

"It's all yours, too, Mom," I said, "with a little touch of me in it."

"Your pancakes are excellent," she said. "Will someone please pour me another mug of coco tea," she laughed. "Now, this is delicious."

Mom told us that one cold afternoon, on her break, she and some colleagues had hot chocolate in the cafeteria. Her friends declared that it hit the spot.

Mom said she told them, "If you think this is good, you should taste my daughter's coco tea."

"Coco tea? What the hell is that, Lisa?" One colleague asked.

"I'll bring you some tomorrow," she said.

The following day, Mom took a large thermos of coco tea to them, and they could not stop praising her.

"Okay, you cocoholics and chocoholics," Mom said she told him. "This is the pure stuff. My mother-in-law sent us the real thing from her home in Montserrat. This is the first and last time you'll have it, so do enjoy it. The volcano has destroyed her trees, and I doubt she'll send me any more."

Mom did not tell them that we had lots of it at home. After that conversation, Mom seemed to be herself again. Dad seized the moment.

Dad said, "Sweetheart, our immediate family is here. We need to talk."

Ejay said, "Yes Mom. I'd like to know what's going on in that head of yours. Let it all hang out, Baby! Mom, you have lost your zip."

She smiled and tapped Ejay on his cheek.

"Honey," Dad said, "Carlota is your mother. You never spoke of her. Naturally, you remember Babs Nixon, because you were older when you went to her."

"That's what's puzzling me, Tunny. I remember Will, but I have no recall of Mama."

We cheered her up, and declared that we would call and visit Abuelita Carlota and Uncle Will. Mom said she had arranged to meet Will for lunch one day and would have a talk with him. I want to know more about my mother.

That afternoon, after she had lunch with Will, she came back with what seemed to be a logical response to the puzzle. Syd Murray was a ne'er-do-well, a coward, and a gambler. Will repeated that his mother was a hard-working woman who did tours with English speaking tourists. Sometimes, she was away for days.

"Will is five years older than I am, so he called her Mamá. Will said that back in Santo Domingo, I did not call her 'Mamá'. I called her 'Tía Lota', the name given to her by our older cousins who shared the family house." Mom paused. "Tunny, Mamá is 'Tía Lota'. I remember Tía Lota's name but not her face. She used to bring us *dulces*." She brushed away her tears with a tissue.

"*Dulces?*" Dad asked.

"It means 'candies,' Dad," I said.

Mom continued, "I told Will I thought she was my aunt. I guess I remembered Will because he was little, too."

Dad said, "Honey, didn't I tell you that somewhere along the way you had some West Indian blood in you? Spanish, French, Dutch, Portuguese or British, our ancestors landed there via the Atlantic crossing."

We hugged Mom, and pledged to support her. Little by little, her childhood memory was awakening. We were happy for her.

I wondered what our lives would have been like if we had met Abuelita Carlota earlier. Would my brothers and I have spent so much time with Maamie and Parpi Daley in Montserrat?

Uncle Will and Abuelita Carlota often visited us and telephoned us. Gradually, we learned more about Uncle Will. He was a divorcé with one son, Walter Pardo Moore, and a stepdaughter who was no longer in his life. Walter lived in Massachusetts. He promised that he would be down to meet us. He was married, but had no children.

Uncle Will taught physical education at a high school in Brooklyn. He had a significant other, herself a divorcée, who had no intention of remarrying. Uncle Will and Abuelita shared a brownstone in the Bedford Stuyvesant section of Brooklyn. His significant other lived in the house behind his. Their affair had started as a backyard romance. Each one had a key to the other's backdoor. Her dog, Brutus, and his dog, Diablo, guarded their properties.

One day, Dad was mowing the lawn. He heard his name, and turned to see Abuelita Carlota walking towards him with two shopping bags. He turned off the lawnmower and ran to meet her. They embraced.

"Tunny, I don't have to depend on Will any more," she said. "I found out how to come by bus."

We were surprised to see Abuelita, but she had brought us paella, and other Spanish goodies. Duke could not stop eating. After we had eaten, Mom and Abuelita Carlota locked themselves up in her room. She never revealed what they spoke about, but they exited the room, laughing. They hugged closely and long when they said goodbye. Duke dropped her back to Brooklyn at twilight.

Dad and Ejay went to Brooklyn to help Uncle Will with some needed repairs. Once, Dad, Duke, Uncle Sol and Ejay painted the entire interior of their brownstone. She made a spread for them. She prepared *bacalao*, (codfish} in the Dominican style with all the West Indian products that were available at the Brooklyn terminal market. She sent a generous portion home for us. Her food was as tasty as the food we had eaten in Montserrat. We wanted her to meet Maamie and Parpi Daley, and she said that she would like to do so.

Although she was past the age of retirement, Abuelita still worked as a seamstress in the basement of her home. She specialized in bedspreads, cushions, curtains, and drapes. A small boutique in Brooklyn sold her work, and she had private customers. She also made the finest baby layettes. She and Auntie Ellie would make a fine twosome.

We telephoned Maamie Daley to tell her that my mother had been reunited with her birth mother. She thanked God that He had answered Lisa's prayers.

"Maamie Daley," I said, "it turned out that Mom was right when she named my brother, 'Syd Murray, hoping that someone would recognize his name some day.' Someone did. It was none other than her biological brother, Uncle Will Moore. We have not met Mom's father, Syd Murray, but we know her mother, Abuelita Carlota. It's a real convoluted story. Maybe you'll hear it some day."

I gave Mom the receiver. She and Maamie Daley had a long talk. Mom ended by thanking her for her prayers. Although I did not ask Mom, I believed that she had abandoned all hope of finding her birth parents. She admitted that she stopped enquiring about them after Ejay was born.

"Maggie, Maamie Daley wants to meet my mother. I would really like to see them put their heads together. That would be wonderful. Don't you agree?"

"Oh yes, Mom," I said hugging her. "That would be great."

The union with my maternal grandmother and uncle did not overshadow my good news. Mom and Dad were happy for Duke and me. After all, it had taken us a long time to conceive. Duke and I had planned two children. Our fraternal twins, Rey Sinclair and Rex Anthony, were born almost seven months after Keith's son, Simeon Keith, whom they nicknamed Simmy.

Mom called her mother to announce the birth of my sons. Days later, Uncle Will and Abuelita Carlota visited us to meet my boys. She cried as she held her great-grandchildren in her arms. She brought them the prettiest layettes that I had even seen, made especially for Rey Sinclair and Rex Anthony by Abuelita Carlota. I told her about Simeon Duberry, II, and days later, she delivered his gifts of baby clothes, made especially for the tropics. She also made Randy Daley the cutest outfits. He had dubbed her " Mamá Lita," and she liked it.

One evening, Duke and I surprised her by taking the boys to her home in Brooklyn. She invited her neighbor and good friend, Mrs. Daphne Thomas, to meet us. Mrs. Thomas played with the boys, and they laughed and cooed with her. Abuelita Carlota was in her glory.

We did not know that Abuelita had called Uncle Will, but he and his girlfriend, Valerie Taylor, came down to see us. Duke liked Uncle Will and Abuelita Carlota, who was a charmer. I realized how much she acted like Maamie Daley. She served us fruitcake and a soft drink, and gave us a fruitcake to take home.

Duke and Uncle Will were die-hard Mets fans, and acted as if they were the owners and managers of the baseball team. "We'll go all the way next year," Duke said. Uncle Will made his comment, and then they argued. They mentioned the names of the players who should stay, and those who should be traded. The names meant nothing to me. I was not into baseball.

One evening Mom was late coming home from work. We had just begun to become concerned, when she called us to say that she had gone to Brooklyn to see her mother. I was elated. Uncle Will dropped her home about three hours later. She had called Abuelita from work, and she had dinner prepared for her when Mom got there. She said that Abuelita told her that she did not like eating alone.

Ejay, Cassandra, and Randy dropped in on Abuelita Carlota when they were in Brooklyn. I supposed that, like Randy Daley, my boys would call her "Mama Lita at first, then graduate to Abuelita," when they receive their full gift of speech. Abuelita Carlota was fast becoming very popular in our lives.

Chapter XX

The Mighty Watchman
Be Damned!"

Duke had applied for and gotten a sabbatical. He wanted to be free to help with our boys.

Naturally, I had telephoned Maamie Daley to tell her our good news. When she heard about our baby boys, she cheered, and shouted, "Congratulations to you Mags, Sweetie, and also to Duke! Congratulate Lisa and my Tunny for me!"

I thanked Maamie Daley. She told me that my great-aunts were twins. She spoke of Christa and Yolanda, Auntie Ellie's twins. She said mine were the first boys.

I sensed when her voice broke. I thought I heard a sob. I asked, "Maamie Daley, are you crying?"

"Damn volcano!" she shouted. "Sweetie, namesake, I may never hold your boys in my arms. The Mighty Watchman be damned!"

She sounded oh so pitiful! It broke my heart. Involuntary tears bathed my face. I did not sob. I did not want her to know that I was also crying. I remembered how she and Parpi Daley had overcome their fear of flying to be at Ejay's graduation.

"You will hold Rey and Rex, Maamie Daley," I said. "Just keep on praying for my family and me."

"Oh, Mags, Sweetie, Boy and I pray daily for all of you, my little darlings and sweeties. He is outside helping a young man he had hired to clean his car. Let me go and tell him that he can add two more to his list of great-grandchildren, Jesse, Vera Rose, Paula, Roland, Jonathan, Randy,

Simmy, Rey, and Rex! Nine, and counting, Mags, Sweetie! Presently, our great-grandchildren exceed Boy's and my total production, but there will be more. Boy and I are so proud of all of you! God bless you! Kiss them for us. We will telephone you soon. So long, Mags, Sweetie."

"So long, Maamie Daley! God bless you, too. Thank you!"

I said, "Duke, the Mighty Watchman be damned! We are going to Montserrat."

"What? Slow down, Duchess!"

When he heard about Maamie's lament, he decided that we must defy the rebellious Watchman and take Rex and Rey to Montserrat to meet their great-grandparents. Since Maamie Daley's childbearing days, it was the custom that all Daley babies be baptized at three months. We had a quiet baptism and left for Montserrat soon after Rex and Rey turned three months.

I was afraid all the way. The airport no longer existed. It, too, had succumbed to tons of ashes, magma and boulders. We took the ferry from St. John's, Antigua, early one morning to Little Bay, Montserrat. The ferry was a large catamaran boat. It was comfortable enough until it entered the rough waters one half hour into the sailing. The babies were uncomfortable, and began to cry. We were happy to see Montserrat's coastline. However, the heat was suffocating. The eruptions had caused a rise in temperature, not only in Montserrat, but also in the entire Eastern Caribbean. Someone likened the heat to "Satan opening hell's gate to provide a vent for his eternal fire."

We finally met Winnie when she, Keith, and Simmy were at the wharf to meet us. She was a beautiful woman with curly dark hair, puckered lips, and a tiny nose. Her eyes were dark brown, and large. When Keith introduced us, she puckered up, and placed a kiss on my cheek and then on Duke's with a "Moi"!. She then kissed our boys while declaring how cute they were. I told her that Simmy was a charmer, too.

When she took Rey from me, I took Simmy from Keith. He was definitely a cute little fellow. He stared at his cousins and reached to touch their faces. At first, they were somewhat cranky, no doubt due to the effects of the short ferry ride.

When we got to the house, Maamie and Parpi Daley just stared at us. We had told them we were coming, but they seemed to be amazed at our presence.

Finally, Maamie asked, "Is it really you, Mags, Sweetie?"

"Yes, Maamie Daley. Duke and I wish to present our sons, Rex and Rey, to you, as we ought. We figured one duke in the family is enough, but two kings would be great. Parpi Daley took Rex and Maamie held Rey. They sat and stared at their newest great-grandsons. They kissed them, and cuddled them closely.

Simmy was wet. Maamie Daley gave Rey to Winnie, took Simmy from me, and changed his diaper. Winnie saw the surprise on my face, and explained that Maamie Daley volunteered to do it. Maamie Daley had made Simmy two dozen diapers, because the disposables were scarce in the island. I gave Winnie a case of diapers, and she hugged me. She had to wash the cloth diapers by hand, and dry them inside to avoid the volcanic dust.

"Thank you, Mags. I can't say I like to wash hippins, because no matter where I hang them, inside or outside, they still collect volcanic dust. Simmy is hardy, but nobody knows what's in those ashes. I hear they are full of chemicals that would irritate his skin. It's difficult to dry clothes when the ashes fall."

"Hippins? I asked.

"Yes. That's what we call diapers, here in Montserrat."

I laughed when I considered that I had not learned much of the island's slang. The furniture was covered with dust, and I wiped them.

"Save your energy, Mags," Winnie said. "This volcanic dust is invasive. It gets in whether we like it or not."

Upon hearing that, I got nervous. I thought, "Even inside; my Lord, am I subjecting my babies to some unforeseen danger?"

When Maamie and Parpi Daley finally accepted that we were truly back with them, we spotted a glimmer of their former selves. It was good to hear "Shug" and "Boy" again. Nevertheless, I thought that Maamie and Parpi Daley had lost their passion for life. They had not mentioned the old house, although Syd's paintings hung in full view.

One day, I stood admiring the painting. Maamie Daley saw me, and joined me. She traced the Big House with her index finger. She stopped her finger journey at the old kitchen and smiled as she stared at the old brick oven.

Speaking of ovens, I saw the old Charley-man oven neatly covered in a corner of Winnie's modern kitchen. I wished I had taken it to America. I was so happy that they had rescued it from the Big House before it was buried deep into the wasteland once called the big yard.

I told Maamie Daley that every morning, after I pray, I run through the parlor to check on our Big House and the animals. They looked so real!

Maamie told me. "I think Boy does, too. The Lord has blessed Syd with the talent that will be our comfort as long as we live."

"I am so happy that you feel comforted, Maamie Daley," I said.

She embraced me. "What more can an old woman need, Mags, Sweetie? She asked. "Tell me a little more about your other grandmother, Mags, Sweetie."

"Abuelita Carlota smiles naturally, but deep down, I think she is sad. She is trying hard to get to know Mom. Mom was somewhat aloof at first. Now, she is warming up. I am going to ask Duke and Dad to let us plan a cruise for them together. Maamie Daley, Mom and Syd look like her and Uncle Will. He sounds exactly like Syd."

I gave Maamie Daley a hug as she admired a photo of Abuelita Carlota, Uncle Will and Syd sitting together on our couch. Ejay had taken it. She studied the photo and declared, "Oh yes, Mags, Sweetie. This is Lisa's mother. Syd is a younger Will. Give her a little time. I do not know if I can give her any advice. I knew my parents all my life until their passing. What could I possibly tell Lisa? I wish she were here so that I could hug her."

One afternoon, I had a long chat with Winnie. Like Keith, she, too, was a divorcee. She had met and married a man from Africa in London. Her cousin, Leonard Martin, who was also raised by her grandfather, had cautioned her not to marry him. When they divorced, they got joint custody of their two daughters, but he asked her permission to take them to Ghana to meet his family. They never returned to London. She said when she asked his friends for her husband and her daughters, they said they had not heard from him. She knew they were lying. She said that she was young and inexperienced, and did not know how to fight back.

About a year after her divorce, her grandfather became ill in Montserrat. She went home to take care of him. When he fell gravely ill, she wrote to Leonard at the old man's request, but he never answered her letter. When her grandfather died, she found out that he had left her his property in the north, and quite a large sum of money in England and in Montserrat. She decided to live in the family house in Olveston. She returned to London, gave up her flat, and went home to Montserrat. She told me she prayed day and night to see her girls again. I listened without prying. Winnie showed me the photos of two little girls. "This is Amina Mariah, and this is Pili

Emma," she said. She planted a kiss on the photos and put them back in her pocket.

I told her they were beautiful, because indeed they were. She told me that Keith had brought her back to the land of sanity.

"And Simmy," she added, holding him tenderly. "I adore him. I'm glad Vera loves him. She accepts me now, because she sees that I love her son.

"Mags, I often wonder what would have happened if my grandparents had not migrated to England when their two sons, Uncle Errol and my dad, Jordan, were small. They separated and then divorced because according to Grandpa, Grandma wanted to return home. Grandma brought her sons back to Montserrat. When she passed away, Grandpa returned home and remodeled his parents' house.

"Errol was the first to marry. His wife left him with their baby boy, Leonard and never looked back. My father also married young. My parents moved to London where I was born, but left for Birmingham when I was a baby, because Dad had many friends there and the work opportunity was better for him.

"Errol left Leonard with Grandpa and returned to England. Grandpa took Lenny to England to his father two years later, but when he saw how his son was living, he went for Lenny. My parents died in Birmingham when I was about five. My grandfather went for me, and took me to London.

"Grandpa was a good carpenter, and a loving parent. He hired someone to do our laundry until I was big enough to do it. Lenny had to help also. Grandpa was a great cook, and he taught both of us how to cook. We went to the market with him on Saturdays. He taught us how to select the best vegetables. He used to send us to church and Sunday school every week, but when the parson visited us and scolded him, he began to attend service with us.

"Grandpa worked hard, and bought a property in Shepherds Bush. I had to fight my cousin, Leonard Martin, because he didn't want me around. However, my parents had designated my grandfather guardian of my inheritance.

"I remember the day when Grandpa told Lenny that his father was living in France with a young mademoiselle. Lenny shrugged his shoulders, indifferently. I tried to locate Lenny when Grandpa died, but he never responded. He turned out to be just as ungrateful as his father.

"Lenny and I grew up together, but he was standoffish and selfish. He used to get furious when people asked him for his sister. He told them in no uncertain term that he was an only child. My grandfather had promised to educate Lenny and me. When Lenny graduated from the university, he didn't bother much with Grandpa, either. He became a licensed social worker. He worked with troubled boys in North London. I also attended the university and became a teacher.

"Grandpa had promised to leave everything for me in his will, because I was an orphaned young woman in London, and Len had had a better rapport with my dad. I met Kofi Amos and married him against my grandfather's wishes soon after Grandpa turned over my inheritance from my parents to me. If Kofi had known about it, he would probably have robbed me.

"Grandpa decided to return to Montserrat after my daughters were born. He offered to take them home with him, but I told him no. How I wished I had accepted his offer. I had deposited most of the money here in Montserrat. Kofi had laughed heartily when he heard of the size of our island.

"Grandpa tried on many occasions to connect with Lenny, but he never replied. Someone told Grandpa that Lenny did not want me around. Grandpa had contacted him to let him know that he was returning to Montserrat, but he never responded. He did not come to Grandpa's funeral. We are the last of the Martins. I would still share the land with Lenny.

"I am a licensed teacher, so I am not stupid. I was foolish once in my adult life. That was when I trusted Kofi Amos with our daughters. I know they steal land here in Montserrat, and the Martin land would be no exception. Its location here in Olveston makes it prime property. Grandpa wrote down the boundaries of our property and left them well marked. With the exodus of teachers and other professionals, I am glad that I had returned to Montserrat. No nation can strive without the education of its young people. I love this little island."

Winnie paused for a while, and then continued.

"I had hired Keith to work on my grandfather's house; now mine. The bastards, who had rented one of the flats, really messed it up. That was how we met. He told me that he was giving me a great price, and asked me never to mention his fee to anyone. I told him that I was only interested in good work, because that was what my grandfather would have expected.

"However, as you can judge for yourself, Keith is a master builder. When I paid him the last third of the money, he thanked me and planted a kiss on my lips. I boxed him real hard. He twisted his jaw, apologized and told me he deserved it. Nevertheless, he kept coming back until he won; but I love Keith. I told him my age, and he told me his. I said, 'The first time you call me 'old', I'll be out of your life.'

"Keith had told me that after his tempestuous affair and marriage to Dionne Marie, what he needed was a mature woman. Mags, he would have been the laughingstock of Montserrat if he had permitted the gossiping to get to him. People said that the Wilkins had paid him off when their saga-girl[23] deserted him for her older man. All I know is that he proposed to me soon after we met. I chased him away, but he did not give up.

"Your Auntie Vee confronted me. She told me that Keith always makes wrong decisions. I told her it was no doubt due to her lack of parenting. I reminded her that her son was no virgin. I asked her, 'Have you forgotten Keith's ex-wife?'

"She said, 'Dionne Marie was wrong for him, and you are no better, Winnie.' I asked her if she had ever heard that I was running after Keith. I let her know that the last thing I needed in my life was her boy and her intrusion. I told her I am a divorcée with two daughters. When Keith comes knocking at my door, I don't see you with him, Mrs. Duberry. That gave me the impression that he is now a man.'

She said I was froward. She told me, 'That does it. I don't want my son marrying a divorcée.'

"I asked her who told her that I want to marry her son. I told her I am a female person, not a cow. I only have two breasts. I advised her to take her baby boy home and nurse him. She glared at me. I saw anger blazing in her eyes. She left in a huff.

"She complained to Keith. He was furious, Mags. Someone told me that he blasted her. He said that his mother was too damn meddling and judgmental. You know our Montserratians; they like to gossip. They declared that my childbearing days were over, and your Auntie Vera believed it. When I got pregnant, she was surprised. I hardly saw her during my pregnancy. One of my colleagues told ne that in times gone by female teachers were automatically dismissed if they got pregnant out of wedlock.

"Keith called Vera to announce the birth of our Simmy. The following day, she came to the hospital without warning,

"She said hello to me, and announced that she came to see her grandchild. Would you know that Simmy looked at her? She picked him up, kissed him, and held him to her bosom for such a long time that it

---

23 playgirl

seemed that they had melted into one. It didn't really surprise me because I know how she adores Jesse and Vera Rose.

"When can my parents come to see Simmy?" she asked.

"You didn't ask permission to visit him, and you despise me, Mrs. Duberry. Maamie and Parpi Daley love me. They're welcome at any time, but we'll soon be home."

She paused for a moment, "Let me tell you something, Winnie. I am a Daley. We Daleys take care of our own."

"I'm glad you do, Mrs. Duberry," I said. "I am a Martin. We Martins are no less caring than you, Daleys. However, remember that Simmy is a Duberry."

"I see that, too, I assure you. To show you how big a woman I am, I apologize to you, and hope you accept my apology. Your lover, Keith, insulted me. He told me I am an old busybody who doesn't know when to keep my big mouth shut."

"I accept your apology, Mama Vera," I said, smiling.

"Just plain Vera, or Vee, is good enough for me, Winnie."

"Okay, Vera. Whatever makes you happy," I said.

"I was so sorry that Vera and Keith had had a misunderstanding. I blamed myself. However, things have run quite smoothly since her hospital visit. Simmy is the glue that has bonded us together. I don't like to hold grudges.

"I adore Maamie and Parpi Daley, and I really mean 'Grandpa' when I speak of Duby Duberry. He reminds me so much of my grandfather. He adores Sadie and Keith, and Sadie's children. Simmy is his heart. He loves Rozy and me, his two in-laws. He is a wonderful old man. People say he's crazy, Mags, but now they see. He predicted the eruption of the volcano. He said that the prophet Isaiah had promised the fire from the mountains in his day, and nobody paid attention to his prophesy. He said he was no prophet, but that he knew the fire that would consume Montserrat would come from the Soufriere Hills."

"Yes. I know," I said. "Duke and I heard that warning one day at the public market. Winnie, are you going to stay here? It is dangerous for you and Simmy; in fact, for everyone. You must always wear your masks. Please, protect little Simmy, too. Volcanic ashes are lethal when inhaled. That's why I make sure that my babies' nostrils are protected. Duke and I wear our face masks."

"Uncle Bern left boxes of masks with us. We share them with neighbors. They are uncomfortable, as you can judge for yourself. Please speak to

Keith, Maggie. I love him, but he is very obstinate. He's making a lot of money. Money is not everything, Mags. Seeing that I'm older than he is, I don't want him to think that I'm bossing him around. We do discuss things. According to Montserratians, Keith is very crabbit. He has good common tense. He taught me not to bother about what people say."

"'You are a grown woman, Winnie. Do not let anybody, and I mean nobody, rule your life. Don't argue with fools, because you'll never win,' he told me."

"He explained why he could never abandon Maamie and Parpi Daley and Grandpa Duby. He offered to send Simmy and me to his Auntie Ellie in Barbados, but I refused. I can't leave him. If we survive, we'll be together, and if we perish, we'll perish together. I can't take another separation. Simmy adores him. I don't want to separate them."

I liked Winnie. She was right for Keith. Simmy was lovable, too. He had his mother's eyes, the largest and brightest eyes that I had ever seen in such a tiny face. They were like black stars, shining. My boys had the fat cheeks of the Randall clan, but they had my pug nose and high forehead. Maamie and Parpi Daley kept the three boys busy with their "Mosquito one, mosquito two," sung in unison and then Parpi Daley buzzed like a mosquito, while he made diving patterns in the air with his open palms. Simmy laughed while my boys watched and listened intently.

While we were there, Syd's painting of the farm arrived. What a joyous time for Shug and her Boy. Parpi Daley kissed it, just as he had kissed his old jackass. After we had examined it, pointing out all its attributes, Keith hung it near the others. Parpi Daley cried like a baby. Keith picked up Simmy. Simmy caressed Parpi Daley's face, as he looked at the painting. Maamie Daley watched her Boy and Simmy.

The eruptions at the Soufriere Hills had reduced Montserrat to one third of its former size, but it was their homeland. Some Montserratians held firmly to their Emerald Isle. Why not? The people, with whom they communicated, spoke with their accent. On clear days, they gathered and gossiped about neighbors and relatives at home and abroad. For some Montserratians, life went on as usual. They worked in the tiny vegetable gardens in their backyards. We ate some of the vegetables that Maamie and Parpi harvested while we were there. The Martin's plot was rather large. The sweet cassavas were huge. So were the sweet potatoes and dasheens. Parpi reminded us that volcanic ashes were very fertile and credited them for the greening of the North.

"Mags," he added, "Montserrat is truly the Emerald Isle. The North is green. Before the eruptions, it was not."

"Mags, Sweetie, Boy is right. If the Lord wanted us to flee our land, would he have provided the new fertility for us? I don't think so, and for his generosity, I praise him from the bottom of my heart."

"Keep on praying, Maamie," I said. "Montserrat needs every prayer that we raise in her name."

ZJB, the Montserrat radio station, started each day with a prayer, and Maamie and Parpi Daley never missed the morning devotion.

Every morning, Parpi Daley rose early and checked the skies in all four directions, but especially in the southwest. He did not listen to the report from the Montserrat Volcano Observatory, *MVO*. He was his own volcanologist. He would announce, "Shug, it looks good today, or "it's not so good today, Shug."

Duke and I were convinced that Mamie and Parpi should not leave Montserrat. We were sure that a final separation from their homeland would kill them. There was a look of yearning in their eyes. We knew that their heart and soul were not in their "safe haven" in the safety zone. I agonized over their longing for their old lifestyle, but I never let them see me sad.

One morning, Keith invited Duke and me for a helicopter flight over the unsafe or "No Go" zone. The volcano had not erupted while we were there. However, they had swarms of earthquakes. Parpi Daley's old Mighty Watchman was in the midst of all the commotion. We saw no sign of life below. There was no evidence that bustling villages once existed there. There were no boundaries. I shuddered as the co-pilot announced our village, the place where Maamie and Parpi Daley had raised their six children and entertained their children's children. There was no sign of the Big House, and I cried. I could feel Duke's hand massaging my shoulders. It felt good. I closed my eyes and rested my head on his shoulder. When I opened them again, we were flying over water, and I stared at the blue waters of the unchanging Caribbean Sea. Its calmness baffled me. I closed my eyes again and did not open them until we landed in the safety zone.

We got back on time to say good-bye to the Matthew brothers. They were lucky to get free passage to England and were on their way. Percy presented his wife, Nancy, to us. She was a State Registered Nurse, *SRN*, who had studied in England, and returned to the island. She would do well back in England. We gave them our blessings. Maamie and Parpi Daley blessed them, and Maamie gave Percy his old pouch with the money that she had put aside for him and his brothers. Duke and I added one hundred American dollars, too. Maamie and Parpi cried silently as they embraced the three young men and Percy's wife. I saw Percy wipe his tears. That scene truly marked the end of an era. The old farm was indeed no more.

That night, Keith took Duke and me to view what the natives and tourists called "the glow". The tourists visited from the neighboring islands to view the volcano in its full display. The Mighty Watchman was not going quietly. He was not at all shy. He gave them a pyrotechnic show to remember. There were "oohs and ahs," as flames and thunder-like noises erupted from the bowels of the Soufriere Hills. The mountains blazed like a bonfire. We heard the clicking of cameras all around us. Some took videos of the awesome spectacle. I wondered how the tourists could demonstrate such joy while Montserrat burned. We left. Duke was very upset with the behavior of the thrill seekers who, no doubt, were oblivious to the pain that the eruptions had brought. Their behavior reminded me of how, after witnessing the blood spurting from the slaughtered animals, I still ate Maamie Daley's stew. I shuddered at the gruesome recall.

"All of us bore our guilt," I thought.

We sat with Maamie and Parpi Daley and the rest of the family on the eve of our return to New York. Maamie and Parpi held our babies. Naturally, Duke got his share of photos. Parpi and Auntie Vee wanted to hear about Mom's mother and brother. We told them all we knew.

I said, "My Abuelita Carlota is a wonderful woman. She said she would like to know Montserrat. I pray that you will meet her some day."

"Does she know about the volcano?" Maamie asked.

"Yes, I think she does, although I am not sure if she knows of the extent of its destruction. I must ask her."

"Duke and Mags, Sweetie, teach your children to love God, because God is love. Above all, teach them to be good to themselves and to one another, and to honor their family. You say that they look like the Randalls, Mags, Sweetie, but they have a lot for the Daleys, too."

"I see that, Maamie Daley. What about the Moores?" Duke asked.

"The Moores?" Auntie Vera asked.

"Yes. Abuelita Carlota is a Moore. We didn't tell you the full story. In fact, Mom had as many aliases as her father. She learned, at the same time we did, that her real name is *Dorotea Pardo Moore* which means Dorothy Browne Moore in English."

"Tunny told me about Lisa's villainous father. Forget that rigmarole, Maggie. As far as I'm concerned, my sister-in-law is Lisa Murray Daley," Auntie Vera said bluntly. "Tell her I say to leave well enough alone."

"That is exactly what Mom has decided to do, Auntie Vee," I said.

Winnie took me aside, hugged me, and whispered. "Maggie, please pray for me. Tell Auntie Lisa I am happy for her. Ask her to pray that I, too, will find my daughters. They are adolescents now. They were born in London. Maybe I'll see them there some day."

I kissed Winnie on her cheek, and promised to pray for her. "I hope your wish will come true, Winnie." I began my silent prayer at that moment.

Our time with Maamie and Parpi and the family went by too fast. Maamie and Parpi Daley said a lazy goodbye to us at the dock. I hugged them, oh so tightly! I felt her lips on my forehead as she whispered feebly "my Sweetie, namesake." I had a strange feeling that I would not see them in life again.

We did not see Keith on a daily basis while we were in Montserrat. They had embarked on a flurry of construction, and he was in the midst of it.

Soon after we returned to New York, Keith called us to say that Auntie Vera had truly mellowed. She had her "Sym" back, and she herself counseled him to marry Winnie. Winnie changed her mind and accepted his proposal. They had a private ceremony. Only Auntie Vera, Maamie and Parpi Daley, Grandpa Duby and Simmy were present when the parson pronounced them man and wife in the tiny chapel of their place of worship.

We were only home for a few months, when we got the sad news that they had rushed Keith to the burn center in the island of Guadeloupe. It seemed he had entered a burning home to rescue an elderly lady. When he pulled her out, she kept screaming "Norman! Norman!" He went back into the house and got burnt. When they pulled him out, they found out that Norman was the woman's cat, and that he had escaped through a rear window.

I listened on the extension as Auntie Vera vented her anger to Dad. "Tunny, that old fart almost made my son lose his life to save her cat. I am bitter! Parpi's Mighty Watchman is not erupting; I am. Duby prayed with me. He asked me to forgive her, but I can't." She sobbed. "He flew with us to Guadeloupe. It was his strong faith that quieted my rage. It was 'touch and go' there for a while. I swore I would have killed that old bitch, if Keith had died.'"

Dad spoke comforting words into the telephone. I wondered if Auntie Vera had heard them. She was truly enraged.

"Vee, it's going to be fine," Dad said. "Keith will be okay. We will pray for him, and for you, too. Maamie and Parpi taught us to be forgiving. You and Sym abandoned Duby in his time of need, but Duby is with you now, and Sym is gone. Life is too short, Sis. Find it in your heart to forgive the old woman. Maybe the cat is the only possession she has left."

"Yes, Tunny," she said. "I'll try. Simmy and Winnie will stay with Keith for the duration of his hospitalization. She is a good wife and mother."

"I'm glad you have accepted Keith's wife, Vee. God bless you, Sis. God will heal Keith."

"Thank you, Tunny. Good-bye."

Ejay and Randy left for Guadeloupe a week after Auntie Vera's call. They spent eight days there. Ejay spoke very highly of Winnie. He and his son went to Montserrat to see Maamie and Parpi Daley and spent six days with them. Naturally, everyone was happy to see Ejay Daley and his son. Ejay told me that he could never have returned to New York and not stopped in to see Maamie and Parpi Daley who were so close to Guadeloupe. Cassandra was nervous. She told me that she got startled every time the telephone rang.

She said, "Maamie and Parpi Daley are not fair, Mags. They decided to stay in Montserrat with a raging volcano, when they knew the family would be worried about them. Ejay adores them. After all, he is their 'Little Boy', but I'm concerned about my baby boy."

I told her that I understood her concern. She was a caring mother. I explained to her why Duke and I thought Maamie and Parpi Daley's decision not to leave was right for them. Ejay and Randy returned home safely.

The first time Keith telephoned us from his hospital room, I screamed. He said, "Maggie, when I saw Ejay and Randy, I cried like a baby. I'm much better. Hey, so I won't wear short pants or bikinis in public any more." I stifled my sobs. "My right leg is badly scarred. Thank God, I did not get burnt about the face.

"Maamie and Parpi Daley are supportive. Grandpa Duby prayed

with me and with all the other patients. He was so convincing that the authorities welcomed him. They called him 'Parson Duberry.' They treat me 'special' because I am his grandson. They even permit me to see Simmy, daily. Winnie and Simmy are holding me together. She's staying with a woman from Montserrat who runs a boarding house a short distance from the hospital. Ejay and Randy also boarded there. Maggie, our sons were together; just like you, Syd, my sister and I were when we were small."

"Yes, Keith, some day, Simmy, my boys, Sadie's two, and Ejay's Randy will laugh and play together. I'm delighted that Grandpa Duby finally got his recognition. 'Parson Duberry,' if you please!" He laughed. "We are praying for you night and day. I thank God for sparing you. Remember that Duke and I are here for you. If you need anything, just say the word."

"Thank you, Mags. I pray every moment, especially when I think of my wife and my son. Thank everybody for me. Tell them I'm fine."

Keith spent five more months in the hospital and returned to Montserrat. After two months of rehabilitation, he returned to work.

Most of us Daleys, and our children went to Montserrat in December, 1999, to celebrate Parpi and Maamie Daley's ninety-fifth birthday. He had turned ninety-five on October 10, and she on December 14. We had planned to have as big a party as circumstances would permit, and then spend Christmas with them. Maamie and Parpi Daley beamed. They knew each of us by name. We numbered forty plus.

Abuelita Carlota, Uncle Will and his son, Walter, also accompanied us. Maamie Daley spent a long time with Abuelita Carlota, telling her what a wonderful woman Lisa was, and how happy she was that they had reunited. We photographed Maamie and Parpi and all the relatives present. Hugo had robbed them of the celebration of their eighty-fifth birthdays back in 1989. The Mighty Watchman was kind to them while they enjoyed their festivity. Syd and Ejay had already begun their recording of the affair.

Syd, Duke, Rozy, Ejay, Keith, James, Vincent, Darius, Marc, Uncle Will and Walter had gone crabbing the night before. They brought back buckets of crabs and crayfish that would delight the "foreigners", while the natives would savor the foreign food: hot dogs, hamburgers, sausages, and cold cuts. All the frozen beef patties, and lasagna, were homemade.

When they were ready to serve the food, they asked Grandpa Duby to bless it. His grace was so long that some began to cough, whisper, and create other distractions. It did not deter him. The islanders, who dropped in, helped to make it a memorable affair. We pledged to return to Montserrat to celebrate their one hundredth birthday.

Ejay whispered in my ear, "Maggie, why didn't they ask me or Uncle Sol to say the grace? Trust me; nobody heard a word Grandpa Duby said." I had to laugh.

Ejay operated the barbecue grill that Keith had set up in the backyard. Someone had donated the goat water, and everyone claimed it was superb. They served the children first. They sat on comforters on the grass. Some of the village children joined them. They were just as hungry or greedy as the adults were. They returned for seconds and thirds. I feasted on the salt fish and dumplings that Auntie Vera had personally prepared.

The diminished state of the island had little effect on our celebration. Alcohol flowed like water. Some folks dropped by just to have a drink and to celebrate my grandparents on their big day. The music was as hot as the alcohol, and the dancing was wild. The littlest Daley offspring danced nonstop. Keith was right. Our children danced together, but not at the Big House.

Upon seeing Simmy's moves, Maamie Daley declared, "My Lord, look at Natty Daley!"

At first, Maamie and Parpi Daley were just spectators, but they tapped their feet to the beat when the music got exciting. Finally, minutes past midnight, Uncle Bern helped Maamie to her feet and waltzed with her slowly around the floor. Auntie Ellie chose Parpi Daley. They waltzed around the floor, also. Uncle Bern then passed Maamie Daley to Uncle Sol, then to Uncle Paul, and then to my Dad, their baby boy, Tunny. Auntie Ellie waltzed Parpi over to Auntie Vera who danced with him, and passed him back to Maamie Daley. Abuelita chose Grandpa Duby, whose moves were classic. They finished their waltz to the wild applause of all of us. We, the younger Daleys, bowed to them, when they took their seat.

Following that special waltz, Auntie Ellie, Yolanda and Christa, and Auntie Vera brought forth the birthday cake. The layout was breathtaking. All of Syd's paintings and photos of Maamie and Parpi Daley in their youth, and their wedding pictures were on display. The birthday cake was the famous Caribbean fruitcake. It was the largest cake I had ever seen**. The caption read, "Blessed 95th Birthday to Our Dearest Maamie and Parpi Daley"*!*"** We sang "Happy Birthday." They cut the cake. Parpi fed Maamie Daley with a golden spoon on which Auntie Ellie had engraved his name. She, in turn, placed a piece in Parpi's mouth with her golden spoon, a gift from Uncle Chris. They kissed, no doubt, as they had done what seemed to have been eons ago on their wedding day. We toasted them, some with champagne, and others with sparkling cider. We savored the cake, which melted in the mouth.

There were mango, coconut, and potato pies, plain cakes, chocolate cakes, and much more. I limited what my boys ate. Winnie and Keith had rescued about one fourth of the birthday cake to distribute among the family.

The musicians turned up the tempo, and the young Daleys went crazy. Ejay got Abuelita Carlota who was ready to get down. She was a smooth and stylish dancer. Dancing was one area where Syd showed no reservation. He was a better dancer than Vincent, James, Ejay, Keith, and all the others. Yolanda, Christa, their father, their husbands and their boys demonstrated dancing, Bajan style. All of us mimicked each other.

Uncle Will and Walter told me they did not think of the volcano while they were having fun. He said some friends had told him he was crazy to take his mother and his only son to such a small island that could be blown to hell in a heartbeat.

"Maggie, I told them, 'Look, not long ago, I found my sister and her Daley family, and I want to get as close to them as I can.' I'm so glad we came."

"I am, too, Uncle Will," I said.

Ejay asked the musicians to play a Merengue and Uncle Will and Abuelita Carlota took to the floor. We simply imitated them. While the music was hot, and everyone was dancing intensely, Maamie and Parpi Daley slipped away.

Mom got on the floor with Uncle Will. They did some wild moves. Dad told him, "Hey, Señor, that's my wife".

Uncle Will said, "Sir, I knew her long before you met her. She is my Baby Sis."

Dad was finally in the groove. Uncle Sol shouted, "That's it, Tunny! Shake your body line, boy!"

"Shake your body line, Uncle Sol," I asked.

"Yes, Maggie," he said. "My brother is too damn stiff. Get down, Tunny."

I thought how strange it was that Mom's favorite dance was the Merengue. She had many Merengue tapes at home.

Dad started dancing wildly, trying to outdo Will Moore and his little sister, Dorotea. Everyone laughed, as Mom paused to look at her Tunny.

We mothers had a rough time rounding up our little ones, but we managed to get them to bed minutes after 2:00 a.m. They went out like a light. The party ended when the cocks crowed to announce the dawn. We simply collapsed.

We woke up late, and had breakfast around lunchtime. Mom said that we were really having brunch. She, Auntie Vera, Auntie Ellie and Winnie were busy in the kitchen. They had large slices of ham, scrambled eggs, eggs sunny side up, bacon, fried fish, pancakes, hot rolls, coffee tea and coco tea. Maamie Daley made cornmeal porridge for the little ones.

"Mommy," Rex said, "This is good stuff. Please make it for us in New York."

"Ask your grandpa, dear," I said.

He ran to my father and said, "Grandpa, please make us cornmeal porridge when we go home. It is good."

"Tell Maamie Daley to teach you how to make it," Dad told him. Rex mumbled something and went to Maamie Daley. I did not hear what he said to her.

Abuelita Carlota told him, "Rex, come to my house, and I will make it for you."

"Thank you, Abuelita," he said, kissing her. "You are nice. I'll come to Brooklyn for my porridge."

One could not be in Montserrat, and not think that more eruptions were still imminent. Grandpa Duby was silent during the celebration. He did not preach any of his public sermons, but after brunch that day, he sermonized among us. One would have thought that he would be puffed up over his prediction that God would strike Montserrat with a flaming fire. He had said that the fire would come from the mountains, but it turned out that they were not mountains at all. They were mere volcanic domes, by all scientific accounts. The last eruptions had taken place four centuries earlier. The growth of all kinds of trees and shrubs camouflaged the domes that had risen from the eruptions, including the island's highest peak, Chances Mountain, or Parpi Daley's Mighty Watchman. No wonder the Caribs fled from the eruptions in their Alliouagana, the island Columbus renamed Montserrat. Were they wiser than our present-day Montserratians? Time would be the best judge.

After the sermon, I reminded Dad of Grandpa Duby's prediction. He said, "Duby got lucky, Maggie."

"Luck had nothing to do with it. He called it right, Dad. Admit it," I said.

"Yes, Maggie. He called it."

"Okay. His was the voice of one crying in the Town. They didn't pay any attention to John the Baptist either," I said.

"People are people, after all," Dad said. "Centuries from now, nothing would have changed."

We did not leave the island together. My immediate family was the last to leave. When we said good-bye at the dock, Maamie and Parpi Daley cried. I could not contain my tears, either. Before long, everyone was crying.

We looked at the faces around us. The émigrés on their way to America, other Caribbean Islands and England, were all sad. They were probably crying not only for what they were leaving behind, but also for the uncertainty of their future. Some bowed their heads in prayer. Others stared at the partly devastated island from the deck of the ferry, until it faded in the distance. I understood their plight. I remember the affinity that the folks of the big yard shared with the coconut palm at which root their umbilical chords 'navel strings' were buried.

The sea was rough. There was little or no conversation among us, as we traveled to Antigua to connect our flights to New York and elsewhere, except for the retching sound of some passengers.

I thought of the natives who had decided not to emigrate. They treated the volcano as if it were invisible, just a mere nuisance. They took care of the ashes as they fell, just as we do our snowstorms. If they were frightened, they were damn good actors. They listened to Radio Montserrat, *ZJB*, got the day's report, and went about their business, as usual.

Mom thought they were remarkable. "Montserratians are hardy folks," she whispered.

It was a pleasure to see Mom, Abuelita Carlota, and Uncle Will sitting side by side on the jumbo jet on our return to New York. They had a lengthy conversation. I did not ask Mom what they had discussed, but I knew it was good. They laughed and smiled all the way home. At one point, I noticed that Abuelita Carlota had dozed and rested her head on Mom's shoulder. That was touching. The flight was smooth.

While we waited to clear customs, Abuelita Carlota told me, "Mags, Sweetie..." I did not hear anything else. I burst into tears. She held me. At that moment, there was no doubt that she was my full-blooded grandmother. We cried together.

When we had regained our composure, she asked, "Do you mind my calling you that? Maamie Daley told me that's what she calls you."

"Oh, no," I said. "It's just that she looked so sad when we said goodbye."

"I know," Abuelita said. "She told me she gets sad when she considers what the volcano has done to the island."

"Yes Abuelita Carlota," I whispered. "I know."

"I've just met Maamie and Parpi Daley, and I didn't want to say goodbye, either." She paused for a bit, and then added, "My Jamaican mother fed us a lot of cornmeal porridge. It was a nourishing but cheap meal, then. Please bring Rex to Brooklyn so I can make it for him. Of course, bring Rey and anyone else who wants to come, too. Sometimes, I'll visit you and make it at your house. My Mother had a great secret. She made her own coconut milk, and used it to enrich that porridge."

"I will, Abuelita Carlota," I said. "Remind me not to eat too much. You see, I, too, like cornmeal porridge. Maamie Daley also used her own coconut milk."

Uncle Will and Walter could not stop talking of the goodtime they had in Montserrat. Walter was a comedian. He said, "Mags, I am going to write a piece called, "Walter, the Crayfish, and the Volcano." Then he showed me his index finger where the crayfish had clawed him. He added, "Don't worry. I didn't let the guys see me cry."

Uncle Will said, "Maggie, the more I look at my son, the more I see my father's face. When Mama did not find your mother after all our searches, she got into a rage one day and destroyed her wedding photos, and everything that had Papa's name and face on it. There was a photo with him sitting with your mother in his lap, and me standing in my sailor suit at his side. I tried to save it, but she snatched it from me and tore it to shreds. She wanted to burn the shreds, but I grabbed her and took the matches away. I whispered, 'Mama, do you want to burn out the apartment?' She broke into sobs."

I sympathized with him, but I never told Mom about her mother's rage.

We kept in touch with Maamie and Parpi Daley. Auntie Vera moved in with Keith and Winnie after Keith added another room to the house. She said she wanted to be near Simmy. I was happy that they were together again. Grandpa Duby visited frequently, but he stayed at the shelter to be near his staunchest supporters.

One day Maamie Daley read me a letter that she had received from Percy. He told her that no matter what anyone said, one of her sons must have been his father. He said as far as he was concerned, he was a Daley. He said no strangers could have embraced him like Parpi and her. She added that they heard from him often, and he sent them the largest greeting cards they had ever received for their birthday, and photos of his family. They were doing quite well. He took a course in fine carpentry to add to what Parpi Daley had taught him, and had a job with a construction firm. His brothers studied the computer, and were doing very well. However, he did not like their social habits. He told Maamie Daley that they were "woman crazy".

I had often heard Maamie Daley say, "It's a sad thing when watchman turns thief."

I thought, "Mighty Watchman, you are nothing but a confounded thief. You have stolen all of my grandparents' land, their house, and their animals, their hope, and their bubbly spirit. Friend and Foe did not survive your eruptions. They have nothing left to leave for their children, and their children's children. I am so happy that you lost your head. Maamie Daley was right. "May you be damned!"

Chapter XXI

Syd Murray Daley, the Introvert

My brother, Syd Murray Daley, was a true introvert. We had entertained Maamie and Parpi Daley and their entire village. We interacted with Syd. We were always in touch with him. Yet, he did not mention his wife, Tabitha. We did not know he was an artist until we received his very fine paintings. Mom spoke to him once a week. He telephoned Uncle Will and Abuelita Carlota regularly. Yet, his last surprise caught all of us unawares.

Early one evening Mom's bell rang. Dad opened the door. Syd entered with an attractive young woman, carrying a baby girl. Duke, my boys, and I were downstairs to have dinner with Mom and Dad. Syd smiled, took the baby from the young woman, and placed her in Mom's arms.

"Mom," he said, "meet my daughter, Dorothy Suzanne Magdalene Daley."

Mom almost dropped the baby. Astonished, Dad, Duke and I observed the scene. Rex and Rey approached Mom and the baby.

"Mom, Dad, Maggie, and Duke, meet my new wife, Ramona Suzanne Daley."

We were still speechless. Mom handed the baby to Dad, went to Ramona and hugged her.

"Forgive us, Ramona," she said, "but your husband has a way of shocking us. Our aloofness is not about you. It is about Syd Murray Daley. We were all in Montserrat not long ago to celebrate my in-laws on their ninety-fifth birthdays…"

"May I call you Mom?" Ramona interrupted.

"Yes. Of course, you may," Mom said, looking at Ramona who seemed awestruck.

She told Syd, "Daley, evidently, you did not tell your family about Dorothy and me. Why? Aren't you proud of us?"

"Mona, don't worry about it. I waited for our baby's birth. If I had told them, I would have to explain my divorce from Tabitha, and this family frowns on divorces, especially my grandparents in Montserrat. I had no intention of dealing with any issues in Montserrat, or in New York for that matter. The focus was on my grandparents' celebration. Besides, there is no love lost between my family and Tabitha."

"Hello Mona," I rushed to say, hoping that she would not think of Syd's remark. "I am Magdalene. Everyone calls me Maggie. Did Syd tell you why he chose Magdalene for Dorothy's middle name?"

"Yes" he said. "Dorothy is your mother's real name, and Magdalene is your grandmother's name. He said his father named you for his mother."

"Thank you for agreeing to give my name to my niece, Syd," I said.

Ramona kissed me. I took the baby from Dad. She squirmed. She looked exactly like Dad, and the Daleys. Ramona said that she was happy to meet Dad, because Syd had told her how much Dee resembles him.

Mom did not hesitate. She asked Syd what had happened to Tabitha. Syd said that he did not want to discuss it. He pulled out his cell phone and called Ejay.

"Hey, Little Boy, this is your big brother, Syd. I am in New York, and I'm coming to see you." He turned to Ramona and said. "I give you permission to tell my family about Tabitha, Mona, since they want to know."

Syd left. Ramona was somewhat apprehensive at first. She declared, "Mom, I am hungry. Do you have any food?"

"Yes, we were just about to eat," Mom said.

We fed Rex and Rey, put Dorothy on a comforter on the floor, and sat to eat. Mom asked Ramona to say the grace, and she did. Ramona spoke of how delicious the food was. She said she was not a good cook, but she knew how to follow simple recipes, and that Daley had taught her how to cook rice and beans. After we had eaten, she spoke.

"Daley and I were colleagues for years, but I changed jobs. I also knew Tabitha. She had attended a few of our office parties. One evening, after my divorce, I ran into Daley at a mutual friend's house party. He greeted me and asked me to dance. I asked him for Tabitha. He told me that they had been divorced for three months. We danced. They announced that the buffet was ready. He asked me for my husband, Bertram. I told him we were divorced, also. He smiled. He told me what led to his divorce. It surprised me, because on the job, we knew Daley to be tight lipped.

"He told me that he found out that Tabitha was cheating on him. She had gone on a cruise with her boyfriend. A friend of his tracked them on board, and got close enough to take some revealing photos. He sent them to Daley, because he could not stand Tabitha. Naturally, Daley confronted Tabitha. She admitted that she had been on another cruise with the same man, and that he had asked her to marry him. Daley said he told her, 'Okay.'

She said, 'Just as easy as that, Syd? Don't you want to discuss it?'

"He said, 'No!' He told her that women were a farthing a dozen, and he would never fight over any woman. I asked him what the hell a farthing was. He removed a brass coin from his wallet and showed it to me. He said that his grandfather had given it to him. He explained its value. It seemed that Tabitha was livid when she found out its true worth. She complained that he never loved her. He told her that she was right. She packed some things, flounced, and left. He changed the lock. Two days later, she returned for the rest of her belongings, accompanied by her cousin and her brother. They divorced amicably. Tabitha's new man is a wealthy businessman, worth about four million dollars."

Ramona paused. We did not say anything.

"Daley told me that he had always wanted children, but Tabitha did not. He said his little brother Ejay and his sister Maggie were already parents. When he heard that she was pregnant for her new man, he was pissed. What a coincidence! I wanted a child, too. My first husband did not. I found out that he had had a vasectomy. I divorced him immediately. He had signed a prenuptial agreement, which gave him no right to my parents' house.

"Daley is your son, so you know him better than I do. He is spacey. I got pregnant the first time he and I were intimate. Isn't our Dee pretty? I am surprised Daley did not brag about her in Montserrat. He adores her.

"When I told Daley I was pregnant, he asked me if I was joking. I said, 'Listen to me, Daley, I want a child, and you do not have to marry me. I have always wanted at least one child. My friends think I am barren.

"He said if the child is his, he wants to be in his life. I asked him what about her life. He said, 'Whatever!'

"I said, Daley, the child is yours. I do not sleep around. I'll tell you what, Daley, go get your DNA, but if you do, that will be the last you'll see of me and my daughter. He shut up. We were not living together, because I did not want to shack up with him. Besides, I had my beautiful home, and he lived in a one-bedroom apartment. He was at the hospital the night that Dee was born, pacing the floor. He just stared at her, and the following day, he returned to take us home. He had a dozen red roses for me.

"I let him name my baby to prove that I wanted him in her life. He named her Dorothy, for you, Mom, and Magdalene for his sister and grandmother. I also added Suzanne for my Mommy, who had not long passed away. Daley said if we must give her a pet name, it should be Dee, not Dottie. He visited Dee and me every day. When he proposed, I made him sign a pre-nupials, too. We got married months ago. He gave up his apartment and moved in with us after the marriage. I love my child, but I trust no man. There you have it in a nutshell."

Mom smiled. Duke squirmed. I nudged him, and whispered, "You see Duke, she trusts no man." He did not react.

Dee woke up, and we heard her voice. Mom covered her ears.

Ramona said, "She is loud, isn't she? She really hollers when she is hungry and wet. Other than that, she is a great baby. Ramona kissed her, changed her hippins, and nursed her. She burped, and smiled broadly.

Syd returned with Ejay, Cassandra, Randy, and Mom Randall.

"Hello everybody!" Ejay announced. "We heard there are two new women in Syd's life, and we' re here to meet them."

Ramona introduced herself and presented Dee to Ejay. "Dad, this girl looks just like you," Ejay said. "Syd is right." He kissed her cheek, and held her in his outstretched arms. Cassandra hugged Ramona, and took Dee from Ejay. She and Mom Randall played with her.

Mom was not finished with Syd. She said, "Ejay, did Syd tell you of his wife and new baby while we were in Montserrat?"

"No, Mom. You know I would have told you. Only Syd can keep a baby a secret. He told us that he and Mona were not married then, and he didn't want to discuss it. I told him, what's done is done, but he should have taken his new family to meet Maamie and Parpi Daley."

Syd apologized, and said he would take his family to meet Abuelita Carlota and Uncle Will while he is in New York, and then take them to meet Maamie and Parpi Daley. Dad had called Uncle Sol, and he dropped in to meet Ramona and Dee. He held Dee and she settled in his arms and fell asleep. I saw the care in his eyes as he cuddled Dee. I read his thoughts. His children were our age, and they, too, must have parented children.

Everyone liked Mona and adored Dee. Syd visited Abuelita Carlota and Uncle Will and told them he came to present his new family to them.

When Abuelita heard the baby's first name, Mona said she clutched her to her breast and cried volumes of tears.

"My baby, Dorotea," she said. Oh, my little Dorotea!"

Syd said, "Uncle Will took Dee, stared at her, sobbed, and said, *"Mi hermanita! Mi hermanita, Dorotea! Eres tú! Eres tú."* (My little sister! My little sister, Dorothy! It's you! It's you)!"

Mona understood a little Spanish. She said that Syd explained Mom's story to her on their way back from Brooklyn. She showed us the outfit that Abuelita Carlota had given Dee, and promised her more.

"Maggie," she said. "I love Abuelita Carlota, and Uncle Will."

"I love them, too," I said. "We are very happy that they are in our lives."

Dad called Maamie and Parpi Daley and told them of his new granddaughter, bragging that she was beautiful because she looked just like him. They also spoke to Syd and Ramona.

Two weeks later, Maamie Daley called to say that Syd was there with Ramona and Dorothy. She remarked how much Dee resembled Tunny.

"Mags, Sweetie, you were right. These are modern times. I'd rather see my Syd happy than to be trapped in an unhappy marriage. When I met Rozy Washington, I knew he was right for my Sadie, Sweetie. I feel that Mona is right for Syd, too. Tunny and your mother always said that Tabitha was not a friendly woman. I love my little Dee. Boy held her just as closely as he held our Ellie and Vera. He loves his sons, but he is crazy about his daughters.

"Mags, do you remember our little chat when you told me how you felt about divorce? I can now see your point."

"Maamie Daley," I said, "thanks for remembering our little chat. Do you know that it was out of respect for you that Syd did not mention his new family. He said it. I am glad that he kept his promise to Ejay and brought his new wife and baby to see you."

"They won't be here long, Sweetie. Syd has to get back to work."

I said a quick hello to Parpi Daley, Syd and Mona. I heard Dee raising hell in the background. Mona asked if I heard her.

I said, "You are kidding, of course. Take care she does not cause the ultimate eruption of the volcano." I could still hear Mona laughing. We said goodbye.

Mom said that she had given birth to three children, but she could not figure out her son, Syd Murray.

"I like Ramona. God has blessed him with a good wife, and my granddaughter is precious. I have no more questions for Syd Murray Daley. Maybe he is like his namesake."

"I like Mona, too, Mom. She loves Syd, and she said she would like to have another child. She said she hated being an only child, and she wants Dee to have a playmate."

"Yes, an only child is a lonely child," Mom agreed.

There was no end to the baby blessings for our grandparents. Yolanda and Christa Ford Best, and their husbands went to Montserrat to present their second born son and daughter to Maamie and Parpi Daley "as they ought." We celebrated them in photos.

Yolanda and Christa declared that they were through with the baby-production business. Yolanda named her son Aaron Christopher, and Christa named her daughter Nia Ellie. I knew that Maamie and Parpi were still counting. They were overjoyed when they called us.

Chapter XXII

The End of an Era

The dawn of the new millennium held no mystery for us, the offspring of the Emerald Isle of Montserrat. The volcano was on all our minds. We, in the so-called advanced society, had shown our fear of that magnificent date in history by hoarding water, dried goods, canned foods, and paper and plastic utensils. Yet, no catastrophic event took place. The earth had survived the advent of the New Year, the new century, and the new millennium. So much for wild predictions and crazy thoughts about the end of the world!

Early on Easter Sunday morning, April 23, 2,000, Auntie Vera called to say that Maamie Daley had joined our ancestors in Heaven. She passed away, peacefully, in her sleep. We spread the news via the telephone and the Internet. Magdalene Elizabeth Daley, I, was no more.

Auntie Vera said it best. "Maamie had reentered the Big House, but it was off limit to us, for a little while."

I closed my eyes and visualized Maamie Daley arranging the pots on the antique stove in her old kitchen. I saw her bronze face under the straw hat that protected her from the blazing sun. I heard her melodious voice calling me, "Mags, Sweetie, go fetch me a cabbage." I cried in spite of myself, because although I had tried hard, I could not imagine that Maamie Daley was dead.

In defiance, I whispered, "No! Maamie is not dead. Not my Maamie Daley."

Ejay, Cassandra, Simmy, and Mom Randall, got a flight on Tuesday morning. The rest of us left on Wednesday. Ejay telephoned us to say that the Mighty Watchman was demonstrating its nasty side, but as Maamie Daley said, "The Mighty Watchman be damned!" We Daleys knew what our responsibility was.

We arrived after they had made the first preparations of the corpse. They had laid out Maamie Daley on her bed in the island's traditional white shroud. To paraphrase her view of Montreal during the snowfall, she resembled a bride dressed to meet her groom. I stood and stared silently at her.

Uncle Bern had arrived on Monday, measured Maamie for her coffin, secured the cedar, and started to work on it. The other brothers helped when they arrived. Auntie Ellie and Auntie Vera lined the coffin with white sateen and made the soft pillow. Keith prepared the brass plate with her name, and date of birth and death. He then etched her nickname artistically on it.

It was the first time that I had seen the Daley craftsmen: Bern, Sol, Paul, and Tunny, Keith, Syd, and Ejay working silently, side by side. They could not have made a more beautiful "house" for the remains of our dear deceased. Parpi Daley sat and admired his sons, daughters, and grandsons, as they put the finishing touches on the coffin.

When they had finished the coffin, they joined hands with Parpi and admired it.

"Boys," he said, "Take it from Shug's Boy. She is pleased. You did not ask for my help, but I could not have done a better job."

They said, "Thank you, Parpi," as if they had rehearsed their response.

I called the others, and they joined me in applauding our men for a job "well done!" Duke praised them, individually.

I did not see when they transferred Maamie Daley's remains from her bed to the coffin. We had gone to our rooms to get ready for the burial service. She looked as if she were asleep. The children were still playing, running in and out of the house, and their voices resounded in Maamie's room. Dee fell, and Simmy and Randy picked her up. I knew Maamie Daley liked that. She had cautioned us to help one another. Her teaching had reached her youngest generation.

I left the room for a little while, but returned to stare at Maamie Daley's remains. I whispered a prayer, and walked over to Parpi Daley, hugged him, and listened as he whispered, "My Shug has left me, Mags, Sweetie."

It was the first time he called me "Sweetie!" His tears flowed. I covered my mouth as unshed tears filled my eyes. I hugged him tightly and left the room.

In an hour, they called us together, and we gathered at her open coffin. It would go on view again at the church. Auntie Becky said she was happy that Maamie Daley went out in the traditional Caribbean manner; from her bed.

She added, "I have lived in North America for many years, but I can never get used to undertakers' parlors. They seem so impersonal. All the children are here. Let them see the end of life. Parents, lift up your children. Let them see Maamie Daley." She covered her mouth. Uncle Bern and her sons placed their arms around her.

Simmy said, "I know what it means to die. Maamie Daley is in Heaven, now. We'll meet her there when we die. Mommy says 'life is short, but she is with the Lord. Grandpa Duby says that everybody must die some day, and we will meet again.'"

"Yes, Simmy," Parpi Daley said. "Life is very short, but you still have a long life in front of you."

"Do I, Parpi Daley?" he asked.

"Yes, Simmy, you and all your little cousins will live for many years, like Shug and I."

We lifted the smaller children, and they viewed Maamie Daley. That done, Grandpa Duby asked that we form a prayer circle. Then he prayed. His prayer was brief. His quivering voice betrayed his stalwart composure. Auntie Vera and Auntie Ellie hugged tightly as they closed the coffin. Keith Duberry, Syd, Vincent, James, Ejay, and Darius Daley, and Marc Ford were those chosen to be the pallbearers. They would take turns bearing the coffin from the house to the hearse, from the hearse to the church, and finally from the church to the burial ground. They placed the coffin in the hearse. The procession began. Those who could walk joined the funeral procession to the church. Those who were physically challenged were driven there.

The St. James Anglican Church was full to capacity. We Daleys, and all our children, had come to bid farewell to our matriarch. Montserrat did the rest. There was a saying among Montserratians that wherever there was a Montserrat party, the uninvited would come expecting to be properly fed. Therefore, the hosts always had a surplus of food to satisfy them. If there were not enough to eat, they would malign the hosts in the village and beyond. The converse was also true. They attended funerals just as willingly, and mourned openly with the families. I was a part of the Montserratian circle in New York, so I was fully aware of that custom.

The Mighty Watchman got in on the act, too, but the pyroclastic flows fell on Tar River and Plymouth. We were all aware of the swarms of earthquakes. We did not let anything deter us from the performance of our final tribute to our dear Maamie Daley.

The parson, Father Cabey, the younger, spoke well of Magdalene Elizabeth Daley, known as Maggie to her friends and Maamie or Maamie Daley to her admirers and offspring.

He said, "Maggie Corbett Daley was a bright young teacher in her youth. She used her teaching skills to raise six wonderful children, who in their turn have nurtured their children. Maggie loved the Lord, and she taught her family to love and cherish Him. She did not send them to Sunday school. She brought them, and taught many of us. I remember how Mr. Anthony Daley, the daydreamer, fondly known as Tunny, was so absorbed in his reverie one Sunday in church, that he missed Father's third Biblical reference. He approached Father nervously after church to ask him for it."

"'Oh, Parson Cabey,' he said, 'please tell me what it was! Maamie will test us when we get home. It's my turn to give the references, and she will punish me if I don't know all of them. He smiled as he added, "Nowadays, Tunny, you would have a printed bulletin."

Dad smiled sheepishly. Ejay eyed him and laughed.

"Father approached Maamie Daley and told her he would like to speak briefly with Tunny after service. She granted him permission to do so. Father took him into his office, scolded him, and told him he saw him dozing. However, he gave him the reference. He made him repeat the verse so many times that he was sure Tunny was unhappy. Do you remember, Tunny?"

Dad straightened himself, and looked at Father Cabey Jr. who was the altar boy on the Sunday in question, at the St. Anthony's Anglican Church, their home church in Town,. It, too, laid buried deep in the tons of magma and pyroclastic flow. Like Maamie Daley, it was no more.

Parson Cabey then asked Dad to repeat the reference and verse with him, because he thought it was appropriate. The parson started to recite

Second Timothy, chapter I, verses 5 and 6. "I know that you sincerely trust the Lord,..."

Dad stood, walked to the lectern, and finished it, "for you have the faith of your mother, Eunice, and your grandmother, Lois. This is why I remind you to fan the flames of the spiritual gift that God gave you, when I laid my hands on you."

Dad returned to his seat, reached for his handkerchief, and dried his tears. Mom slipped her hand in his.

"Yes, friends, we can easily substitute Magdalene Elizabeth Daley's name for Eunice and Lois in this passage. May the Lord continue to bless you as you mourn your faithful matriarch! May your spiritual gifts be abundant!

"Now, friends, I call upon Magdalene Elizabeth Daley Randall, fondly called Mags, Sweetie, by her grandmother. She has requested to recite a poem she wrote in homage to her grandmother."

All eyes were fixed on me, as I rose and walked steadfastly to the lectern. My parents were quite surprised, and so were Duke and my boys.

I greeted the clergy, my family, and all those present. I smiled broadly at Nancy Farrell Cumberbatch whom I spotted from the lectern, then unfolded the paper on which I had written my poem in honor of Maamie Daley. I recited it slowly and deliberately.

Dear Friends, Maamie Did Not Die

The Lord has silenced Maamie's voice,
And you're here to say good-bye.
Remember friends, you must rejoice,
For you see, she did not die.

She has ended her earthly sojourn,
To go home to her Lord on high.
It's a better place than she has known,
Dear friends, she did not die.

Do not speak of her in the past tense,
Just look to the brightest stars in the sky,
You'll see her smile in their light, hence
You'll know, she did not die.

Remember the good times she has had,
And how she set her goals so very high?
You know of her triumph; don't be sad.
For dear friends, she did not die.

Do not speak of death and dying,
And above all, please do not sigh.
Let there be no regrets and fainting,
For dear friends, she did not die.

So, do not mourn for her, dear friends,
Though her tongue in silence may lie.
Her view of Heaven all joy transcends,
I tell you friends, she did not die.

Tell all who knew Maamie that I say,
They'll meet her in Heaven by and by.
Tell them to wipe their tears away,
And they'll see clearly she did not die.

Mom jumped to her feet, and applauded me. The Daleys rose, and the congregation did likewise. I thanked them before I left the lectern. My parents, Duke, my sons, and those who sat in the first mourners' row hugged me. I felt grateful that they had appreciated my poem, because as I had said before, Maamie Daley would never die for me. How could she, when I will carry her name for the rest of my life? Thank you Dad," I whispered, "for naming me Magdalene Elizabeth!"

No one else got up to speak, because such speeches were not customary in Montserrat. The parson and his ministers repeated the commendation. They sang the recessional hymn.

Some family members broke down when Parpi Daley, supported by Uncle Bern and Uncle Sol, stood, and planted a kiss on Maamie's Daley's closed coffin.

"Oh Shug," he lamented. "Why didn't you wait for me? You knew if you called me, your Boy would come."

He then turned around with the help of his sons, and returned to his seat. Minutes later, he insisted on being one of the pallbearers. Uncle Bern whispered something in his ears. I do not know what he told him, but Parpi Daley led the mourners to the burial ground.

They buried Maamie Daley on a hill overlooking a deep valley, called a ghaut in Montserrat. In the distance, the Caribbean Sea, clothed in the splendor of golden and fiery reflections, glistened in the afternoon sun. All around us, the emerald green shrubs and trees glistened for my grandmother. Parson Cabey recited the committal. We threw our roses on the coffin, as they lowered it in the deep hole. Auntie Vera broke down. Sadie and I comforted her. She had kept the islanders' promise and stayed with her mother until the end. I felt, deep in my heart, that she would not abandon her father. For the first time, she seemed older than her years. I hugged her tightly. We walked away from the scene. Neither Auntie Vera nor I wanted to see the filling of the grave.

The Mothers' Union had prepared the repast, and we thoroughly enjoyed all that they had done for Maamie Daley. Nancy Farrell Cumberbatch had evidently volunteered to help them. She served us after embracing us individually. She said she was a little apprehensive given the situation with the volcano, but she had to be there, for "Teacher Maggie".

Whenever we suffered a loss, it seemed that we received some good news, and the passing of Maamie Daley was no exception. When we returned home from the funeral, there was a handsome young man sitting on one of two large suitcases under a mango tree in the yard. Grandpa Duby stared at him.

He told Keith, "That young man resembles your grandmother. I think he's looking for us."

Keith approached the stranger and said, "Excuse me. I am Keith Duberry. May I help you?"

"Yes," he said, staring at Grandpa Duby. "My name is Alexander Waring, and I'm looking for Sebastian Duberry, but I know I've found him. My brother, Sebastian, looks just like him."

He approached Grandpa Duby and said, "Sir, I am your grandson, Lex. I'm Lydia's older son."

Grandpa Duby stared at him, then fell into his arms, sobbing. "God bless you," he said, repeatedly. "God bless you." Grandpa Duby paused, then sobbed some more. "You look just like your grandmother," he finally said. "Tell me your name again."

"Alexander Waring, but please call me Lex."

Grandpa Duby introduced Lex to everyone. "Meet my grandson," he said proudly, "my Lydia's boy."

Parpi Daley agreed that Lex resembled Duby's wife whom we did not know. Keith and Sadie hugged their newfound cousin.

After they had greeted Lex, they invited him to enter into the house. The living arrangement was tight. They would have to find a space for the new-arrival. In the meantime, we shared in the second repast that Mom, Auntie Alexandra, Auntie Becky, and their helpers had prepared. They had enough food for a small army.

We told Lex how wonderful Maamie Daley was, and he offered his condolences to us, before and after supper.

Lex said that his mother had never spoken of her family. He said that Lydia became alarmed when she heard about the eruptions at the Soufriere Hills. When the family questioned her ongoing concern, she told them that she was a Montserratian and that her family still lived there. He started to monitor the disaster in Montserrat. According to Lex, he grilled his mother until she revealed the names of her relatives, Sebastian and Simeon Duberry. He decided to visit the island. He wanted to know his relatives, and to find out if they were safe.

After he met the family, he asked for Uncle Sym. Auntie Vera bowed her head. Keith told him that his father had died in hurricane Hugo back in '89. For the first time, I saw the extent of the damage to Keith's injured leg when he sat and pulled his pants leg up. The scars were deep. He had lost some flesh near his calf. I grimaced because I thought of the pain he must have endured.

Grandpa Duby, Keith, Sadie, and Lex spent hours talking. Afterwards, Keith told me that Lex swore he would reunite his mother and his grandfather. He, too, had lost his father, Constantine Waring. He had a sister, Deirdre, who was married with four children, and lived in Westchester, New York. He said that Lydia spent much of her time with Deirdre and her family. She had retired from teaching to help Lydia with her grandchildren. His brother, Sebastian, was a free spirit, who contacted them occasionally. The last time they heard from him, he was in Alaska. Lex did not know that Lydia had named Sebastian for their grandfather.

Lex told them that he was a divorcé. He hoped to get married again. He had no children. He told Keith that he would invite his grandfather and him and his family to the United States. He said he knew his paternal

219

grandparents. Unfortunately, they, too, had passed away. He was surprised to hear that Duby had already been to New York.

Lex spent much time with Grandpa Duby. He accompanied him to the Shelter where he read the Bible verses on which his grandfather based his sermons. They spent time walking about and hitching rides. Then Keith arranged for Lex to get a temporary license. He did, and he drove his grandfather around in Parpi Daley's car.

Lex loved Sadie and Auntie Vera, and adopted the Daley family. We exchanged telephone numbers. He resided in Hoboken, New Jersey. I thought that I would introduce him to my friend, Melissa Fields, but he said he had a special person in his life, Maya Smith, with whom he shared an apartment. He beamed when he showed us her photo. She was short, but very slim and pretty.

Lex had brought all kinds of supplies for use in times of disaster. We helped him to distribute some among the people who needed them most. He promised to raise funds for the folks at the shelter from his friends and colleagues when he returned home.

We invited Parpi Daley to New York, but he said he was weary and would not leave the island again. He said he was just waiting on God, and was ready to join his Shug in Paradise.

"I'm waiting for my glorious day, Mags, Sweetie, and you know Shug will be there to welcome me home. Do you know that Sym escorted Shug to her eternal home? She whispered, 'Boy, I must leave you soon. Sym Duberry is waiting for me.' I could see Sym rowing the boat."

He chuckled. "I thought she was talking in her sleep as she often did. Sym, our fisherman, rowed the boat, Mags, Sweetie." He seemed pleased.

I had often heard Maamie and Parpi Daley speak of the river between Heaven and earth. They explained that good souls crossed that waterway on their journey from earth to Heaven. An ancestor waited there to escort the new arrivals to Paradise. If a family member were present at the bedside of the dying, just before the person breathed his last breath, he would learn who the escort was. Although I never questioned Maamie Daley about it, I liked the concept. In the case of Maamie Daley, it was no wonder that her shepherd was Simeon Duberry, the joker with the split between his front teeth. He was more like a son to her than a son-in-law.

It was marvelous to see how Maamie Daley's children supported each other. Auntie Vera called a meeting with her siblings and invited me to join them on the morning after the funeral, while Winnie and Keith were busy frying fish for breakfast. "Sym's boy" always got the fish he wanted at the bay. The fishermen treated him well, in deference to his father who had taught his fishing skills to many of them.

Auntie Vera had singled out her brothers and sister, Simmy and me, and told us that she wanted to speak to us. We sat in the shade of a cluster of coconut palms and drank young coconut water while she spoke. Dad and Uncle Paul broke some of the coconuts open, and we scooped the jelly out with the "makeshift spoons" that they had made from the husks.

"Brothers, Ellie and Mags, I want to tell you what Maamie said about my daughter-in-law, Winnie. Mags, I invited you to sit with us, because you appreciated Winnie from the moment you met her. I didn't realize how much I had taken her for granted, until Maamie gathered us together for a "scolding" the night before she passed.

"Parpi, Keith, Winnie, and I had wondered why she wanted to speak to us. Simmy sat on his father's lap, and absorbed every word. If Maamie were ill, or felt any pain, she never complained. We had no clue that she was so near death. At first, she whispered, but her voice got stronger as she continued.

'Winnie, Boy and I are so sorry for the way we have treated you. I, personally, am quite ashamed.'

"Winnie tried to interrupt her, but she raised her hand, and said, 'Please do not interrupt.' She then took command of her voice and spoke forcefully."

'Winnie, we are so caught up with what we have lost that we have forgotten what we have gained. I know now, in my heart, that I must number you among my children. I am lucky, aren't I? Everyone knows that seven is the luckiest number. Thank you for having a kind heart and a giving spirit. When Duberry tells me of the folks we know who are very despondent in the shelters, I shudder. Their children and grandchildren have made no provision for them. You have opened your heart and your home to us, and Boy and I will be eternally grateful to you. I thank you, Keith for choosing this good woman. A good wife is a blessing from the Lord. Winnie, I want you to forgive our negligence. I love you very much.'

Auntie Vee said Maamie opened her arms widely, and Winnie fell sobbing into her embrace.

"I started to cry, and Maamie scolded me."

'Vera Duberry,' she said, sternly, "and Tunny, you know when she added our surname to her call, we were in for it. I expected to hear her say, 'Go, and fetch me the strap!" We laughed.

"She continued, 'I sense a strain between you and your daughter-in-law. It has to be you, Vera. You are too judgmental. Since you have moved in, you see for yourself that Keith is lucky to have Winnie. Look at your grandchild!'

"Simmy left his mother's side, and sat next to me."

'Children know when they are happy. I know you love him. Vee, I want to hear you thank Winnie from the depths of your heart. Yes, you have friends in high places here in the north. They welcomed you into their homes, but they didn't provide a shelter for your poor old parents. Please let me see the Vera whom I raised to be loving and grateful.'

"I started to cry. Keith put his arms around me. My lips trembled and I could not speak. I stood over Maamie, gathered Winnie, Keith and Simmy, and hugged them. My tears fell on Maamie's white hair. I heard Parpi's voice.

"'To tell you the truth, Winnie, I feel so at home here, that every morning when I rise, I think that I am on holiday, and that one day I will go home to the Big House, but when the ashes fall, and darkness covers the daylight, I remember the revenge of my Mighty Watchman. Shug is right. Thank you! I am so glad that you have rescued Shug and me."

Auntie Vee continued, "I stood and stared at Winnie. She cast her eyes down.

"Winnie, you heard my mother and my father. They raised us to be loving and grateful. I am so grateful to you, Winnie. You have been more than kind to me. Maamie is right. Thank you. May the Lord bless you at this moment and always!

"I once told you that you were wrong for my son, but I watched you at his bedside in Guadeloupe, and I have observed you together here in your home. You love my son, and that is all a mother could ask. I love you, and I beg you, 'please forgive me!' Please let us not dwell in bygone times. Let us raise our hope for tomorrow.

"Keith stood and hugged me. Winnie hugged Simmy, drew closely to Keith and me, and shared our hug. I closed my eyes, but I knew that my heart would be open to Winnie for the rest of my life."

Uncle Bern said, "Vera, little sister, I know you are a good woman. You are just hasty. Maamie left you with sound advice."

"Yes Bern. I know. Thank you for listening. I just thought I should share some of Maamie's last thoughts with you."

Just then, we heard Keith's voice, announcing that the breakfast was ready. Maamie Daley was right. There is no substitute on earth for fresh food. The fish was delicious. Keith had filleted some fish for the children. I admired Ejay as he ate his fish head. When I smiled at him, he flexed his muscles.

Rey said, "Uncle Ejay is very strong, Mommy."

"The power is in the fish head, Rex," Ejay said.

"Yuck," Rey said. "You eat fish head! Uncle Ejay that is yucky."

"Try it, Rex. You'll like it and you'll be strong like me."

"Uncle Ejay, I am Rey. Rex and I are not identical."

"Whoever!" he said. "I give up. Sadie, please tag them."

Duke said, "I know my boys, Ejay. Check them out carefully."

Vincent and James were on their very best behavior. Darius lamented that he had not visited the island while the Big House and the hideaway at the farm still existed. Alexander Warring stayed on. Keith told us that he had gotten to know his cousin better, and they pledged to stay in touch. Sadie had already arranged to contact her Auntie Lydia in New York.

The Daley clan left Montserrat and returned to their respective homes.

Uncle Sol and Dad had called it right. They said that it would not be long before we return to Montserrat to bury Parpi Daley. They said he had lost all interest in this world. In September, we, Daleys, returned to Montserrat to bury Parpi Daley next to his Shug. He, too, had passed away quietly. He looked as if he were sleeping. He wore a pronounced smile. As I listened to the offers of condolence, I hoped that I had honored my grandparents for all they had done for me. I made a silent vow to pass their legacy on to my children, and my children's children if I were fortunate enough to be alive when they come along. First, I would make sure that Rey and Rex remember them.

Abuelita Carlota and Uncle Will had accompanied us to Montserrat. Abuelita Carlota was not well when Maamie Daley passed away. During the procession, she stood at my side, and I placed my hand in hers. She and Uncle Will sat among us, mourners, at the church, and I sat next to her, while Rex sat at my right side.

I heard the parson's eulogy, and it made my heart feel good. "Gabriel Emanuel Daley, fondly known as 'Boy, Parpi Daley and Gabe,' has fought the good fight, run the race and has won his reward. Oh, my friends, there is joy in Heaven today. 'Boy' has been reunited with his beloved 'Shug' and with Sym, the fisherman, their dear son-in-law.

"Let us remember Gabriel for all the good things he has done. We will miss him, but anyone who has attained the promised seventy years, has achieved an impressive age! Gabriel lived ninety-five plus years.

"May the Lord bless all the Daleys and your offspring who have come again, in spite of the ongoing eruptions at the Soufriere Hills volcano, that Gabriel Daley had nicknamed 'The Mighty Watchman,' to pay homage to your patriarch. Gabriel, you sowed good seeds, and you have reaped a bountiful harvest."

Rex tapped me and whispered, "Mommy, what's a patriarch?"

"Hush," I whispered, placing my index finger on my lips. "Later, Son!"

The service ended with the rousing hymn, "When We All Get to Heaven," one of Grandpa Duby's favorite songs. The people surrounded us. They praised Parpi Daley for his generosity and his good ways. The family was the last to exit the church. Someone mentioned his "Shug," while praising him.

One elderly woman said, "Gabe Daley always had a kind word for everyone. Maggie Corbett was one of the luckiest women in Montserrat. She got the last of the good men."

While we waited outside to join the funeral march to the grave, I said, "Rex, a patriarch is the beloved senior male of a family."

I thought his next question was very intelligent. "Mommy, when the patriarch dies, who takes his place?"

I said, "Ask your Daddy when we get home, dear." My legs grew weak as I walked the final steps behind my grandfather's coffin. I held Rex's hand tightly. I told myself, 'Uncle Bern is the patriarch now.'"

They sang "Jesus Lover of My Soul." Grandpa Duby sang loudly. They continued to sing it as we followed the pallbearers, all grandsons and Lex Waring, who bore Parpi Daley to his final resting-place beside his Shug. While the parson reminded the gathering that death has no victory and no sting, because God has given us the victory through our Lord Jesus Christ, I bowed my head and prayed for my family as he pronounced the committal. I peeked through my half-closed lids and noted that all present had closed their eyes.

I closed my eyes tightly, hoping to shut out the thought that my grandfather's remains were in the box. I visualized Parpi Daley alive and well, beckoning us to go with him to the candy store to get our sweeties on Saturdays, after he had received his pocket money from Maamie Daley.

I opened my eyes at the shout of "Amen". The parson nodded to the gravediggers. I heard the cranking sound as they lowered the coffin into the grave.

I thought I heard Maamie Daley's voice rising above all the others, "Forever with the Lord."

"Mags, Sweetie, where is my Boy?" I closed my eyes.

I heard Parpi Daley's answer, "Here I am Shug! Shug, I am right here." The coffin made its final descent into the cruel pit.

"Oh there you are Boy. What took you so long?" Maamie asked plainly.

"I came as quickly as I could, Shug," he said.

"You go on with you, Boy!" She chuckled.

I saw them embrace and walked slowly away.

I opened my eyes to see an elderly man, whom I did not recognize, throw his rose into the open pit. "So long Desperate," he said. He turned and walked away, aided by a young woman. I knew that he had known my grandfather since his childhood.

It was strange to see how the children found their parents, and held their hands or stayed by their sides. They had just witnessed the burial of their patriarch, and they saw the silent tears that we shed for him. As we walked away from the gravesite, a cool breeze caressed our faces, and dried our tears. I looked up and saw two black birds in flight, one flying slightly ahead of the other. They then headed in the southwest direction.

They had a light supper for us at the church hall after the burial. I looked around the room at all of the descendants of Maamie and Parpi Daley. I saw our grandparents' faces on many of them. I looked at Mom and Dad. Their once black hair was intermixed with gray and Sadie and I had a number of gray hairs, too. My boy's question filled my head, again. I asked myself, 'When the matriarch and patriarch die, who can replace them? My answer now, is "No one among the Daleys." Maamie and Parpi Daley were unique, and I am so glad that I knew them."

However, my Rex stood, approached Dad, and asked, "Grandpa, are you the patriarch of the family, now?"

"No, Son," he said. "I bow to my brother, Bern. He is the eldest."

Uncle Bern smiled, and added, "Yes, I am the patriarch, although I never thought of it, and you, Ellie, my dear sister, are now the matriarch. If Montserrat is still standing, let us return to celebrate the one hundredth anniversary of our parents' birth."

Everyone present agreed that we would be back for that occasion.

225

Chapter XXIII

Memories, the Sweetest
parts of Dreams

When we returned to the house, I found a quiet, cool place in the shade of a mango tree, and reminisced about my experiences in Montserrat. I was happy that Syd and I had begun to go there at a much younger age than Caroline Donoghue. She took her first trip to Montserrat when the artificial glitter of the cement jungle had already beguiled her. I thought of the things I could never forget about the tiny island that had become much more than my father's birthplace to me.

How could I forget Maamie and Parpi Daley, when I see them in all my experiences, not only through copies of Syd's photos and paintings, but also in that motion picture that is forever turning on my mind's screen? How could I forget Parpi Daley, who did not say, "I love you," every day, but whose love for us far exceeded any word that he could have uttered? How could I forget Maamie Daley, whose very presence meant "Mother, and teacher", with all the caring that came with those appellations? I hear her voice every day since her passing, asking me to fetch a cabbage, when she was about to cook, or her Bible, when she sat to read silently in the evening. How could I forget the first person who actually taught me the art of penmanship? The trick was in the holding of the pen. She did not beat me on my knuckles, as Dad said she had done to him. However, Syd, Sadie, Keith, and I have fine handwritings, but Keith has since added his own style to Maamie Daley's basics. God knows, she had tried with Ejay. Although his handwriting improved, it never quite measured up to Syd's and mine. She did not catch him when he was young enough.

How could I forget the original kitchen, which reminded me of a little countryside diner? We gathered there to satisfy our hunger or to help to prepare the delicious foods. Maamie Daley's unwritten recipes are printed on my mind, forever. How could I forget dining there with the family? How could I forget the letters she wrote to me from Montserrat, Montreal, and Barbados, when they are such a treasured part of my inheritance?

How could I forget our potato-baking seminars, when Syd and I learned to use the dry cow dung, "one of the greatest fuels on earth", and the hot ashes that they swept from the stone oven? How could I forget fishing for crayfish under the rocks in the running streams that meandered past the farm on their way to bathe the thirsty land?

"How could I forget the Big House with the large calabash and clay goblets of fresh spring water that must have replenished themselves, because they were never empty? How could I forget sitting with a basket of mangoes, and enjoying each one's unique flavor? How could I forget the calabash tree, when we have so many of its utensils in our home? Hugo had destroyed it, but Parpi Daley told me it would grow again. It would be such a pleasure for me to see the tree in bloom again with its shiny baby calabashes!

"I will always remember the pigeon peas shelling hours that were the prerequisite to the largest pot of pigeon-peas soup that I had ever seen. We salivated as we waited for the treat, because Maamie Daley was famous for letting food simmer quite slowly, thereby pulling out every ounce of its flavor. I remember the corned pork, the dasheen, the cornmeal, or "moosha" (cassava) dumplings, the sweet potatoes and "tire seed", (*yautias in America, tanyas in some Caribbean Islands*), that made the soup so delicious that we ate and ate, until the pot was empty, disregarding the amounts we had consumed, and we could hardly move.

It was strange that Maamie Daley prepared pigeon peas soup on moonlit nights. We sat around and savored our soup. There was no pause for idle chat. Those who spoke most, got less soup. Syd and I learned that early on, and simply nodded in acquiescence. I wondered how I returned to New York weighing the same or less than when I left home. Weight or no weight, I ate as many of Maamie Daley's dumplings as I could.

The first time I mentioned the pigeon peas soup to my Dad, he told me that Maamie Daley used to prepare it on dark nights. He said that before they began to raise pigs, they bought the corned pork from other butchers. Maamie Daley could afford just one small piece of corned pork for the whole pot of soup. He said that he got it one evening, and he ate it without saying a word. The rich brown soup lent its color to everything, so that the pork could easily have been mistaken for a dumpling or any vegetable.

"Maamie had told us if we got the pork, to give it to her, and she would divide it into eight pieces for the family. I felt so guilty, that I did not sleep a wink that night. Maamie said since we could not be trusted, she would never make pigeon peas soup on dark nights again."

"Dad," I said, "You didn't. No wonder Maamie Daley told me, 'Your father, my boy, Tunny Daley, was the most mischievous of all my children.'

After hearing Dad's confession, I tried to duplicate the soup at home with frozen (dead) pigeon peas from Montserrat. Since Maamie and Parpi Daley were no longer with us, we had no corned pork. I used ham hocks. My soup was good. At least, everyone said so, but although I thanked them, I knew deep in my heart that it was not as good as Maamie Daley's soup. My mother called hers 'pigeon peas porridge,' because it was thick. She liked my soup. She had learned the word "porridge" from Dad, because she especially liked his rich cornmeal porridge.

When I had conjured up many of my Montserrat reminiscences, I felt sorry for folks, like Caroline Donoghue, who found nothing to like in the Island. She had spent her time in Montserrat longing to be back in the Bronx. How sad! Although she told me that she would be a student at Hunter, I never saw her again.

I had fallen asleep under my favorite mango tree. No one woke me. When I opened my eyes, Winnie was sitting at my side. Simmy was running with his cousins and some other village children. I thought of how easy it was for children to return to normal. I knew that mine understood what death was, but they were getting on with their lives.

Winnie said, "Mags, Simmy and I will be going to England for a month or two, and Syd would join us there. My cousin, Leonard Martin, who was upset when my grandfather left everything for me, has forgiven me. He said he wants to put all that mess behind him. I told him that I've gotten many offers to sell some or all of the Martin land, but I will never do that. I told him he is welcome to share it with me, because there's enough for all of us. We are a small family. Lenny has a wife and two children. They are still toddlers. He married late. He has his own home, and owns another property in England. He is doing quite well.

"Lenny said he has some friends from Ghana who may be able to help me find my girls. Keith wants me to leave right away. I'll take Simmy with me. Lenny said we can stay with him and his family."

"Winnie, I am so happy for you! I hope you will find your children. I will pray for you. In fact, let us ask Grandpa Duby to lead us in prayers for you."

"Let me check with Keith, first." Winnie said.

"When are you planning on leaving?"

"In two weeks," she said, running to search for Keith.

She returned saying he said 'that prayers would be okay.'"

"Mags, I want to thank you. I didn't tell Vera anything, but she should be happy for me. She adores her children and her grandchildren, especially my Simmy, because he is here with her."

Later, Winnie told me that she had spoken to Auntie Vee immediately after our conversation, and not only did she agree that she should go, but she also volunteered to go with her. Winnie was surprised. However, she concluded that it was because of Simmy. She said that Auntie Vera asked Uncle Paul if she could stay with them. Naturally, he said yes, so they would leave for England in two weeks.

That evening, after dinner, while the children played in the moonlight, the family gathered on the back porch to chat. I told them about the two doves I had seen in flight. They agreed that Maamie Daley was the lead dove.

I stood and faced them. I said, "Family, by now, you know of Winnie's predicament. Her first husband kidnapped her daughters and returned to Ghana with them. Her cousin, in England, has some friends from Ghana who think they can help her to find them. I want to ask Grandpa Duby and all present to pray for her safe trip to England and for her success in finding her daughters.

"I know that prayers work because Maamie Daley told me that she prayed daily for my mother to find her family. You know she has, because you have met and welcomed my Abuelita Carlota, and my Uncle Will. I took Abuelita to Mom, and she sat beside her. Uncle Will could not be here with us, but he has spoken to all of us and offered us his condolences. Some day, Grandpa Duby will see his beloved Lydia, because of his grandson, Alexander Waring. Lex came here in spite of the erupting volcano. Family ties are stronger than the Mighty Watchman. We Daleys are bound by the love of Maamie and Parpi Daley. All my life, I heard how our matriarch and patriarch taught their children to love and help one another. That love has been extended to their grandchildren and great-grandchildren.

At the end of our eleventh trip to this island, Maamie and Parpi Daley knelt beside Syd and me, and prayed for us. I can feel their presence here tonight. Let us pray for Winnie. She needs our prayers. Grandpa Duby, the floor is yours."

Grandpa Duby entered on cue, as if he were forewarned. "Winnie Martin Duberry," he said, "from the moment I heard your story, I have been praying for you to be reunited with your children. I am sure that God has always been on your case. You are a little closer to finding them today than you were a month ago. Thank God for his loving kindness. Pili and Amina, no matter where you are tonight, may the Lord put the need to find your mother in your hearts! May He reunite you, in His time!

"Dear Lord, please bless this gathering. Please listen to the silent prayers of all who come before You. I have lived for years with the absence of my daughter, Lydia. She left me because I was addicted to the spirit of the bottle. Now, the Holy Spirit has overpowered me, and sent me as a messenger to reach out to those who have not yet seen the Light.

"Winnie, God will grant your wishes, because He is a merciful God. As unworthy as I am, He has granted mine. I met my grandson whom I did not know existed. Pray earnestly, and believe in your prayers. Pray that the prayers we offer up tonight will touch your daughters wherever they may be.

"May the Lord bless your travels. Lord, please grant that all here present, will return safely to their homes abroad. Dear God, please grant these favors, we pray. Amen."

Everyone said, "Amen."

Grandpa Duby sat. I stood next to Abuelita Carlota, bowed my head closed and squeezed my eyes tightly, and began. "Dear loving God, you have blessed Grandpa Duby with the gift of Your Light. Please let Your Light shine on all of us tonight. Amen"

Uncle Sol spoke next. His prayer was compassionate. "Mags, thank you for your request for prayers. Some years ago, I lost touch with my children when my ex-wife remarried. I know the feeling, Winnie. I hope to see mine again, some day.

"Dear family, you are as important to me as the breath I breathe. While we pray sincerely for Winnie's reuniting with her family, please pray that I, too, will find mine! I cried the last time my mother asked me for them, because I had no answer for her. Maamie and Parpi, please be our angels and ask the Lord to help Winnie and me. You now dwell with Him in the spirit. Amen!"

Dad hugged Uncle Sol while he sobbed, and sat beside him. "Please forgive me," Uncle Sol said.

The children had stopped playing, and sat among us.

Rey asked, "Mommy, why is Uncle Sol, crying?"

"He is crying, because he hasn't seen his children for a long time. Auntie Winnie is not in touch with her daughters either. That's why we are praying for them to be reunited."

Abuelita spoke loudly from her seated position, "Winnie," she said, drying her tears, "God will return your children to you. Trust this old lady, whose heart is now lighter, because I have found not only my daughter, but many other sons and daughters, including you. God has the balm for the brokenhearted, and the tender voice to comfort those who call on Him. May God bless you in your search!" She hugged and kissed Winnie, whose tears flowed silently.

Simmy hugged Winnie, and kissed her wet cheeks. "I love you, Mommy," he said. "I know you'll find my sisters. Maamie Daley told me so." Everybody paused, and looked at him.

Did she, Simmy?" I asked.

"Yes, Auntie Mags, Sweetie."

That was the first time he called me 'Sweetie.' I shivered, because it confirmed that Maamie Daley's spirit was with us.

"I didn't know Maamie Daly was going to die. I went into her room, and climbed in the bed with her. She told me to be a good boy, and to tell Mommy that she will find her girls. Then, she died, and I forgot to tell Mommy."

Grandpa Duby stood with Simmy and asked us to stand. "It's alright Sym," he said, kissing him. Now, family, let us free our hearts and minds from all doubts! Please answer 'We do,' to all of my questions.

"The Good Book states, 'A child shall lead them.' Do you believe that my little Simmy received a message for his mother from Maggie Corbett Daley?

Everyone answered, "We do."

"Do you believe that our greatest detective, the Holy Spirit, our Counselor is already on this case?"

"We do."

"Do you believe that our Counselor will find those two young ladies and reunite them with their mother?"

"Let us end by saying, 'We do, and we know that God will answer our prayers.'"

Our voices filled the void as we said, "We do, and we know that God will answer our prayers."

"Then, who am I, this mere mortal man, to stand in the way of this gathering of believers? The Lord, our Holy Spirit, will grant the wishes of those who have prayed aloud and silently here tonight." He walked over to Winnie, and she stood.

"Winnie, you are the mother of Simeon, II, the seed of the Duberrys. I prayed for this child, at his birth, and even now, because I know the trouble that the volcano is causing. You are a good wife to my grandson, and a good mother to my great-grandson. Maggie Daley told me that she loved you, and she told you so on many occasions. She said she was happy that you are one of us. You know that I love you. You will find your children. Now family, let us put our hands together and applaud this courageous mother."

He hugged Winnie. We applauded her, and she cried. With teary eyes, she embraced every member of the family that evening.

"Dearest family," she said. "Only my husband, Keith, and I, know what I am about to tell you. I am three months pregnant with our second child. I have listened closely to your prayers, and I thank you. It is so good to belong to a family who cares. I am privileged to be a part of yours."

"Solomon, you, too, will find your children. Get on your knees, and pray for their return. The Lord will answer your prayers, if you only believe."

"I believe, Duby," Uncle Sol said. "I have no other choice. Maamie and Parpi taught us to believe."

Grandpa Duby started humming "Jesus Loves Me." No one sang a syllable, but the humming of that sweet tune remained in my head all through the night. I would never forget that moment.

When the humming ended, Auntie Ellie said, "Yes, Winnie, you are precious to all of us. Look how willingly you shared your home and your property with us. I tend to be very private, but beginning today, I shall be more openhanded. Keith, you are a very lucky young man. Cherish your wife, or you'll hear from me, your Auntie Ellie."

"Auntie Ellie, the last thing I need is another Daley woman on my tail. Winnie, please tell them that you are my special gift from God. I knew it the first time you slapped my face."

Winnie blushed. Keith hugged her.

I said, "Winnie, I got to know you a little more on this sad occasion. You shared your home with Maamie and Parpi Daley, and they were grateful. Your action was the wad that lightened the load of their loss of the Big House and the farm. If you had never welcomed another Daley, that would have been good enough for me. However, you also welcomed my Mom's mother and her brother. You are most generous. When you leave London, please return to Montserrat by way of New York so we can entertain you." I kissed her cheek.

"Do not forget Rozy, our children and me, dear sister-in-law. We love you, too," Sadie said.

Winnie raised her hand, "Please stop all of this adulation, family. You are making me blush. We know that we love one other. I adore all of you."

We hugged, and cried, and declared our love for one another. Of course, Maamie and Parpi Daley looked on approvingly. I saw them as clearly as the moonlight that shone on us that night. I heard Maamie whisper, "Boy, they love one another." I heard Parpi Daley's chuckle.

On the eve of our return to New York, I walked back to the burial ground, alone, to bid farewell to Maamie and Parpi Daley, privately, although I knew that their souls had been set free, and only their flesh lay decomposing in the pitiless grave. Someone had pushed the faded wreaths aside. A rose bush on Maamie Daley's grave had begun to take root.

I said, "Maamie and Parpi Daley, I know you can hear me. I came to say so long, never good-bye. You heard what Uncle Bern said. We will be back to celebrate your century. Tomorrow morning, I will return to America. I was not sure that I would ever be back in Montserrat, what with the unpredictable eruptions of The Mighty Watchman. To put it simply, I was afraid of the volcano. However, I remembered how you overcame your fear of flying to join us in celebrating Ejay's graduation from high school, and then later for the celebration of my marriage. You are no longer with us in the flesh, but I have memories of you that will last forever. The farm, the market place, and the old house are also living memories of my childhood, and Syd has preserved them in his paintings. I suppose it is only fair that Auntie Vera get the original paintings. She honored both of you by keeping her vow of caring for you to the end.

"You enriched my childhood, and gave me advice that I shall always cherish. My regret is that my boys will no longer have you to come home to. I will make sure that you will live forever in their hearts. I will tell them regularly about your marriage of the vegetables, Maamie Daley. I will show them how to make wads, both physical, and spiritual, to lighten their loads in life. I am sure you know my secret that I have never shared with anyone. I have two of your farm dresses, one of your pinafores and your straw hat. I close my eyes, and there you stand tall and proud in my memory.

"Parpi, I will tell them how you kissed your old jackass good-bye before we put him in his grave on the edge of the farm, and how you embraced Syd's painting of your farm. Of course, we now have Syd's photos and his paintings to give them a graphic view of everything. I will tell them how The Mighty Watchman turned on you, and swallowed up the farm that it had protected all those years. It was a confounded thief. It stole all your land, Parpi Daley. I will tell them how you decked a youngster in Montreal with a snowball, because he had dared to hit you with one. I will tell them how their Uncle Rozy first knew you as "Desperate" when he was ten years old.

Tell you what, Maamie and Parpi Daley! I will spend the rest of my life letting them know that they had the greatest great-grandparents who ever lived, and that I had the most wonderful grandparents. We will meet again, but please visit me in my dreams. I would like that so much! I would then brag of my messages from Heaven. No grave can rob me of your presence."

I stooped and picked up a banner with its golden message, "To our dearest Parpi, from Bern, Ellie, Sol, Paul, Tunny, and Vee, with love." I folded it and held it in my hand.

When I left the gravesite, I saw two blackbirds in flight again. They circled the area above the grave and then flew towards Parpi Daley's Mighty Watchman. They were only a short distance away from the Big House. I knew the lead dove was Maamie Daley, because everyone had agreed that Parpi always seemed to lag behind.

"So long Maamie Daley! So long Parpi Daley!" I shouted into the open void. Then I whispered to myself, "You see Maamie Daley, I remember."

We returned to our homes in Barbados, St. Croix, Canada, England, and America. Winnie and Auntie Vera went on to England two weeks later. Winnie kept in touch via the Internet, and by telephone. She had overstayed her visit, but Leonard's friends had found no trace of her daughters. Keith told her to stay on and have the baby in England. He delayed his trip there until a week or so before the birth of their second son, whom they named Emanuel Daley Duberry. They had honored Parpi Daley. They nicknamed him Eman.

Uncle Paul's children, Darius and his new bride, Evangeline, Verona, and Winnie's cousin, Leonard Martin, were Eman's godparents. They said that Auntie Vera spoke glowingly of her daughter, Winnie.

They returned to Montserrat by way of New York when Eman was three months old. They said that they could only spend three weeks in the United States. Auntie Vera and Keith took Winnie to many sites of interest in the city. They took Eman with them. Rozy came for them, and they spent a few days with Rozy, Sadie and their family and one day with Syd and his family in Georgia. Winnie returned with the happy news that Syd and Ramona were expecting their second child, and it would be a boy. His name would be William. They had not yet determined what his middle name would be.

While they were in Georgia, Mom got a brilliant idea. She had truly embraced the party spirit. She was excited as she outlined her plan.

"Maggie, do you remember how Winnie and Syd fried fish for us and entertained all of us Daleys? It is time for us to reciprocate. I want to give them a party they will not soon forget. That is reality. I want to steal Eman Duberry. He is adorable. I can forget that. Now, I want you and Tunny to do your West Indian cooking. I will ask Mamá to do her Dominican thing. I will prepare my ham. Marianne will make the breadfruit salad. She hardly makes potato salad any more. It turned out that Mom Randall really had a thing for Eman. She took care of him while his parents were sightseeing and shopping.

On their last weekend, Dad took Keith, Winnie and the boys to New Jersey to visit Uncle Sol. They had no idea that we were preparing a bash for them. Ejay got the latest calypsos, and set up his music.

Yolanda, Christa and their husbands were also in New York. They were on their way home to Barbados after visiting their brother, Marc, who had married and lived in Barcelona, Spain. They stayed with Ejay and Cassie. We included them in our surprise bash. They had left their children with their grandparents much to their delight.

Vincent and James, the confirmed bachelors, joined us. Vincent had fathered two sons and James a son and a daughter with their live-in girl friends, but they had not taken the plunge into wedlock. Their parents were not pleased. Of course, the big question was, "What would Maamie and Parpi Daley think of that kind of behavior?" We hoped to meet their children, some day.

Syd, Ramona and Dorothy, joined the Washingtons and surprised us on the evening of the bash. Rozy told Dad, "Naughty Daleys! How could you plan this party without thinking of us? I'll see what Maamie and Parpi Daley have to say about that, Tunny."

Dad said, "Rozy, please don't tell Maamie and Parpi. It won't happen again."

"Okay, Uncle Tunny," Rozy said. "I forgive you this time."

We laughed hysterically. We had a mini family reunion with all the noise and gaiety of the Daley clan. We ate, and danced. The elders, Uncle Sol and Tunny spoke of their childhood in Montserrat. Uncle Sol wound up sobbing, no doubt for his children. I wished I had the gumption to ask him what had caused the rift between him and his wife.

Of course, Abuelita Carlota and Uncle Will were also there. They had become an essential part of our family. Mom shared some secrets with her mother. I was happy to see how they had cemented their mother-daughter relationship.

Jesse, Vera Rose, Dee, Simmy, Randy, Rex, and Rey, ate and danced like champions. Dee got down, too. She kept asking for more goatwater. At one point, she said to Mom, "Grandma Lisa, keep the goat. Just give me the water." Everyone burst out laughing. Eman Duberry was bouncing so high from his seated position that Mom Randal had to hold him tightly. The music had no doubt captivated him. I could see Maamie and Parpi Daley covering their mouths and laughing at the actions of their newest offspring. They would probably speak of how crabbit Dee and Eman were.

We needed a full day's rest after that bash. I took Winnie, Yolanda, and Christa on the shopping spree of their lives. Ejay took Jonathan and Roland Best and Keith shopping at a "Men's Clothing Outlet" in New Jersey. Abuelita showed up with her babies' and children's clothing for the new arrivals. They thanked her and applauded her expertise.

Auntie Vera hung with Mom Randall. She would not return to Montserrat with Keith and his family. They would embark on their long promised ten-day Caribbean cruise together from Miami.

The Bests promised to visit often with their babies. Jonathan, who was a history buff, appreciated the Museum of Natural History. Roland just liked everything about New York. Everyone left New York, feeling happy. Of course we, their American cousins, had an open invitation to their homes in Barbados.

They returned home with many packages, bragging that they had a wonderful time.

Rozy got Duke and Ejay to agree to let our boys spend the summer in Georgia. Cassie and I agreed. Cassie had just received the confirmation that she was pregnant with her second child. Ejay was ecstatic. It suddenly struck me that in less than one year, we would add many more babies to the Daley clan, taking into consideration any multiple births.

The last time I checked, the members of our family, in Barbados, Georgia, New Jersey, New York, Montreal, Canada, Christenstead, St. Croix, London, Paris, Barcelona and Montserrat, were fine. The family prayed, and waited to hear Winnie announce that she had found her daughters. She wanted them to know their brothers.

She said they had bought Simmy a set of drums in London, and she regretted the purchase until one day when she heard his song above the hullabaloo. "I have sisters in Africa! Yeah! Yeah! I have sisters in Africa! Oh yeah!" She said that although the tune was catchy, she ran to her room and let her tears flow.

The last call I received from Winnie, she told me, "Mags, Eman is a tyrant. He is giving my Simmy a hard time. I'll fix his little red butt."

"You and Keith must not spoil him," I told her.

"No, the boy is just a terror. He is not three yet, but he is big, eats like a pig, and talks like a parrot. He is very demanding. Vera loves him. She thinks he is spunky. I think he is just like her."

"There you go, Winnie," I said. "Remember what Montserratians say, 'Sheep can't bring goat.' Then I paused and said, "My Lord, he is just like my brother, Ejay was, when he was two. Syd wanted to strangle him."

"I want to strangle Eman. I'll deal with Eman, but he could be so damn loving and cute."

"I repeat, 'Don't spoil him, Winnie.' Cute becomes rude, before you know it. When Mom had enough of her baby son, she wore out his butt."

"It's me he takes advantage of, Maggie. It takes only one look from Keith, and he melts."

"Little people are not stupid, Winnie," I told her."

I figured that the Lord must have given Eman to Winnie as a distraction. She hardly mentioned her daughters ultimately.

Auntie Vera and Mom Randall had pledged to have a ball on their cruise. Duke was happy with the friendship that had blossomed between his mother and my aunt. Uncle Sol took one week off to drive them to Miami where they would board their cruise ship. Upon seeing he ship glistening in the afternoon sun, Uncle Sol telephoned Dad to say that he wished he had booked to accompany the women on their cruise.

"Tunny," he said, "The ship is bigger than Montserrat."

However, he pulled a Syd stunt on us, after he had sworn Auntie Vera and Mom Randall to secrecy. Uncle Sol had promised to stop off in Georgia to visit Syd and Sadie and their families, but he returned home, saying that there was an emergency at his house. Three days later, he called Dad, and invited us to his house for a family moment that Friday evening. Ejay and Duke drove us there. Mom wanted to bet Dad that "Sol was ready to tie the knot again."

Dad wrinkled his nose, and said, "I hardly think so, Lisa. Sol likes being single. When I suggested that, it often reminds me of our Montserratian saying, "Tunny," he said, 'one fall down's good enough for monkey; two are too much.'"

I thought Uncle Sol had already gotten married. When we arrived, I secretly looked at his ring finger, but he wore no wedding band. We wondered if the relationship between him and his girlfriend had ended, because she was seldom around any more. They put the children in the den to watch t v, and left the door open so we could monitor them. The aroma from the kitchen was good, because Uncle Sol always had food for us when he invited us to his home.

He had made his famous lasagna, braised chicken breast, sweet and sour chicken parts, mixed vegetables, sliced ham, and tossed salad. I took the mango pie he had asked me to make for him. He had also made a good ginger beer and sorrel.

After we had eaten, he opened his bar, and asked the adults to help themselves. We sat comfortably. Uncle Sol pulled out his video camera, set it up, and turned on the television. He turned on the VCR. We saw the first shot of the cruise ship in the port at Miami, and then he zoomed in on Auntie Vera and Mom Randall walking towards it to board. The next scene was that of a young couple. The young man wore a T-shirt with the name **COREY**, and she one with the name **ROSY DAY.** I stared in disbelief.

"Rosalie! Mom, it's Rosalie," I screamed. She still resembles the Daley's."

Upon hearing my scream, the children joined us. Uncle Sol pressed the pause button.

"Yes, Maggie. It's Rosalie and her husband Corey Arnold." He paused to sob. "I have found my daughter."

By then he was sobbing loudly, and Dad sat next to him and placed his arm around his shoulder, while the rest of us said how happy we were for him.

"Uncle Sol, how come you're crying? Isn't that what you wanted?" Randy asked.

"Yes, Randy," he said. "But it's overwhelming."

"Sol, Rosalie was a chubby little girl with buckteeth. Look at her now! She is gorgeous, and Corey is a handsome young man," Mom said.

"Thank you, Lisa," he said. He whispered something in Dad's ear, and Dad went to the bar and returned with Uncle Sol's drink.

Rey said, "Dad, don't you think it's time Randy, Rex and me get our first drink?"

"No, Rey," I said.

"Why not?" he asked defiantly. "Mommy, I was speaking to Daddy."

"Rey, have some sorrel or ginger beer," I said, "and stop your nonsense now!"

"Okay, Mommy, but I'll have my first drink when I am thirteen. I'll be a man then."

Duke stared at him, and he poured himself a full tumbler of ginger beer. "Uncle Sol," he said, sipping it, "now, this is ginger beer! It's strong. Ah! Ah!"

"Rey, cool it," Duke said.

"Okay, Daddy."

Uncle Sol sipped his drink slowly, and then announced, "Family, Anne and Nathaniel have passed away."

Our mouths fell open. Uncle Sol drew many deep breaths.

"Rosalie told me that my boy Natty made the ultimate sacrifice to these United States of America. He died in Afghanistan." He paused to breathe deeply again. "Anne died of complications following a surgical procedure three months ago. Rosie Day said her stepfather, Gerald Carpenter, was a very possessive man. He had convinced Anne to change the children's name to Carpenter. She told them that I did not care enough to support them after she told me of her intention to remarry, so what the heck!

"'Gerald will take care of you, but we must change your name. One family, one name!" Mom repeated. Gerald is kind enough to want it, so we will make it official.'

"My Rosy Day said he was not kind to David and Nathaniel, and when the boys became of age, they fought him, and he threw them out. He died two years ago. Anne had been ill for a while, before she had the surgery from which she did not survive.

"I tried to defend myself, but, she stopped me. "'Daddy, Mommy confessed everything to David and me. We were at her bedside when she passed. She told us that we'd find you. She asked you to forgive her, please. David and I were going to come to New York to find you. He is in Aruba right now with his family. They have a timesharing there. My kids, Melissa and Vern, and Nathaniel's younger son are with them, too. Corey and I had been booked for this cruise for a year, so here we are.

"We wrote you two letters at our old address in Harlem, but they returned them stamped, Addressee Unknown", and you were not listed in the telephone book. We knew that Uncle Tunny also lived in Harlem, but we supposed that he too had moved. How are our cousins? I can't wait to see them. Mommy had one brother, as you know. He has a son and a daughter. They live in Kansas.'"

"Oh Sol, we are so sorry to hear of your loss," Mom said.

"Thanks for your support, Lisa and family. I figured I would give you the bad news first. The good news is that I have six grandchildren. Rosalie has two children, Melissa and Vern, Timothy and Andrew. David has a girl and a boy, Deidre and Charles, and Nathaniel had identical twin boys, Joseph and Jeremy."

While Uncle Sol ruminated, we waited patiently.

Suddenly his face lit up. "Tunny, I am a great-grandfather. Natty's boy, Jeremy, is the daddy of an infant son, Jedee."

Uncle Sol and Dad locked in a Daley embrace. Dad said, "Sow the Daley seed, Sol! Just sow the Daley seed!"

"Let's continue," he said, rolling the tape again.

Uncle Sol focused the camera on Auntie Vera and Mom Randall walking towards the ship. The afternoon sun painted the western horizon. Suddenly, a young woman dressed in blue jeans and a white blouse came into view. She stared at Uncle Sol, and ran towards him shouting "Daddy! Daddy! Daddy, it's me, your 'Rosy Day'"

A young man followed her. Uncle Sol stopped the video to tell us that Mom Randall grabbed the camera and captured the moments as he and his daughter hugged, leaving Corey and Auntie Vee to stare at them.

Uncle Sol broke his embrace, and stared at Rosalie. Then he spread his arms open to invite Corey and Auntie Vera who spoke suddenly.

"I am your Auntie Vee," she said.

Uncle Sol introduced Mom Randall to Rosalie, who introduced Corey to everyone. Uncle Sol took the camera again and continued to video Rosalie, Corey, Mom Randall and Auntie Vera. At one point, Rosalie asked for Syd and me, by name. I could not wait to see my cousins again She did not mention Ejay. She did not know of him.

Uncle Sol was quite happy, the happiest I had seen him in years. I had sensed his sadness when we gathered together, especially when the Daley clan was surrounded by their children.

Uncle Sol spoke again. "My Rosy Day promised to send me the e-mail addresses, home addresses, and telephone numbers of my grandchildren. Of course, they are known as Gardeners for now. My great-grandson is six months old. I thank you family, for all your prayers. I have been humbled. Rosy Day could not wait to be in touch with you again. She used the computer on the ship to forward all this information to me. She declared that she could not have waited a moment later."

He distributed all the information in envelopes addressed to all of us, individually. Ejay was surprised when he did not get one.

"What about me, Uncle Sol?" he asked.

"You were not around when they left, Ejay," he said.

"Ejay, I told her about you, and she asked me to give you all the information."

"Thank you, Uncle Sol," Ejay said.

There was a long pause. Then Uncle Sol spoke again. "I'll have it for you soon, Ejay," he began. "I took my wife and family to Montserrat once for Christmas, when the children were little. I know my parents were not pleased that Anne and I divorced, but things happen. I was a damn good father. What does a man do when a woman declares that she has no more feelings for him, and asks right away for a divorce? I tried everything to save my marriage; one full year of counseling. Anne had shocked me. How was I supposed to know she had reunited with her first boyfriend, and that he was waiting for her in North Carolina? I visited my kids while they were in North Carolina, and you know I supported them. Then, her dear husband took them to California, and ended my communication with my kids. Naturally, he was a man of means.

"I sat on the porch of their abandoned home in North Carolina and cried like a baby. Their ex-neighbors saw me, and told me they had moved to Virginia. Before I could thank her, she jumped in her car and sped away. A few minutes later, a little boy whom I recognized told me that they had moved to California. I never heard from my kids again. However, I forgive Anne. Why not? According to Rosy Day, she had asked for my forgiveness on her deathbed.

"After Parpi passed, I prayed and begged him and Maamie to be my mediators and ask the Lord to reunite me with my kids. I knew they would have a close relationship with the Lord. Now, I learn that my Natty is dead."

He sobbed and paused to wipe his tears. Mom placed her arms around him.

"I can't wait to meet his kids, Joseph and Jeremy. I can't wait to meet all my grandchildren. Thank you Lord," he shouted. "Thank you Maamie and Parpi. Thank you, family, for your support."

He told us that he had already written to Grandpa Duby to thank him for his prayers. We ended our evening with Uncle Sol by praying that Winnie would find her daughters. All of us gathered around him, and we prayed that God would protect us while we were absent one from another.

Our communication with Rosalie and her family began after they returned from the cruise.

One era had not long ended for the Daley clan when another began. I told Duke that many new offspring had been born since Maamie and Parpi Daley's transition. I wondered if he and I would have the pleasure of knowing our children's children.

Mom and Dad were happy as their second generation multiplied. They were elated to see that Syd and Ejay were closer than they had ever been. Syd had asked Ejay to suggest a middle name for his son, William.

"Ejay, I heard Syd asked you to name his baby," I said quizzically one evening.

"Yes, Maggie. Syd and I are tight. He named him William, in deference to Uncle Will and Abuelita. I was glad when he asked me to suggest a middle name. I told him Anthony, in honor of Dad. Don't you like the name, William Anthony Daley?"

"Of course," I do, but you told me you would bear Randy's load, so he won't need a wad, but you gave one to your little nephew, William."

"What are you saying, Maggie?"

"William Anthony Daley! Check out the initials, Ejay!"

Ejay seemed puzzled for a while. "Maggie, I had no clue. Can you see Maamie Daley in this?"

"There's no doubt about it," I said. "When William reaches the age of understanding, I'll explain his WAD to him."

The Daley offspring of North America was fully in touch, one with another. We were not in walking distance from each other as Maamie

Daley had suggested, but modern contraptions called the computer and the cell phone, had made our communicating far easier. It went as easily as, 'Hello Rosa Daley! Long time no see!' Rosalie echoed her greeting, and we were together again, as if no time had been lost in our relationship.

Rosalie, David, Jeremy and Joseph would use some of the money they had inherited from Gerald Carpenter to change their family name back to Daley. They planned to have a grand family reunion at Uncle Sol's place when the lawyers advise them that their petition had been approved.

I am happy to report that a new generation of Daleys and their offspring are doing fine. One third of the island of our origin, that survived the eruptions, still stands. Montserrat is blooming and buzzing with the fervor of its courageous people who refuse to stop living. The Mighty Watchman may some day reestablish its dominance as the highest peak in the island, new owners will plow the fertile land that it oversees, and appreciate their harvests. Superstitious folks may talk of the "jumbies" that keep watch over the Daley property. Yes, maybe Boy and his Shug will roll a few pebbles down the hill to scare intruders away from their sacred land. They will do everything possible to protect it, and we'll join them in our turn, some day.

By the way, readers, Lydia, Alexander and Sebastian wrote to invite us to their Grandpa Duby's welcome back to the U.S.A. Lex admires his grandfather, and wants him in his life. His sister declares that she will accompany him to Montserrat to learn more about his homeland. We have shared many fine moments together. Rozy, Sadie and their children visit often, and we reciprocate.

Readers, by no means have we forgotten Keith and his family, the keepers of the homeland flame. Unfortunately, Winnie has not heard anything about the whereabouts of her daughters'. However, she has refused to give up her search, and we stand by her, prayerfully. Leonard Martin has become her detective in England.

We plan to return to Montserrat after Uncle Sol's family wins their petition to return to their true last name. Winnie, Keith, Simmy and Eman will entertain us.

Auntie Vera has become a world traveler, visiting her extended family in the United States, Europe, Canada, and in the Caribbean. She and

Mom Randall continue to cruise together. Neither has expressed any desire to remarry.

Occasionally, the volcano still erupts, no doubt as a reminder that it is still in control. Many Montserratians have returned to the island, built their dream homes, and are silently and openly saying, "The volcano be damned! A ya be barn, a ya me rear, and a ya me a go dead."[24]

I say to all the Daleys and the descendants of Daleys whom I may never have the privilege of meeting, "Yours is a rich heritage. Seek out your elders and learn from them. Remember, wisdom comes with age. For those of you whom I've had the privilege of knowing, please keep the Daley Candle burning, because it is a light that should never grow dim. Your ancestors have paved a road for you. Your generation and those who will follow you must use education as a means of climbing the ladder to success, but please acquire manual skills as well. Until your hair begins to turn a little gray, you still have a lot to learn. Stand firm in unity, for there is strength in its bond. In our Lord's prayer, we ask our Lord Jesus to "Give us this day our daily bread." I implore you to keep in touch daily with our Daley seniors, and listen to them. Their wisdom may help you to overcome just one more hurdle.

Dearest Maamie Daley, long ago, I promised you that I would write about all the things you and Parpi taught me, and that you would live forever in our hearts and on the pages of a book. You were an inspiration, and two of my first and finest teachers. In reality, you taught me new things every moment I spent with you.

Maamie Daley, I have named my piece, *Maamie and Parpi Daley of Montserrat*. Like Auntie Vera, I, too, have kept my promise. My grandfather, your Boy, will always be the champion of the Daley mystique. Maamie and Parpi, if I were to keep count of the times we
speak of you, the calculation would be astronomical.

I, too, damn the volcano that caused you so much woe, so here is my take on the Mighty Watchman: So Maamie, you may brag among our ancestors that your Maggie Sweetie is also a poet.

---

24   See #1

Please, Mr. Volcano

"Please Mr. Volcano, no more eruptions!
If you must erupt, do leave us some options.
Please no more invasions of the 'Safety Zone'!
Remember, that's where folks still call 'Home'!

"Some visit our homeland to see your glow.
Their 'oohs' and 'ahs' prove they do not know,
That your gaseous emissions can be dangerous,
May the Lord have mercy on them, and on us!

"Scientists say that our land is being reborn.
But, its rebirth is leaving our people forlorn.
Dear Mr. Volcano, listen to our fervent pleas,
We want all your explosions to cease, please.

"Dear Mr. Volcano, do not bellow any more.
You have already proven your amazing power.
We are very cognizant of your devastation,
That has depleted our homeland's vegetation.

"Our little Island is famous for its green smile.
It is known as the Caribbean's "Emerald Isle.
It matters little what naysayers may do or say,
Montserrat will smile verdantly again, we pray.

"So please Mr. Volcano, do go back to sleep!
Your ashes have buried some of our land so deep,
That our disoriented jumbies are forced to roam,
Because they cannot find their way back home."

With all my love, Magdalene Elizabeth Daley, II, your Mags, Sweetie, also known as Magdalene Elizabeth Daley Randall. I will always be second to you.

The end.